FARMHOUSE KITCHEN Book 3

A third book of recipes based on the Independent
Television series presented for 12 years by Dorothy
Sleightholme and now by her successor Grace Mulligan

Edited by Mary Watts

**YORKSHIRE
TELEVISION**

First published in Great Britain 1982 by

YORKSHIRE TELEVISION ENTERPRISES LTD

Television House, 32 Bedford Row, London WC1R 4HE

© Yorkshire Television Enterprises Ltd, 1982

ISBN 0 946064 00 8

Reprinted 1985
Reprinted 1986 (twice)
Reprinted 1987 (twice)
Reprinted 1988 (twice)
Reprinted 1989

Cover Illustrations: Mary Evans Picture Library

Text Illustrations: Mary Evans Picture Library, pages 28, 61, 84, 94, 145, 148, 180, 187; The Mansell Collection, page 13; Peter Newark's Historical Pictures, page 117; John Topham Picture Library, page 101.

Printed in Great Britain by Richard Clay Ltd, Bungay, Suffolk

CONTENTS

ACKNOWLEDGMENTS

In this third collection of recipes, which will be used in our television programmes for the next 4 or 5 years, I have once again been delighted to receive contributions from all over the British Isles and some from abroad. Many viewers have sent in their family favourites, many others have written with requests for traditional county fare, for vegetarian recipes, for oriental dishes.

It has given Grace Mulligan, Graham Watts and me much pleasure to visit the Women's Institute of Cornwall, Devon, Dorset, Gloucestershire, Gwent, East and West Kent, Somerset, West Sussex and Worcestershire. Each of these federations presented a wonderful array of local delicacies and traditional dishes and many of their recipes have been selected for this book. Through the Dorset W.I. I discovered The Piddle Valley Cookebook and I am indebted to the Piddletrenthide Parochial Church Council for permission to print John Firrell's version of Mackerel with Gooseberries, known to him as Portland-style Mackerel. The work of individual W.I. members in seeking out old recipes, bringing them up to date and preparing them for us to taste was remarkable and is greatly appreciated.

Sarah Brown, who began the Terrace Project in Scarborough 4 years ago, which numbers amongst its activities a wholefood restaurant and shop, has offered me many of her successful dishes and will demonstrate them in the programmes. Some of the other wholefood recipes have been contributed by Janet Horsley, who has recently published through Prism Press a book of her own called Bean Cuisine. Permission to use Elizabeth Shears' recipe has been granted by the Nutrition Science Research Institute, Brookthorpe, Gloucester.

Priya Wickramasinghe is Sri Lankan, is much travelled and has lived in this country for 15 years (her 3 young children are all English-born). She was introduced to me by Messrs. J. M. Dent & Sons Ltd with whom she has published Spicy and Delicious and Oriental Cookbook. Her recipes, which are examples of everyday and special-occasion oriental cookery, are written with the western cook in mind and will allow you to make at home many dishes which you may hitherto have only tried at Indian, Sri Lankan, Indonesian or Chinese restaurants.

Without the help of some of our old friends and programme participants I could not present this book to you confident that every recipe has been tried and tested. The recipes do work and have been tried out on husbands, families and friends of Judith Adshead, Margaret Heywood, Liz Mickery, Sybil Norcott, Dennis Rouston and Anne Wallace, who have also given us many of their own recipes.

I am indebted also for much help and advice to the Home Food Science Section (M.A.F.F.) Long Ashton Research Station; the Prestige Group p.l.c., for information concerning pressure cooking; and last but not least to Joyce Town who has organised the typing of every recipe and typed many herself two or three times over.

Mary Watts
Summer 1982

INTRODUCTION

Compiling a cookery book brings one face to face with the need to make cooking not just an everyday necessity but an exciting challenge to stimulate all the senses. There is no point in having a highly nutritious meal if it looks and tastes dull.

Dorothy and I have tried very hard to show that good food is not necessarily expensive food. We want to encourage you to experiment with wholewheat flours, raw vegetables and fruit, herbs, spices, pulses and grains so that you eat for your health's sake too.

Traditional cooking has not been forgotten and we have many recipes from counties north and south. From the East there are recipes with exciting aromatic ingredients to tempt you. Superb cakes, buns, fruit breads, preserves and drinks are all here.

With four children of my own I know well the need for substantial, filling and nutritious dishes for bleak winter days but we have also tried to remember those of you who live alone and your need for an elegant, light but nutritious meal.

We hope this book, with its contributions from many others besides Dorothy and myself, will convey to you our enthusiam for cooking of all kinds so that it becomes a pleasure for you too.

We also hope you will take one or two steps in other directions, away from your regular old standby recipes, and possibly find some things which in time will become new firm favourites.

Grace Mulligan   Dorothy Sleightholme

Yorkshire Television's Farmhouse Kitchen series is produced and directed by Mary and Graham Watts.

5

Chapter 1

Soups and Starters

Stock from a piece of meat or a whole chicken has the most flavour. The following recipe uses an excellent broth derived from cooking a piece of lamb or beef which is removed after about 2 hours and served as a main course with vegetables. Remember to start the night before.

DUNDEE BROTH

50 g/2 oz dried green peas
50 g/2 oz barley
2·8 litres/5 pints cold water
675 g/1½ lb piece of beef or lamb, tied with string
225 g/8 oz diced carrots
125 g/4 oz diced turnip
125 g/4 oz chopped cabbage
2 whole leeks, chopped
Extra carrot and turnip cut in chunks to serve with the boiled meat
1 tablespoon chopped parsley
Salt and pepper

1. Wash and soak the dried peas overnight.
2. Put peas and barley on to cook in a large pan with the water.
3. Tie meat with string so that it can be carved as a joint. Put it into pan when water is hot.
4. Add diced and chopped vegetables. Put lid on pan.
5. Cook steadily for about 2 hours.
6. 30 minutes before the soup is to be served add the extra vegetables.
7. When the time is up and the meat and vegetables cooked, lift out meat and remove string. Lift out vegetables. Keep hot.
8. Add salt and pepper to soup as required. Add parsley and serve.

Mrs Grace McGlinn
Dundee, Scotland

CLEAR BEEF SOUP

25 g/1 oz dripping or more
1 large onion, chopped
A clove of garlic, chopped
1 teaspoon sugar
225 to 350 g/8 to 12 oz shin of beef, cut small
225 g/8 oz ox liver, cut small
1 pig's trotter or calf's foot
1 small carrot, scrubbed and chopped
1 large tomato, halved and grilled
A bouquet garni (a sprig of thyme, parsley and 1 bay leaf tied together)
1·7 litres/3 pints water
Salt and pepper
1 large egg-white
2 to 3 tablespoons sherry or madeira (optional)

1. Melt dripping in a frying pan. Fry onion and garlic until soft. Sprinkle with sugar and stir. Leave to cook without stirring until sugar caramelises (i.e., browns) but do not allow onion to burn.
2. Lift onion and garlic out of frying pan into a large saucepan or flame-proof casserole.
3. Now brown beef and liver in frying pan, adding a little more fat if necessary.
4. Put beef, liver, trotter, carrot, tomato and herbs into the saucepan with onion and garlic. Pour in water.
5. Bring to the boil, season with salt and pepper, put on lid and simmer for about 2 hours either on top of stove or in a moderate oven, Gas 3, 325°F, 160°C.
6. Strain off liquid and leave overnight so that fat can rise.
7. Next day scrape off the fat and put jellied stock into a large saucepan over gentle heat.
8. When it is liquid and warm but *not* hot, add egg-white. Start to whisk with a hand rotary egg-beater or an electric whisk so that surface of soup is covered in a white froth. Allow to boil for 2 or 3 minutes.
9. Turn off heat and leave for 10 minutes. A brownish scum will cling to the egg-white, thus clearing the soup underneath.
10. Now pour contents of pan very gently through a sieve lined with muslin or thin cloth.

11. Re-heat soup and adjust seasoning. Taste it and if flavour is not strong enough boil it uncovered, reducing water content and so increasing flavour.

12. Take pan from heat and add wine just before serving. Although it is given as optional there is no doubt that this traditional ingredient adds to the flavour.

Serve with Sippets (*see page 12*) or some cooked pasta, or parsley.

Also delicious served chilled as a jelly. It will set in a jelly if the pig's trotter or calf's foot has been well cooked.

Freezes well.

Potted Meat

Using the remaining cooked shin of beef and pig's trotter, strip away fat and gristle. Mince the meat, beat into it enough softened butter to give a thick, creamy, spreading consistency. Season to taste. A little of the clear jelly may be added at this time to help the consistency. Press into pots and pour on a covering of melted butter.

Keeps for 3 or 4 days in a fridge, or a month in a freezer.

HAM SHANK

There are many ways to use an inexpensive shank. A smoked bacon or ham shank can also be used.

From 1 shank you should get 2·25 litres/4 pints of rich stock, 225 g/8 oz ham pieces and some ham fat

To cook shank and make stock

1. Put shank in a large saucepan with 2·7 to 3 litres/4½ to 5½ pints of water. Cover pan, bring to boil and simmer 1½ hours until meat and fat is falling off bones. Or, pressure cook for ¾ hour adding only the maximum quantity of water indicated in your pressure cooker manual.

2. Strain liquid into jugs. Allow to cool. Then put in refrigerator or wait until fat has risen and stock is set to a firm jelly.

3. When shank has cooled remove meat and separate fatty bits, skin and bones.

4. Lift fat off jellied stock to use for frying, etc.

Skin and fatty bits from meat can be rendered down to produce more dripping. Put them into a small pan, cover with water and put on lid. Simmer for 1 hour, then pour into a small bowl. As it cools fat will rise and when set can be lifted off liquid beneath.

Stock freezes well.

Ham may be chopped into white sauce and used on toast or in Vol-au-vents (*see page 112*), or pancakes (*see page 93*).

Try these dishes too: Ham Soup (*below*), Ham, Egg and Onion Flan (*page 108*), Ham Rissoles (*page 31*).

HAM SOUP

For 6 or more people

Using stock from ham shank take care to taste before using. It may be very salty and require diluting with water.

175 to 225 g/6 to 8 oz yellow split peas
2 medium-sized carrots
2 medium-sized onions
1·7 litres/3 pints ham stock

Other vegetables can be used— e.g., cabbage, leek, parsnips, turnips—400 to 450 g/14 to 16 oz vegetables is about right.

To serve

A little finely-chopped ham
2 tablespoons chopped, fresh parsley

1. Soak split peas in water for 3 hours. Then drain. If pressure cooking it is not necessary to soak first.

2. Scrub and chop carrots. Peel and chop onions.

3. Put split peas, vegetables and stock in a saucepan with a lid and simmer for 1 hour. Or pressure cook for 30 minutes taking care not to exceed maximum quantity of liquid indicated in your pressure cooker manual.

4. Add ham, parsley and seasoning if necessary and cook for 5 minutes.

Serve very hot.

This soup can be liquidised before parsley is added. It is then particularly delicious served with Sippets fried in ham fat (*see page 12*).

HOT BEETROOT SOUP

This soup freezes well.
A liquidiser is needed.

450 g/1 lb raw beetroot
450 g/1 lb potatoes
2 onions
50 g/2 oz butter or margarine
1·5 to 1·75 litres/2½ to 3 pints strong chicken stock
Salt
Freshly ground pepper

To garnish: yoghurt or soured cream

1. Peel and dice beetroot and potatoes. Peel and chop onions.
2. Melt butter in a large saucepan and cook vegetables gently with lid on pan for about 5 minutes.
3. Stir in the stock, bring to the boil and simmer until beetroot is cooked.
4. Cool the soup and reduce it to a purée in liquidiser. Return to pan. Adjust seasoning.
5. Just before serving, bring soup to boiling point and serve with a swirl of yoghurt or soured cream in each bowl.

Freeze before yoghurt or soured cream is added.

CARROT SOUP

2 onions
40 g/1½ oz butter
1 clove of garlic
A pinch of salt
450 g/1 lb carrots
Pepper

1 dessertspoon coriander seeds
1 glass of sherry
600 ml/1 pint chicken stock
600 ml/1 pint milk
To garnish: chopped parsley

1. Peel and slice onions and cook carefully in butter in a large pan until transparent.
2. Crush garlic with salt and add to onions.
3. Scrub carrots, slice thinly and add to pan.
4. Season with salt and pepper. Add coriander seeds and sherry. Cover and cook gently until vegetables are soft, about 10 to 15 minutes.
5. Add stock and cook a further 15 to 20 minutes. Allow to cool.
6. Liquidise or sieve the soup, then strain into a clean pan.
7. Add milk when ready to serve. Reheat carefully. Adjust seasoning.
8. Sprinkle parsley in each bowl of soup.

CREAM OF LEEK AND POTATO SOUP

4 medium-sized leeks
50 g/2 oz butter
4 small potatoes
150 ml/¼ pint water
600 ml/1 pint chicken stock
Salt and pepper
150 ml/¼ pint thick cream

1. Wash and trim leeks and chop into small pieces, using both white and green parts.
2. Melt butter in a saucepan and add leeks. Cover pan and reduce heat so that leeks cook slowly without browning, for about 5 minutes. Shake pan occasionally.
3. Meanwhile, peel potatoes and cut into small cubes.
4. Add potatoes to leeks with water and stock. Season to taste.
5. Bring to boil, cover pan and simmer soup for 25 minutes.
6. Sieve or liquidise soup and return it to the pan.
7. Add cream. Heat, but do not boil.

Mrs Eileen Trumper
Llanvair Kilgeddin, Gwent

10

SPICED RED LENTIL SOUP

This soup is a flaming orange colour.

4 large or 6 good helpings. Easy to make less.

1 medium-sized onion
1 red pepper
2 sticks of celery
225 g/8 oz marrow or courgettes
125 g/4 oz red lentils
1 tablespoon oil
1 teaspoon paprika
1 teaspoon turmeric
A pinch of cinnamon
A pinch of cayenne pepper
A 400 g/14 oz can of tomatoes
1 teaspoon basil
1 bay leaf
About 750 ml/1¼ pints water or vegetable stock
Salt and pepper
1 tablespoon shoyu (*see page 80*)

1. Chop vegetables finely.
2. Wash lentils and pick them over for stones.
3. Heat oil and fry spices—i.e., paprika, turmeric, cinnamon and cayenne.
4. Add vegetables and lentils. Stir well so that oil and spices coat the vegetables. Cook about 5 minutes, stirring occasionally.
5. Cut up tomatoes, put them in a measuring jug and add enough water or stock to make 1·1 litres/2 pints.
6. Add this with basil and bay leaf to pan of vegetables. Bring to boil and simmer for 40 minutes or until lentils are cooked.
7. Add salt and pepper to taste. Add the shoyu. Add more water or stock if necessary.

Sarah Brown
Scarborough, Yorkshire

MINTY GREEN SOUP

For this you need a liquidiser.

At least enough for 6 but freezes well

175 g/6 oz green split peas
1 medium-sized onion
225g/8 oz carrots
2 small potatoes
2 sticks celery
1 small parsnip
1 tablespoon oil
1·1 litres/2 pints light stock or water
½ to 1 tablespoon dried mint or chopped fresh mint to taste
Salt and pepper
1 tablespoon shoyu (*see page 80*)
Milk (optional)

To garnish: 2 tablespoons cream, sprigs of fresh mint

1. Wash the split peas.
2. Peel and finely chop onion.
3. Scrub and finely chop carrots, potatoes, celery and parsnip.
4. Gently fry onion in oil until translucent.
5. Add other vegetables and fry gently for 5 minutes, mixing well so that oil coats vegetables and seals in flavour.
6. Add green split peas and stock or water. Bring to boil and simmer for about 40 minutes until peas are cooked.
7. Put soup through liquidiser, adding mint, seasoning and shoyu as it blends. Return to pan.
8. If soup is too thick either stock, water or milk may be added. Heat gently, check seasoning.

Serve with a swirl of cream and sprigs of mint floating on surface.

Sarah Brown
Scarborough, Yorkshire

SIMPLE ONION SOUP

For 4 people

4 large onions, about 675 g/1½ lb
40 g/1½ oz butter or margarine
900 ml/1½ pints well-flavoured chicken stock
Salt and Pepper Mix (*see page 44*)

1. Cut up onions very fine.
2. Melt butter or margarine in a saucepan. Add onion, stir well and put on lid.
3. Turn heat down very low and allow onion to sweat for 10 minutes. Shake

11

pan from time to time but avoid taking off lid.
4. Add stock, season to taste, bring to the boil and simmer for 3 minutes or until onion is tender.

CREAM OF TOMATO SOUP

Freezes well, but do so before milk or cream is added.

1 medium-sized carrot, scrubbed
1 onion, peeled
2 sticks of celery, washed
75 g/3 oz butter or margarine
A 400 g/14 oz tin of tomatoes
1 teaspoon sugar
600 ml/1 pint light stock
Salt and Pepper Mix (see page 44)
25 g/1 oz plain flour
1 tablespoon tomato paste or purée*
150 ml/¼ pint top-of-milk or single cream

To garnish: chopped parsley

(*See: To keep tomato purée fresh, page 45)

1. Slice carrot, onion and celery finely.
2. Soften 40 g/1½ oz of the butter or margarine in a large saucepan. Add vegetables, put on lid and cook gently until soft, shaking pan occasionally.
3. Add tomatoes with their juice, sugar, 300 ml/½ pint of the stock, salt and pepper to taste. Simmer for 5 minutes.
4. Sieve contents of pan into a bowl. Rinse out pan.
5. Melt remaining 40 g/1½ oz butter or margarine in pan. Stir in flour and cook for 1 minute. Stir in rest of stock and tomato paste. Cook for 1 minute. Stir until boiling and simmer for 1 minute.
6. Add tomato mixture from bowl, and the milk or cream. Check seasoning. Heat to nearly boiling point, but do not actually boil or the soup may curdle.

Serve sprinkled with chopped parsley.

WHITE FOAM SOUP

Enough for 6 but easy to make half quantity

1 onion
1 stick of celery
A clove of garlic
40 g/1½ oz butter
25 g/1 oz flour
1·1 litres/2 pints of milk
A blade of mace
2 eggs
Salt and pepper
50 g/2 oz finely-grated cheese
1 tablespoon chopped parsley

Serve with tiny cubes of bread fried in butter or margarine. (*See Sippets, below*)

1. Chop onion and celery very fine. Crush garlic.
2. Melt butter in a 2 litre/3 pint saucepan. Stir in flour, then add milk slowly, stirring thoroughly till smooth. Bring to the boil and cook for 2 minutes.
3. Add onion, celery, garlic and mace. Let the soup barely simmer for 20 to 30 minutes until it is well flavoured.
4. Cool slightly, then add beaten yolks of the eggs.
5. Reheat without boiling. Then add salt and pepper to taste, and grated cheese. Do not allow to boil.
6. Beat egg-whites to a stiff froth. Fold half into the soup. Pour the rest into a hot tureen and pour soup over. Sprinkle with chopped parsley.

Mrs Irene Mills
For Leckhampton W.I., Glos.

SIPPETS

Fry cubes or small triangles of bread in hot bacon, or ham fat, or butter until brown and crisp, turning often.

Delicious if a clove of garlic, chopped into 2 or 3 pieces, is first fried in the fat. Try these also cold surrounding salads with soft ingredients.

SOUP NUTS

To accompany soup, 12 to 15 portions

Using half the quantity of choux pastry given on *page 106*, bake tiny raisin-sized pieces of the paste on a greased baking tray in a moderately hot oven, Gas 6, 400°F, 200°C, for 10 to 12 minutes until pale golden brown and dry.

Store in an airtight container. Or freeze.

Anne Wallace,
Stewarton, Ayrshire

MELBA TOAST

1. Cut slices of bread for toast—not too thick.
2. Toast lightly brown on both sides.
3. Cut in half diagonally to make triangles. Then slice the bread through the centre between the toasted sides to make two pieces from one.
4. Place in a large roasting tin and dry off at the bottom of the oven until crisp.

5. Store in an airtight tin.

Goes well with hot or cold soup.

MARINATED SMOKED MACKEREL

For 4 people

Buy two 125 g/4 oz fillets of smoked mackerel, cooked

Marinade

1 small onion, finely-chopped
2 tablespoons salad oil
1 tablespoon wine vinegar or lemon juice
¼ teaspoon dry mustard

To serve: chopped fresh parsley

1. Skin mackerel and divide into portions in a shallow dish.
2. Mix marinade ingredients and pour over mackerel.
3. Cover with a lid or greaseproof paper and foil and put in refrigerator or a cool place for about 3 hours.
4. Lift mackerel on to separate plates. Sprinkle with parsley.

Delicious with crusty French bread.

13

FRESH MUSSELS WITH PARSLEY

For 2 people

450 g/1 lb fresh mussels in the shells*
15 g/½ oz butter
½ a large clove of garlic, crushed
1 dessertspoon parsley

*Try to buy mussels on the day you mean to use them. If it is necessary to keep them overnight put them in a flat dish in a cool place with a sprinkling of water, or cover with a wet cloth.

1. Wash and scrub mussels, pull off the beards. Using the back of an old knife knock off any barnacles. Discard any open mussels.
2. Put mussels in a large pan with the other ingredients. Put on lid and cook over a high heat. Shake pan from time to time. Cook for only enough time to open the mussel shells. Shake again so that the liquor gets into the mussels. Not more than five minutes in all.
3. Serve immediately with crusty French bread to mop up the delicious soup.

AVOCADO AND SALMON MOUSSE

Best eaten the day it is made.

225 g/8 oz tinned salmon
15 g/½ oz gelatine
3 tablespoons water
2 avocado pears
½ teaspoon salt
A dash of pepper
2 teaspoons anchovy essence
3 tablespoons single cream
2 or 3 drops of green food-colouring
2 egg-whites

To garnish: 1 stuffed green olive, chopped fresh parsley

1. Drain salmon. Reserve juice. Remove bones, skin and flake the flesh finely.

2. Put gelatine in 3 tablespoons water in a cup or small bowl. Set the cup in a pan of hot water and heat gently until the gelatine is completely dissolved. Stir well.
3. Split, stone, skin and cut up the avocados. Scrape as much pulp as possible from skin as this will give the mousse a deep green colour.
4. Liquidise the avocados, salt, pepper, anchovy essence and salmon juice. Or, if you do not have a liquidiser or food processor, mash thoroughly and beat until smooth.
5. Place in a large bowl, strain in the dissolved gelatine. Stir in cream and flaked salmon adding green colouring if needed.
6. Whisk egg-whites until they will stand up in peaks. Then fold into salmon mixture.
7. Turn into a fish or ring mould which has been rinsed in cold water and leave to set.
8. Turn out into a serving dish. Garnish with the stuffed olive, for eyes, and parsley.

This recipe would make excellent individual ramekins too.

SMOKED COD'S ROE PÂTÉ

225 g/8 oz smoked cod's roe
Juice of 1 lemon
150 ml/¼ pint double cream or 75 g/3 oz soft butter mixed with milk made up to 150 ml/¼ pint
A pinch each of ground ginger, cayenne pepper and paprika

Do not use an electric mixer or blender for this as it would break up the tiny eggs.

1. Remove skin from the cod's roe and empty into a bowl.
2. Put in half of the lemon juice and mash well with a fork. Add rest of lemon juice and beat again.
3. Gradually beat in cream, or the butter and milk.
4. Season to taste with the ginger and cayenne pepper.

5. Transfer to serving dish. Sprinkle with paprika and refrigerate.

Serve with hot buttered toast.

SMOKED MACKEREL PÂTÉ

For this you need a liquidiser or food processor.

350 g/12 oz smoked mackerel
2 thick slices wholemeal or brown bread
45 ml/3 tablespoons wine or cider vinegar
Half a tart eating apple, about 100 g/4 oz peeled and cored
Black pepper to taste

1. If using home-smoked mackerel proceed straight to step 2. Otherwise proceed as follows. Soak fish in water for an hour or two to relieve strong smoky taste. Wash thoroughly and cook in water just to cover, simmering for 5 minutes. Drain.
2. Remove bones and skin from fish.
3. Soak bread with vinegar.
4. Place all ingredients in liquidiser or food processor and switch on until all is blended and smooth.
5. Press into a ½ kg/1 lb loaf tin or a 13 cm/5 inch round tin or a soufflé dish. Chill.
6. Turn out on an attractive plate to serve.

Serve with Melba Toast (*see page 13*) and butter, a nice salad or plain watercress.

Anne Wallace
Stewarton, Ayrshire

LIVER PÂTÉ

For this you need a liquidiser or a food processor.

As a lunch or supper dish, enough for 5 people. As a starter, 10 portions.

150 ml/¼ pint thick white sauce made with 20 g/¾ oz butter, 20 g/¾ oz flour, 150 ml/¼ pint milk, salt and pepper
250 g/8 oz chicken, calf or lamb liver

15 g/½ oz butter
A clove of garlic, crushed
125 g/4 oz fat bacon pieces
Half a sour apple, peeled, cored and sliced
4 anchovy fillets
1 egg
125 g/4 oz streaky bacon rashers
1 bay leaf

1. Make white sauce. Melt butter, stir in flour and cook 1 minute. Add milk gradually, stirring till it is thick, and boil gently for 2 minutes. Season with salt and pepper.
2. Trim skin and gristle from liver if necessary and cut it into 2·5 cm/1 inch pieces.
3. Fry it quickly in butter, just to set it. Put into liquidiser.
4. Add garlic, bacon pieces, apple, anchovy, egg and sauce to liver in liquidiser with salt and pepper to taste. Switch on and blend till mixture is smooth.
5. Line a ½ kg/1 lb loaf tin or oven dish with streaky bacon.
6. Pour in liver mixture and lay bay leaf on top.
7. Cover closely (greaseproof paper and foil will do) and put it in a roasting tin half filled with water.
8. Cook in middle of a moderate oven, Gas 4, 350°F, 180°C, for 2 hours.
9. Remove from oven and roasting tin. Press the pâté with a weight on top until it is cold.
10. Turn out on a plate and serve in slices with salad, Melba Toast (*see page 13*) or hot toast and butter.

Can be kept in refrigerator for a week or in freezer for 6 weeks, but long freezing is not suitable because garlic flavour tends to get a bit strong.

Anne Wallace
Stewarton, Ayrshire

SUSSEX FARMHOUSE PÂTÉ

Freezes well.

450 g/1 lb belly pork
225 g/8 oz bacon pieces

15

225 g/8 oz pig's liver
1 medium sized onion
2 teaspoons chopped fresh
herbs, such as parsley, thyme,
sage, marjoram, etc., or 1
teaspoon mixed dried herbs
Salt and black pepper
125 g/4 oz wholewheat
breadcrumbs

1. Remove all skin, white bones, etc.,
from pork and bacon and any pipes
from liver.
2. Put meat through mincer twice
with onion, herbs, seasoning and
breadcrumbs.
3. Put the mixture into a greased
½ kg/1 lb loaf tin. Cover with greaseproof paper and foil and place in a
baking tin with enough water to come
halfway up sides.
4. Bake in the centre of a slow oven,
Gas 2, 300°F, 150°C for 1½ to 1¾ hours.
5. Do not strain fat or juices off but
leave to get cold in tin with a weight
on top.

Mrs Janice Langley
Shoreham-by-Sea, West Sussex

PORK SPARE RIBS IN A BARBECUE SAUCE

*This recipe makes a good first
course with, say, 3 ribs per person.
There is enough sauce for 4 people.*

About 1 dozen meaty spare ribs
of pork, split into singles

Sauce
300 ml/½ pint dry cider or dry
home-made white wine
1 dessertspoon cornflour
2 tablespoons cold water
1 large teaspoon dry mustard
1 tablespoon soya sauce
1 level tablespoon brown sugar
125 g/4 oz tinned pineapple
pieces, drained and cut in half

1. Cook the spare ribs. Either roast in
a moderately hot oven, Gas 6, 400°F,
200°C, for 30 minutes until brown and
crisp. Or put them in a saucepan,
cover with water and boil until meat is
tender. Drain well and put ribs into a
roasting tin or oven dish.

2. Heat cider. Slake cornflour with
the water and add to pan. Stir as it
thickens and cook for 2 minutes.
3. Mix mustard into soya sauce and
add to pan with sugar and pineapple.
4. Pour sauce over spare ribs and put
in oven to heat through, reducing
temperature to moderate, Gas 4, 350°F,
180°C, for 15 minutes.

Best eaten with your fingers.

APRICOT AND ORANGE

A simple and refreshing starter to a
meal, or a sweet, or even for breakfast.

125 g/4 oz dried apricots
Boiling water
3 oranges
A sprig of mint, for decoration

1. Cut apricots into small pieces. Easy
with kitchen scissors. Put them in a
bowl or jar and cover with boiling
water.
2. Squeeze oranges. Add juice and
pulp to apricots.
3. Leave in a cool place or refrigerator
overnight or longer so that flavours
blend and apricots are really plump.

Serve in separate glasses or little
bowls with a mint leaf to decorate.

Anne Wallace
Stewarton, Ayrshire

CUCUMBER AND GRAPEFRUIT SALAD

Nice as a starter or a salad.

2 grapefruit
¼ cucumber
50 g/2 oz diced Cheddar cheese
150 ml/5 fl oz natural yoghurt

1. Cut grapefruit in half and remove
segments. Discard all pith and chop up
the fruit.
2. Dice the cucumber.
3. Mix all ingredients together with
the yoghurt and fill the halved
grapefruit shells.
4. Serve chilled.

Judith Adshead
Mottram St. Andrew, Cheshire

CHEESE STRUDEL SLICES

For 6 people

A 225 g/8 oz packet of frozen puff pastry or use home-made rough puff pastry (*see page 106*)

Filling

1 large beaten egg
125 g/4 oz Cheddar cheese, finely-grated
225 g/8 oz curd or single cream cheese
1 level tablespoon chopped parsley or chives, or a mixture
A pinch of garlic salt
Pepper and salt

To decorate: sesame seeds

1. Roll out pastry on a floured board to a rectangle about 31 by 23 cm/12 by 9 inches.
2. Prepare filling. Keep aside 1 tablespoon of the egg and mix all other ingredients together.
3. Spread filling over pastry to within 2·5 cm/1 inch of edges.
4. Turn edges in to hold filling in place and then fold three times to make a flattened Swiss-roll shape about 8 cm/3 inches deep.
5. Lift roll on to a baking sheet, brush with remaining egg and scatter sesame seeds over top. Cut six shallow slits through pastry top.
6. Bake near top of a hot oven, Gas 7, 425°F, 220°C for 10 minutes. Then reduce heat to moderately hot, Gas 5, 375°F, 190°C for a further 15 minutes.
7. Cut into slices and serve hot.

Judith Adshead
Mottram St. Andrew, Cheshire

HUMUS

A dish from the eastern Mediterranean and the Middle East.

Enough for 8 people—easy to make in small quantities

225 g/8 oz dry chick peas
150 ml/¼ pint stock (use cooking water from chick peas)
4 to 5 tablespoons tahini*, white if possible
Juice of 1½ lemons
A teaspoon shoyu (*see page 80*) or soya sauce
A clove of garlic, crushed, or 1 teaspoon garlic powder
½ teaspoon salt
¼ teaspoon paprika
Black pepper

*Tahini is a paste made from crushed sesame seeds, similar in texture to creamy peanut butter. It's purpose is to thicken the chick pea paste as well as to add flavour. White tahini is made from hulled sesame seeds, brown tahini is from whole seed. Both have a nutty flavour, but the brown type has a much stronger flavour.

To serve

Slices of lemon
Parsley
Wholemeal bread or pitta (*see page 139*)

1. Soak chick peas in water overnight.
2. Next day drain them, discarding water. Rinse, re-cover with about 1·5 litres/3 pints water, put on lid and boil hard for 25 minutes. Then reduce heat and simmer until soft but not mushy.
3. Meanwhile prepare other ingredients.
4. Drain chick peas, reserving liquid for stock and grind them to a fine powder. This can be done in a food processor or through a mincer or mouli-grater. If chick peas are cooked for about 2 hours until really soft they can be mashed by hand.
5. Add enough of the reserved liquid to make a stiff paste. Mix in all other ingredients.
6. Put humus in a shallow dish garnished with lemon slices and parsley.

Serve with bread. Traditionally served with Pitta bread (*see page 139*).

Will keep 4 or 5 days in refrigerator.

Sarah Brown
Scarborough, Yorkshire

STUFFED RINGS OF RED AND GREEN PEPPERS

For 6 or more people

A very pretty and delicious dish.
For this you need a liquidiser or food
processor.

2 small red peppers
2 small green peppers

Stuffing

This is a pâté of chicken livers which
can be made in larger quantities to
serve on its own. Can be frozen, but
only for 1 or 2 weeks.

125 g/4 oz chicken livers
25 g/1 oz butter
1 tablespoon oil
1 onion, finely-chopped
A clove of garlic, finely-chopped
**½ level teaspoon chopped fresh
thyme, or ¼ level teaspoon dried**

**2 tablespoons medium-sweet
sherry**
125 g/4 oz cream cheese
Salt and pepper

To serve: hot buttered toast

1. Cut a lid off each pepper with its
stalk and hollow out by removing core,
seeds and white membrane.
2. Prepare chicken livers by scraping
out core and cutting away any part
tinged with green. Chop, but not
small.
3. Melt butter with oil and fry liver,
onion, garlic and thyme, gently
turning all the time, about 5 minutes.
Cool.
4. Add sherry to the pan. Then blend
in a liquidiser or food processor.
5. Add cream cheese, salt and pepper.
Continue processing until well
combined.
6. Fill this mixture into the hollowed-
out peppers. Chill.
7. Just before serving, cut in 1 cm/½
inch rings.

Serve with hot buttered toast.

Chapter 2

Fish

COCKLE CAKES

A recipe from Gwent where they are called Teisen Gocos.

Enough for 4

4 dozen cockles in their shells, or 350 g/12 oz shelled cockles, fresh or frozen
Salt
A little oatmeal
Deep oil for cooking

For the batter

225 g/8 oz flour
A pinch of salt
2 tablespoons oil
1 egg, separated
300 ml/½ pint tepid water

To serve: brown bread and butter, lemon wedges

1. If the cockles are in shells try to use them the day they are bought or gathered. Scrub well, rinse and put in a saucepan with 1 teaspoon salt. Pour boiling water over to cover and boil cockles for 3 minutes. Then drain and leave to cool.
2. If using shelled cockles, wash very well to remove grit and soak for 1 hour in cold water.
3. Meanwhile, start the batter. Put flour and salt in a basin, add oil, beaten egg-yolk and water. Beat well and leave in a cool place.
4. Remove cockles from shells.
5. Beat egg-white stiffly and fold it into batter.
6. Take 3 or 4 cockles at a time on a dessertspoon. Fill spoon with batter and drop into hot oil. Fry until golden.
7. Drain on kitchen paper.

Serve with brown bread and butter and lemon wedges.

Mrs Eileen Trumper
Llanvair Kilgeddin, Gwent

SPANISH COD

A delicious dish for a special occasion.

For 4 people

4 cod steaks, allow 150 to 175 g/5 to 6 oz per person

Sauce
25 g/1 oz butter or good margarine
25 g/1 oz plain flour
150 ml/¼ pint white wine
150 ml/¼ pint water
Pepper and salt

Topping
50 g/2 oz chopped onion
1 tablespoon olive oil
50 g/2 oz sliced mushrooms
1 tablespoon chopped green pepper
2 tomatoes, peeled (see page 72) sliced and seeds removed
50 g/2 oz prawns
1 tablespoon chopped parsley
Pepper and salt

1. Prepare a moderately hot oven— Gas 6, 400°F, 200°C.
2. Start with sauce. Melt butter or margarine over low heat, stir in flour and let it sizzle for a minute. Pour in wine and water gradually, stirring as it thickens and let it boil gently for 3 minutes. Season with pepper and salt.
3. Pour sauce into an oven dish. Use a dish in which cod steaks will fit side by side.
4. Wash and dry fish and place on top of sauce.
5. Fry onion in oil till soft but not brown.
6. Add mushrooms and green pepper and continue cooking for a moment longer until pepper starts to soften.
7. Stir in tomato, prawns, parsley, pepper and salt. Spread this topping over fish steaks.
8. Cover with a piece of greased paper and bake for about 30 minutes. Test fish by using the point of a knife in the centre of steaks. Fish loses its translucent appearance when cooked.

Anne Wallace
Stewarton, Ayrshire

COLEY WITH A HOT CUCUMBER SAUCE

Coley is very like haddock but is dark in appearance when raw. It cooks easily and turns very white.

4 small fillets of fresh coley, skinned
About 300 ml/½ pint milk
A little lemon juice

Sauce

1 small unskinned cucumber
Salt
A 142 ml/5 fl oz carton of single cream
142ml/5 fl oz plain yoghurt
1 teaspoon castor sugar
Pepper

1. Put coley in a shallow pan, barely cover with milk and poach gently either under grill or on top of stove for 15 to 20 minutes until done.
2. Drain off milk and keep fish hot in a serving dish.
3. Meanwhile make sauce. Grate the entire cucumber coarsely. Spread out the pulp in a flat shallow dish. Sprinkle with salt and leave for 20 minutes. Strain.
4. Turn pulp into a small saucepan. Stir in cream and yoghurt. Add sugar and pepper.
5. When mixture starts to bubble turn it into a jug to serve separately with the fish.
6. Sprinkle chopped parsley and a squeeze of lemon over fish.

FISH AND MUSHROOM PIE

Makes about 6 portions
275 g/10 oz rich pie pastry (*see page 105*)
125 g/4 oz mushrooms
150 ml/¼ pint water
450 g/1 lb white fish—e.g., cod, coley, haddock, whiting, etc.

Basic white sauce

50 g/2 oz butter or good margarine
50 g/2 oz flour
About 300 ml/½ pint milk
1 teaspoon chopped fresh tarragon, or ¼ teaspoon dried
Salt and pepper

1. Roll out two thirds of pastry to fit an 18 cm/7 inch pie plate and roll out the rest to fit top.

2. Stew mushrooms gently in the water in a covered pan for 5 minutes.
3. Drain liquid into a measuring jug. Slice mushrooms.
4. Meanwhile remove and discard skin and any bones from fish and cut it up into small pieces.
5. Now make the sauce. Melt butter or margarine over low heat, stir in flour and let it sizzle for a minute.
6. Add milk to mushroom liquid to make 450 ml/¾ pint. Add to pan gradually, stirring as it thickens and comes to boil. Let it bubble for 3 minutes.
7. Season sauce well with tarragon, salt and pepper.
8. Add fish and mushrooms to sauce. Allow to cool.
9. Fill the prepared pastry case. Damp edges and fit on lid pressing to seal. Do not make holes in top yet or filling may boil over and spoil top.
10. Bake near top of a moderately hot oven, Gas 6, 400°F, 200°C, for 45 minutes, moving pie to middle as it begins to brown. When it is done remove from oven and cut slits in top in one or two places, to let out steam and keep pastry crisp.

Serve hot or cold. Nice with green peas or beans.

Anne Wallace
Stewarton, Ayrshire

HADDOCK AND TOMATOES

With a crisp cheese topping

For 4 people
450 g/1 lb haddock fillets
Salt and Pepper Mix (*see page 44*)
2 teaspoons lemon juice
1 small onion, finely-chopped
4 tomatoes, skinned (*see page 72*) and sliced
2 tablespoons finely-grated cheese
4 tablespoons fresh breadcrumbs

1. Wipe and trim fillets, cutting into portions if too large, and arrange them in a shallow oven dish.

2. Sprinkle fish with salt, pepper and lemon juice.
3. Scatter onions on top and then make a layer of sliced tomatoes.
4. Mix together cheese and bread-crumbs. Sprinkle over tomatoes.
5. Cook at top of a moderate oven, Gas 4, 350°F, 180°C, for 30 minutes.

HADDOCK PUFFS

A Devonshire recipe. Very light and especially tasty with smoked fish. An economical alternative to scampi.

Enough for 4 as a starter, 3 as a main course

225 g/8 oz haddock, fresh or smoked
150 ml/¼ pint milk
50 g/2 oz self-raising flour*
1 tablespoon chopped fresh parsley, 1 teaspoon dried
Cayenne pepper
Salt
2 beaten eggs
Deep fat for frying

*Wholewheat flour can be used. If you cannot get self-raising wholewheat mix in ¼ level teaspoon baking powder.

1. Poach fish in milk almost to cover. It will take 10 to 15 minutes depending on thickness of fish. Then drain fish, saving the liquid.
2. Flake fish in a basin with 2 table-spoons of the liquid. Mix in flour, parsley, cayenne pepper and salt to taste. Salt will not be necessary with smoked haddock.
3. Mix in beaten egg and 2 to 3 table-spoons of the cooking liquid to make a soft consistency.
4. Deep-fry in hot fat, dropping mixture in a teaspoon at a time. Fry until golden brown, turning from time to time, about 3 to 4 minutes.

Serve very hot with brown bread and butter and tartare sauce (*see below*).

Mrs Becky Blackmore
Exeter, Devon

TARTARE SAUCE

300 ml/½ pint mayonnaise (*see page 64*)
1 tablespoon chopped capers
1 tablespoon chopped cucumber
1 teaspoon chopped parsley
½ teaspoon chopped onion
1 teaspoon vinegar

Prepare mayonnaise then mix into it all the other ingredients.

SMOKED HADDOCK IN SCALLOP SHELLS

Or in a fish pie.

1 kg/2 lb boiled and creamed potatoes
700 g/1½ lb smoked haddock
700 ml/1¼ pints milk
50 g/2 oz butter or margarine
50g/2 oz flour
75 g/3 oz grated cheese, Parmesan and Cheddar mixed
Pepper and salt
125 g/4 oz lightly-cooked green peas

1. Prepare potatoes.
2. Cook haddock gently in the milk. Strain, saving milk for the thick white sauce.
3. Melt 40 g/1½ oz of the butter, stir in flour and sizzle for 1 minute.
4. Gradually add milk, stirring as sauce thickens. Cook 3 minutes.
5. Stir in 50 g/2 oz of the grated cheese. Remove from heat.
6. Meanwhile flake the haddock, removing skin and any bones.
7. Fold the haddock and peas into the thick white sauce and adjust the seasoning.

To make a fish pie
Pour the fish mixture into a greased pie dish and top with the creamed potato. Smooth the potato then score across in a rough pattern. Dot with remaining 15 g/½ oz butter. Sprinkle on remaining cheese and brown under the grill.

Reheat when required in a moderate oven, Gas 4, 350°F, 180°C, for about 30 minutes.

To serve in scallop shells

Using a piping bag with a large star nozzle, put in the potato and decorate the border of each shell generously with stars. Fill centre of shells with haddock mixture. Sprinkle on remaining cheese and dot potato with last 15 g/½ oz of butter.

Reheat near top of a moderate oven, Gas 4, 350°F, 180°C, for about 20 minutes.

PILAFF OF SMOKED HADDOCK

For 4 people

350 g/12 oz smoked haddock
1 tablespoon oil
25 g/1 oz butter
1 onion, chopped
175 g/6 oz brown rice
1 green pepper, chopped
2 tomatoes, skinned (*see page 72*) and chopped
1 pint chicken stock
1 teaspoon turmeric
Pepper
Chopped parsley

1. Trim fish, removing any skin and bone. Cut it into bite-sized pieces.
2. Melt butter in oil and fry onion lightly. When soft but not brown stir in rice and dry for a minute.
3. Add fish, green pepper, tomatoes, stock, turmeric and pepper.
4. Bring to boil, cover pan, lower heat and cook gently until rice is almost tender—about 20 minutes.
5. Sprinkle liberally with chopped parsley just before serving.

Anne Wallace
Stewarton, Ayrshire

SMOKED FISH AND EGG ON TOAST

A snack for 4 people but a smaller quantity could easily be made

350 g/12 oz smoked fish fillet
150 ml /¼ pint milk
150 ml/¼ pint water
2 eggs
25 g/1 oz butter or margarine
25 g/1 oz wholemeal or white flour
Black pepper
2 tablespoons chopped parsley
Pieces of freshly-toasted crisp wholemeal bread
Mustard and cress

1. Put fish in a saucepan, pour over it the milk and water. Bring to the boil, cover pan and simmer for 10 minutes.
2. Put eggs in water to boil for 10 minutes.
3. When fish is done, remove from liquid and flake into largish pieces. Save the liquid.
4. When eggs are done, plunge them into cold water and remove the shells. (Held under running cold tap the eggs will not burn your fingers while you shell them.)
5. Roughly chop eggs and put them with flaked fish.
6. Melt butter or margarine in a pan, add flour and let it sizzle for a minute without browning.
7. Stir in 150 to 300 ml/¼ to ½ pint of the fish liquid. Stir over low heat until sauce is thick and let it simmer 2 or 3 minutes.
8. Add fish, egg, a grating of black pepper and the parsley and heat gently.

Serve on or with crisply-toasted wholemeal bread and have mustard and cress with it.

SAVOURY PUFFS

These are light and crisp with a moist centre. Good as a supper dish for 4 or 5 people or on cocktail sticks as hot savouries for a party.

Makes 40 bite-sized puffs

Can be frozen.

Choux pastry, quantity given on *page 106*
About 175 g/6 oz flaked smoked fish or any canned fish
Deep fat to fry
Chopped parsley
Paprika pepper

1. Prepare choux pastry paste and mix fish into it.
2. Have fat heated and drop small teaspoons of mixture into it, turning if necessary, so that they brown evenly. They puff up as they cook.
3. When golden brown, remove with a draining spoon on to kitchen paper. Keep hot while cooking rest of puffs.
4. Pile on a hot dish, sprinkle with parsley and paprika pepper.

Anne Wallace
Stewarton, Ayrshire

MUSTARD HERRINGS

For 4 people

4 fresh herrings
Salt and freshly-ground black pepper
40 g/1½ oz butter
50 g/2 oz onion, finely-chopped

Mustard sauce

15 g/½ oz butter
15 g/½ oz flour
1 large teaspoon made English mustard
A pinch of sugar
300 ml/½ pint water
4 tablespoons milk
25 g/1 oz grated cheese

1. Scale, gut, wash and trim heads, tails and fins from herrings. Cut each one open from belly to tail. Press out flat, skin side uppermost, and press along backbone. Turn fish over and lift out backbone from tail to head.
2. Lay in a large flat oven dish, season with salt and pepper. Cover with foil or a lid.
3. Bake in a moderately hot oven Gas 6, 400°F, 200°C, for 15 to 20 minutes.
4. Meanwhile melt butter in a small pan and cook onions until tender. Lay aside.
5. Take another pan to make the sauce. Melt butter, remove from the heat and beat in the flour and mustard.
6. Add sugar and blend in water gradually.

7. Return to heat and bring to boiling point. Simmer for 4 to 5 minutes, stirring often. Remove from the heat.
8. Add milk and half of the cheese.
9. Take dish out of oven, scatter cooked onion over herrings. Pour sauce over. Sprinkle with rest of cheese and brown under a hot grill.

FRESH MACKEREL SPICED IN CIDER

6 small mackerel
Wholewheat flour seasoned with salt and pepper (*see page 44*)
300 ml/½ pint apple juice, sparkling or still, or cider
½ level teaspoon pickling spice
2 bay leaves
1 medium-sized onion

1. To fillet the fish, follow instructions in Portland-style Mackerel (*see below*).
2. Sprinkle inside fish with a little seasoned flour.
3. Roll up fish loosely from tail to head and place them close together in a fairly deep oven dish.
4. Pour over apple juice or cider. Then sprinkle with pickling spice and add bay leaves. Peel and slice onion and spread over fish.
5. Cover dish with a lid or greaseproof paper and foil and put in a cool oven, Gas 1, 275°F, 140°C, for 1½ hours.
6. Remove from oven and allow to cool in the liquid.

Serve with boiled potatoes or brown bread and butter.

Sybil Norcott
Irlam, Nr. Manchester

PORTLAND-STYLE MACKEREL

For 4 people

4 fresh mackerel
Wholewheat flour, seasoned with salt and pepper (*see page 44*)

Gooseberry Sauce

225 g/8 oz gooseberries, fresh or frozen

30 ml/2 tablespoons water
50 g/2 oz sugar
25 g/1 oz butter
A pinch of nutmeg

1. If you have to bone mackerel yourself this is the way to do it. Gut and clean, removing head and tail. Cut open to backbone from belly to tail. Open out slightly and place on a board, cut side down. Bang hard with a rolling pin along the backbone until mackerel is flat. Turn fish over and backbone just pulls out, bringing most of the other bones as well. Pull out any long rib bones remaining. Trim off fins and tiny spines. Wash fish and pat dry.
2. Simmer gooseberries in the water until tender.
3. Put gooseberries through a sieve and then return purée to the pan.
4. Add sugar and stir well over gentle heat till it is dissolved.
5. Add butter and nutmeg and simmer for 5 minutes.
6. Dust mackerel with seasoned wholewheat flour.
7. Grill until golden brown, 4 to 5 minutes each side. Time varies according to size of fish.

Serve sauce separately.

John Firrell
Piddletrenthide, Dorset

SALMON MOUSSE

It is nice to use a fish-shaped mould for this.

A 212 g/7½ oz tin of salmon
1 dessertspoon tomato purée*
15 g/½ oz gelatine
2 tablespoons water
1 tablespoon vinegar
1 egg-white
A 175 g/6 oz tin of evaporated milk, refrigerated for 1 hour before using
1 teaspoon lemon juice

Decoration

A little paprika pepper
1 stuffed olive
2 gherkins

*See To keep tomato purée fresh, p. 45

1. Lightly oil a suitable 850 ml/1½ pint mould.
2. Flake salmon, removing bones and dark skin. Mash it with tomato purée.
3. Using a small basin which will fit over a pan of very hot but not boiling water, put gelatine to dissolve in the water and vinegar. Stir once and leave until it becomes clear.
4. Whisk egg-white until firm.
5. In another bowl whisk cold evaporated milk until thick, adding lemon juice to help it thicken.
6. Stir gelatine into salmon. Fold in whisked milk, and then egg-white. Mix all together gently.
7. Pour into mould and leave 3 to 4 hours to set in a cool place. Goes a bit tough if it sets too quickly.
8. Turn out on to a flat dish. Sprinkle a little paprika pepper down the centre, place half a stuffed olive for the eye, and gherkins, sliced part-way and fanned out for fins.

A GOOD IMITATION ASPIC JELLY

Gives a shining finish to pieces of cold chicken set out for a salad. Can also be used to top a savoury mousse by decorating with slices of cucumber and tomato and then covering with jelly to a depth of 7 mm/¼ inch. Spectacular used to coat a large salmon or ham for a special meal. Try it for Avocado and Salmon Mousse (see page 14), or Salmon Mousse (see above), Fresh Trout with Herb Mayonnaise (see page 26), Poached Chicken (see page 38).

For this you need 1 or 2 refrigerator trays of ice-cubes.

25 g/1 oz gelatine
25 ml/1 fl oz water
A 300 g/11 oz tin of consommé
3 tablespoons sherry
Juice of half a lemon
425 ml/¾ pint water

1. Put the 25 ml/1 fl oz of water in a cup or small bowl, sprinkle the gelatine over the surface.

2. Set the cup or bowl in a pan of warm water. Heat gently, stirring all the time until the gelatine dissolves.
3. In a pan mix consommé, sherry, lemon juice and 425 ml/¾ pint water. Stir over low heat until it is liquid.
4. Strain in the gelatine and stir.
5. Now stand pan on a baking tin full of ice. Stir until the aspic is syrupy. It is now ready to use.

SOLE ON A BED OF PASTA SHELLS WITH PRAWNS AND CREAM SAUCE

For 4 people

100 g/4 oz butter
Salt and pepper
8 small fillets of sole
½ litre/¾ pint milk
175 g/6 oz pasta shells
50 g/2 oz flour
4 tablespoons dry sherry
150 ml/5 fl oz single cream
1 teaspoon anchovy essence or sauce
50 to 100 g/2 to 4 oz frozen prawns

To garnish: 2 tomatoes, lemon slices

1. Use 50 g/2 oz of the butter and divide it into 8 little pieces.
2. Shake a little salt and pepper on each fish fillet and roll it up around a piece of butter.
3. Place fish in an oven dish. Pour round 150 ml/¼ pint of the milk. Cover dish with greased paper or foil.
4. Cook in middle of a moderate oven, Gas 4, 350°F, 180°C for about 20 minutes until fish is cooked.
5. Meanwhile, put pasta on to cook in slightly salted water, allowing for it to be done when fish comes out of oven.
6. Then make a roux of remaining butter and flour. This means melting butter in a pan, stirring in flour and allowing it to sizzle for 1 minute without browning.
7. Stir in remaining milk and then liquid from fish. Stir over low heat until thick, and boil for 2 minutes.

8. When fish is done lift it carefully out of dish on to a plate for a moment.
9. Drain pasta and put it in fish dish. Set fish on top and keep it warm.
10. Return to the sauce. Add sherry, cream, anchovy essence and prawns. Bring it back to boiling point so that prawns are well heated.
11. Pour sauce over fish and garnish with slices of tomato and lemon.

Anne Wallace
Stewarton, Ayrshire

FRESH TROUT WITH HERB MAYONNAISE

A liquidiser is needed.

4 fresh trout, about 275 g/10 oz each
Wine vinegar
Salt

Mayonnaise

A bundle of fresh herbs, parsley, chervil (or fennel), chives, tarragon, spinach and water-cress (or sorrel), about 50 g/2 oz herbs altogether
1 very small onion or small shallot, very finely chopped
2 anchovy fillets
1 dessertspoon capers
1 small pickled gherkin
1 hard boiled egg-yolk
1 fresh egg-yolk
1 teaspoon lemon juice
25 ml to 50 ml/1 to 2 fl oz sunflower oil
Salt and freshly-ground pepper

To garnish: lettuce, cucumber slices

1. Leave heads and tails on trout, gut them, wash and wipe out with salt and kitchen paper.
2. Take a large pan, big enough to lay trout out flat. Try them for size and cover with water.
3. To each pint of water add 1 tablespoon vinegar and ½ teaspoon salt. Now remove trout.
4. Bring water to the boil, then slip in each trout. Bring back to the boil and at once remove pan from heat. Allow

the trout to get quite cold in the pan of stock.

5. Now for the mayonnaise.
Wash herbs.

6. Chop the onion or shallot very finely and put it in a pan of boiling water. Boil for 1 minute. Drain into a sieve and run under tap.

7. Put herbs, onion, anchovy fillets, capers, gherkin, both egg-yolks and lemon juice into a liquidiser.

8. Liquidise for 10 seconds at high speed. Then start to dribble in the oil, a little at a time until the mixture thickens and emulsifies.

9. Season with salt and pepper and more lemon juice if necessary.

10. Lift cold trout out of stock. Pat dry and lay it on a nice dish with lettuce and cucumber.

11. Serve mayonnaise separately, giving each person a little pot.

TUNA FISH CASSEROLE

For 2 people, or can be served in ramekins as a starter for 6 people.

1·2 litres/2 pints water
Salt
125 g/4 oz wholewheat pasta
A 100 g/3½ oz can of tuna fish
1 tin of condensed cream of
mushroom soup
50 g/2 oz butter
Pepper
A squeeze of lemon juice
(optional)
1 tablespoon chopped parsley

1. Bring the water to the boil. Add a little salt, then the pasta, and bring back to simmering point. Stir to make sure pasta is not sticking together then partly cover the pan and simmer for 7 minutes or more. Cooking time will depend on the type of pasta you use. It should be not quite done when you drain it.

2. Meanwhile, remove bones from the fish and flake it.

3. Drain the pasta and add to it the fish with the soup, butter, pepper and

lemon juice. Mix well. Taste for seasoning and return pan to heat.

4. As soon as it is hot stir in most of the chopped parsley. Turn the mixture into a warmed oven dish and brown it under the grill.

Sprinkle the rest of the parsley on top just before serving.

Anne Wallace
Stewarton, Ayrshire

TUNA TART

225 g/8 oz self-raising flour
½ level teaspoon salt
40 g/1½ oz butter or margarine
150 ml/¼ pint milk
200 g/7 oz can of tuna fish
2 teaspoons vinegar
225 g/8 oz tomatoes, fresh or tinned
75 g/3 oz grated Lancashire cheese
Stuffed olives (optional)

1. Sift the flour and salt into a bowl.

2. Rub in the butter or margarine until mixture is like fine breadcrumbs.

3. Mix to a soft dough with the milk.

4. Roll out on a floured board to 25·4 cm/10 inch round and lay this on a lightly-greased baking sheet, or use a loose-based flan tin of the same size. However, as this is like a pizza, roll dough to fit bottom only, not sides.

5. Drain oil from tuna, break it up and mix in vinegar.

6. Skin tomatoes (*see page 72*) and slice. If using tinned tomatoes, drain well before slicing.

7. Arrange the tomato slices on top of dough. Then cover with tuna.

8. Sprinkle on the cheese and decorate the top with sliced, stuffed olives.

9. Bake in a moderately hot oven, Gas 6, 400°F, 200°C for 30 minutes.

Eat hot.

Sybil Norcott
Irlam, Nr. Manchester

27

WHITING WITH MUSHROOMS

Enough for 2 or 3, but can be made in any quantity

Quick to make.

40 g/1½ oz butter
3 or 4 fillets of whiting
50 g/2 oz mushrooms, sliced
1 tablespoon chopped fresh parsley
25 to 50 g/1 to 2 oz fresh bread-crumbs

White sauce

15 g/½ oz butter or margarine
15 g/½ oz flour
150 ml/¼ pint milk
Salt and pepper

1. Start with sauce. Melt the 15 g/½ oz butter or margarine, stir in the flour and let it sizzle for 1 minute.
2. Gradually add milk, stirring as it thickens. Then cook for 2 minutes. Season to taste with salt and pepper.
3. Use some of the 40 g/1½ oz butter to grease an oven dish. Melt rest of butter in a pan.
4. Spread white sauce in dish.
5. Lay whiting fillets on sauce. Cover with mushrooms, and pour over melted butter.
6. Sprinkle parsley over mushrooms and finish with a layer of bread-crumbs.
7. Bake in a moderately hot oven, Gas 5, 375°F, 190°C for 15 to 18 minutes.

Chapter 3

Poultry, Game and Rabbit

BONED AND STUFFED ROAST TURKEY

For 5 to 6 people

The thought of carving a boned and stuffed turkey or chicken is very appealing, especially if you are doing it with a hungry family watching. Boning isn't really as difficult as it sounds. All you need is an extremely sharp, short-bladed knife, a steel to keep it sharp and some nimble finger work.

A 1·8 to 2·3 kg/4 to 5 lb turkey, with giblets

Stuffing

200 g/7 oz prunes, soaked overnight
75 g/3 oz butter
1 large onion, finely-chopped
125 g/4 oz fresh wholewheat breadcrumbs
50 g/2 oz sultanas
50 g/2 oz chopped walnuts
Grated rind and juice of 1 lemon
2 tablespoons chopped fresh parsley
Salt and pepper
1 beaten egg

To roast

75 g/3 oz bacon fat or good dripping
225 g/8 oz streaky bacon, cut off rinds

Gravy

Giblets
A piece of onion
A piece of carrot
1 bay leaf and 4 peppercorns
600 ml/1 pint water
25 g/1 oz flour

To bone the bird

1. Lay it breast down on a board. Cut right down the back from neck to tail, or parson's nose.
2. Now start cutting the flesh from the carcass, working down and completing one side at a time. Very short cutting movements are needed. In some places by careful manipulation with the fingers the flesh can be pushed off the bone. Continue cutting, keeping close to the bones all the time and taking care not to puncture the skin.
3. Cut through wing and thigh joints and continue cutting to release flesh up to the breast-bone.
4. Do not work on thigh bones or wings yet.
5. Now work round other side of carcass.
6. When both sides are clear, cut up and along the breast bone. Take care not to break the skin as the flesh is very thin along the ridge.
7. The whole carcass should now be free. Pull it out gently (and be sure to boil it later for a good full-bodied stock for soup).
8. Working from inside, remove thigh bones cutting carefully between bones where drumstick joins.

For this recipe leave the bones in the drumsticks and wings as this will give the stuffed bird a better shape. However, they can be removed and the cavity stuffed but it may be necessary to cut through the skin and flesh on the inner side—i.e., breast side.

Stuffing

1. Remove stones from prunes and chop flesh.
2. Melt 25 g/1 oz of the butter and fry onion until soft but not brown.
3. Combine prunes, onions, breadcrumbs, sultanas, walnuts, lemon rind and juice, a little of the parsley, salt and pepper. Mix with beaten egg.
4. Now cream remaining 50 g/2 oz butter with parsley, salt and pepper and use half of it to rub inside of bird.
5. Pack stuffing into all the corners of the bird and make the rest into a large wide sausage for the middle.
6. Using a large needle threaded with fine string, sew up the skin, with large overcasting stitches, reshaping the bird as well as possible. For safety, tie bird up with 2 strings around its middle.
7. Rub remaining parsley-butter over outside of bird.

To roast

1. Melt fat in a roasting tin. Put in the bird and baste it before it goes in oven. Cover with foil.

2. Roast in a moderately hot oven, Gas 6, 400°F, 200°C, for 1¼ to 1½ hours, or until done. 15 minutes before end of cooking time remove foil and spread bacon across bird.

To test if it is cooked, pierce thigh with a skewer. If juice is pink then it needs further cooking. If juice is clear it is done.

Cooking time is calculated at 15 minutes to the ½ kg/1 lb plus 15 minutes. Weigh bird after stuffing.

3. Meanwhile put giblets, onion, carrot, bay leaf, peppercorns and water in a pan. Put on lid and simmer for 40 minutes.

4. Remove bird from oven on to a warm serving dish and keep hot. Make gravy in roasting tin.

5. Pour off as much fat as possible from tin, leaving the residue of turkey juices.

6. Work flour into juices. Put tin on top of stove over low heat.

7. Gradually stir in strained giblet stock and extra water if necessary. Stir until gravy thickens. Let it boil for 1 minute.

8. Pour into a warm jug or serving boat and keep hot.

Try Cranberry and Orange Preserve (*see page 171*) with this.

AUNT POLLY'S PIE

A way to use left-over turkey, chicken, stuffing and stock.

225 g/8 oz bacon rashers
225 g/8 oz left-over chicken or turkey
225 g/8 oz pork sausage-meat
50 ml/2 fl oz stock from boiling chicken carcass
Left-over stuffing

1. De-rind bacon, lay rashers on a board and, using a knife with a wide blade, press out rashers to stretch and widen them.

2. Line a deep pie-dish with bacon rashers, saving 1 or 2 for later.

3. Add chicken or turkey cut up into bite-sized pieces.

4. Cover with a layer of sausage-meat.

5. Pour over the stock.

6. Bake in a warm oven, Gas 3, 325°F, 160°C for 10 to 15 minutes. Then remove pie from oven and press stuffing over top. Cover with remaining bacon. Bake a further 20 minutes.

Can be eaten hot from the dish or cold, turned out and sliced.

Sybil Norcott
Irlam, Nr. Manchester

RISSOLES

Chicken or Turkey and Bacon

125 g/4 oz cooked chicken or turkey, finely-minced
1 rasher of bacon
50 g/2 oz fresh brown bread-crumbs (*see page 33*)
Salt and pepper
1 tablespoon basic white sauce (*see page 94*) **or 1 egg-yolk**
1 beaten egg
Dried breadcrumbs to coat rissoles (*see page 33*)
Deep fat or oil to fry

1. Prepare chicken.

2. De-rind bacon, fry it until really crisp, then crush into small pieces.

3. Mix chicken, bacon and fresh breadcrumbs with enough white sauce or egg-yolk to bind it together.

4. With floured hands, shape mixture into short fat sausages. Leave aside to firm up.

5. Dip rissoles in beaten egg, then in breadcrumbs. Leave aside to firm up.

6. Heat fat or oil until really smoking. Fry rissoles until golden. Drain on kitchen paper.

Ham

125 g/4 oz cooked ham, finely-minced
50 g/2 oz fresh brown bread-crumbs
1 teaspoon chopped fresh parsley
Salt and pepper

1 tablespoon basic white sauce
(*see page 94*) or 1 egg-yolk
1 beaten egg
Dried breadcrumbs to coat
rissoles
Deep fat or oil to fry

1. Mix ham, fresh breadcrumbs and
parsley. Season well with salt and
pepper.
2. Bind mixture with sauce or egg-
yolk.
3. With floured hands, shape mixture
into short fat sausages. Leave in
refrigerator to firm up.
4. Dip sausages in beaten egg, then in
dried breadcrumbs. Refrigerate for 1
hour.
5. Heat fat or oil until nearly smoking
hot. Fry rissoles until golden and
crisp. Drain on kitchen paper.

ROAST DUCKLING WITH WALNUT SAUCE

For 4 people

A 2 kg/4 to 4½ lb duckling
Salt

Sauce

2 tablespoons duckling dripping
1 medium-sized onion, chopped
50 g/2 oz walnuts, chopped
1 level tablespoon plain flour
300 ml/½ pint duckling stock
Grated rind and juice of 1
orange
2 tablespoons sherry
2 teaspoons chopped parsley

To serve and garnish

1 tablespoon duckling dripping
25 g/1 oz walnut halves
Watercress
1 orange, cut into slices

1. Wipe duckling dry inside and out.
Place on a rack in a shallow roasting
tin. Prick the skin all over with a fork.
This allows the fat to flow out during
cooking and bastes the bird without
any attention. Sprinkle well with salt.
2. Place in a hot oven, Gas 7, 425°F,
220°C and immediately reduce heat to
a moderate, Gas 4, 350°F, 180°C. Roast

for 1½ to 1¾ hours or until tender and
well browned, and the juices run clear
when the thickest part of the leg is
pierced with a skewer.
3. To prepare sauce. Heat duckling
dripping in a pan, add chopped onion
and walnuts and cook gently until
lightly browned.
4. Stir in flour and cook 1 minute.
5. Gradually blend in stock, orange
rind and juice and simmer gently for 2
minutes, stirring throughout.
6. Stir in sherry and chopped parsley
and season to taste.
7. To serve. (a) Gently fry walnut
halves in duckling dripping then drain
well on kitchen paper.
(b) Put duckling on a hot serving dish
and garnish with watercress, fried
walnuts and orange slices. Serve
walnut sauce in a separate bowl.

For a party

ROAST DUCKLING WITH 3 SAUCES

Apricot

A 425 g/15 oz tin of apricot
halves in syrup

Apple

2 large cooking apples
1 tablespoon lemon juice
2 tablespoons water
15 g/½ oz butter
1 tablespoon sugar

Redcurrant Jelly Sauce

3 to 4 tablespoons redcurrant
jelly
1 tablespoon water
Finely-grated rind and juice of ½
lemon
A good pinch of nutmeg

To serve and garnish

2 to 3 teaspoons redcurrant jelly
1 rosy dessert apple
A little lemon juice
Watercress

Apricot Sauce
1. Reserve 8 apricot halves for
decoration and heat through in oven
10 minutes before end of cooking time.

2. Press remaining fruit and syrup through a sieve, or liquidise. Heat through in small pan.

Apple Sauce
1. Peel and core apples then slice into a saucepan.
2. Add lemon juice and water and simmer gently until soft and pulpy.
3. Beat in butter and sugar.

Redcurrant Jelly Sauce
Place all ingredients in a small saucepan and stir over gentle heat until jelly has dissolved. Simmer 2 minutes.

To serve
Fill apricot halves with a little redcurrant jelly. Cut fine slices of unpeeled apple and sprinkle with lemon juice. Arrange these on a warm serving dish around the duckling and decorate with sprigs of watercress.

Serve the three sauces in similar containers so that guests may help themselves.

Any remaining sauces may be mixed together to make a tasty sauce to serve with grilled sausages or cold meats.

Audrey Hundy
Abbots Morton, Worcestershire

BASIC STUFFING FOR POULTRY AND MEAT

This can be made in bulk and frozen without its main seasoning or flavouring ingredients.

700 g/1½ lb onions
350 g/12 oz fresh breadcrumbs, wholewheat or white
50 g/2 oz butter or margarine
50 g/2 oz shredded suet
2 lemons
1 beaten egg
Salt and pepper
A variety of flavourings, some of which combine well with each other:
Chopped prunes, soaked in water overnight
Chopped apricots, soaked overnight
Chopped apples
Chopped celery
Chopped herbs like sage, parsley, marjoram, thyme, etc.
Chopped nuts

1. Peel and finely chop onions, fry in butter until soft.
2. Cool, mix with the rest of the ingredients. Season well.
3. Divide into four: freeze in separate bags.
4. To use, defrost and add the selected flavouring ingredients. The stuffing is then ready to use.

TO MAKE DRIED BREADCRUMBS

1. Lay slices of stale bread in a dry roasting tin and place in the bottom of the oven while something else is cooking. Remove when dry and brittle.
2. Now crush, using a rolling pin.

If really well dried they should keep in airtight jars for months.
Use for coating fish, chicken, rissoles, etc., before either shallow or deep frying.

Fresh breadcrumbs are made from semi-fresh bread using an electric coffee grinder, blender or food processor. Or by hand with a grater. Most sliced bread is unsuitable because of its foam plastic nature.

Keep in a fridge for a few days. Freezes well.

For stuffings, treacle tart, etc.

CHICKEN KEBABS
For 2 people

This makes a very nice main course when served with Yoghurt and Tahini Dip (*see page 65*), Stir-fried Vegetables (*see page 77*) and hot Greek Pitta Bread (*see page 139*).

2 chicken portions, breast and wing pieces

It is cheaper to buy the chicken this way, although only the boned breasts are required for this recipe. Cut off the wings and with a sharp-pointed knife

33

cut bones away from breast flesh. The butcher will do this for you. Save the wings for another meal, like Chicken and Honey (*see below*).

Marinade

3 tablespoons corn oil
2 tablespoons soya sauce
2 heaped teaspoons coriander seeds or 2 level teaspoons ground coriander
A clove of garlic, crushed
1 tablespoon lemon juice
1 teaspoon brown sugar
$\frac{1}{2}$ teaspoon ground ginger
Salt and pepper

1. Start this the night before it is to be eaten. Prepare the chicken breasts, cutting flesh into bite-sized pieces.
2. Mix all the marinade ingredients, grinding the coriander seeds in a mortar or a mill.
3. Mix chicken into marinade and leave it overnight in refrigerator.
4. Next day Yoghurt and Tahini Dip can be made. (It is best made without garlic when accompanying this dish.) Vegetables for stir-frying should be prepared close to the time of the meal.
5. Finally, preheat grill to hot.
6. Thread chicken pieces on to skewers and grill about 5 minutes on each side until browning a little and cooked through. Any remaining marinade can be used to baste chicken as it cooks.

If serving with hot pitta bread cut each piece in half and open it like a pocket. Put in a little of the stir-fried vegetables, then some kebabs and finally the cold dip. Eat it like a sandwich.

Can also be served with well-flavoured brown rice.

Elizabeth Mickery
Pudsey, West Yorkshire

CHICKEN AND HONEY

For 3 people
Delicious with cold Yoghurt and Tahini Dip (*see page 65*).

6 chicken wings, thighs or legs
50 g/2 oz melted butter
2 tablespoons oil
2 teaspoons soya sauce
A little clear honey
Salt

1. Preheat grill to high.
2. Trim chicken, but leave skin on.
3. Mix butter, oil and soya sauce and brush this all over chicken. Put under grill.
4. Turn grill down to moderate heat and cook chicken for 15 minutes, turning several times.
5. Brush with any remaining oil mixture. Smear each wing with honey and sprinkle with salt.
6. Return to grill for another 10 minutes until cooked and the skin is dark brown and crisp.

Elizabeth Mickery
Pudsey, West Yorkshire

CHICKEN COOKED IN WHITE WINE WITH TOMATOES

This is the well-known Poulet Chasseur.

1 chicken, jointed, or 6 chicken pieces
2 tablespoons seasoned flour (*see page 44*)
50 g/2 oz butter or 2 tablespoons oil
1 large onion, chopped small
A clove of garlic, crushed
450 ml/$\frac{3}{4}$ pint chicken stock
Salt and pepper
A 400 g/14 oz tin of tomatoes
1 tablespoon tomato purée*
1 teaspoon soya sauce
A dash of Worcestershire sauce
A small glass of white wine, dry home-made wine is useful

See page 45 for a tip on how to keep tomato purée fresh

1. Roll chicken pieces in seasoned flour and brown in the fat in a frying pan. Remove from the pan.
2. Fry onion and garlic and remove from the pan.

3. Add 1 tablespoon of remaining flour to pan, stir in the chicken stock carefully and allow to thicken on a low heat.
4. Add seasoning, tomatoes, purée, soya sauce, Worcestershire sauce and wine.
5. Lastly, add chicken pieces, put on lid and cook gently on top of the stove for 1 hour. Or, transfer to a covered casserole and cook for 1 hour in a moderate oven, Gas 4, 350°F, 180°C.

Mrs Patricia Chantry
Hook, Goole, N. Humberside

CHICKEN CASSEROLE

For 4 people

65 g/2½ oz butter or margarine
4 chicken joints
1 onion, finely-chopped
2 sticks celery, finely-chopped
225 g/8 oz long grain brown or white rice
A 400 g/14 oz tin of tomatoes
600 ml/1 pint stock
1 teaspoon mixed herbs
1 level teaspoon sugar
125 g/4 oz mushrooms, sliced

1. Heat 50 g/2 oz of the butter or margarine and brown the chicken joints. Lift them out of fat into a casserole.
2. Fry onion, celery and rice gently for 3 to 4 minutes.
3. Stir in tomatoes, stock, herbs and sugar. Bring to the boil, stirring.
4. Pour rice mixture over chicken. Cover the casserole and cook in a moderately hot oven, Gas 6, 400°F, 200°C, for 1 hour.
5. Heat remaining butter and fry mushrooms quite briskly for 2 minutes. Add to casserole.
Freezes well.

CEYLON CHICKEN CURRY

For 4 people

2 large onions
2 tablespoons ground coriander
2 teaspoons ground cumin
1 teaspoon chilli powder
½ teaspoon turmeric
¼ teaspoon cardamom powder
A 5 cm/2 inch piece of cinnamon bark, or ¼ teaspoon ground cinnamon
2 teaspoons salt
4 cloves of garlic, finely-chopped
4 tablespoons vegetable oil
A 1·4 kg/3 lb chicken, jointed
50 g/2 oz creamed coconut
350 ml/12 fl oz hot water
Juice of 1 lemon
2 tablespoons finely-chopped fresh coriander leaves, if you can get them

1. Grate one of the onions and mix with the spices and salt.
2. Finely-slice second onion and fry with garlic in the heated oil until golden brown.
3. Add grated onion and spice mixture and stir for about 5 minutes until heated through.
4. Add chicken joints and fry for another 5 minutes until well-coated in mixture in pan.
5. Dissolve creamed coconut in the hot water and add to chicken.
6. Bring to the boil, lower heat, cover pan and simmer for about 1 hour until chicken is cooked.
7. Before serving, add the lemon juice and garnish with the coriander leaves if available.

Serve with Boiled Rice (*see page 86*) or rice sticks or noodles.

Priya Wickramasinghe
Cardiff

FRIED TARRAGON CHICKEN

For 2 or 3 people

225 g/8 oz chicken pieces, breast, wings or legs
1 beaten egg
1 to 2 tablespoons dried breadcrumbs (*see page 33*)
20 g/¾ oz butter
20 g/¾ oz lard

Marinade (*see page 52*)

2 tablespoons oil
2 tablespoons white wine, or
cider vinegar, or lemon juice
1 large teaspoon finely-chopped
fresh tarragon or ½ teaspoon
dried
A clove of garlic, crushed
½ teaspoon dry mustard

Sauce

150 ml/¼ pint chicken stock
1 teaspoon cornflower
1 tablespoon water
Salt and pepper

1. Remove skin from chicken.
2. Mix marinade ingredients.
3. Lay chicken pieces in a flat dish.
Pour over marinade and leave for 2 or
3 hours. If you like tarragon flavour
leave overnight.
4. Remove chicken and pat dry. Save
marinade for the sauce.
5. Dip chicken pieces in beaten egg
and then in breadcrumbs.
6. Heat butter and lard and fry
chicken until crisp, brown and cooked.
7. Meanwhile, make sauce. Put
marinade in a pan with chicken stock.
8. Slake cornflour in water and add to
pan. Bring to the boil, stirring as
sauce thickens. Simmer 2 or 3 minutes.
Season to taste.
9. Put chicken on a warm dish. Serve
sauce separately.

HUFFED CHICKEN

In this old Sussex recipe a chicken was
stuffed, then wrapped in suet pastry
and probably a pudding cloth, and
boiled for several hours. This is an
updated and delicious adaptation.

4 chicken breasts

Stuffing

100 g/4 oz prunes, stoned and
chopped
100 g/4 oz cooking apples,
peeled, cored and chopped fine
1 large onion, finely-chopped
25 g/1 oz fresh wholewheat or
white breadcrumbs
Rind of half a lemon
Pepper and salt
1 small beaten egg

Suet Pastry

450 g/1 lb plain flour
½ level teaspoon salt
225 g/8 oz shredded suet
225 to 275 ml/8 to 10 fl oz cold
water
Beaten egg, to glaze

1. Remove skin from chicken and bone
it if necessary. Cut a pocket in each
breast.
2. Mix stuffing ingredients and fill the
pockets.
3. Prepare suet pastry. Mix flour, salt
and suet, then mix with water to make
a firm dough.
4. Using a floured board, roll out
about 7 mm/¼ inch thick.
5. Cut pastry to wrap around each
piece of chicken. Damp edges and press
together. Put on a greased baking tray
with pastry join underneath.
6. Make pastry leaves to decorate and
stick them on with water. Brush with
beaten egg.
7. Bake in a moderately hot oven, Gas
6, 400°F, 200°C, for 30 minutes, when
the pastry will be golden brown and
crisp.

Mrs Janice Langley
Shoreham-by-Sea, West Sussex

INDONESIAN CHICKEN SATE

For 4 people

A 2 kg/4 lb fresh chicken

Marinade

2 tablespoons soya sauce
2 tablespoons cooking oil
2 tablespoons hot water

Peanut Sate Sauce

175 g/6 oz roasted peanuts
4 dried red chillis
2 tablespoons shallots, chopped
2 tablespoons soya sauce
1 tablespoon brown sugar
1 teaspoon salt
1 tablespoon oil
125 ml/4 fl oz water

To garnish: lime wedges, if
possible, or lemon

1. Skin the chicken, remove flesh from bone and cut it into bite-sized pieces.
2. Take 8 skewers and thread a few pieces of meat on to each skewer.
3. In a shallow dish mix the marinade ingredients.
4. Lay skewered meat in this marinade for at least 3 hours, turning from time to time.
5. While the meat is marinating, prepare the peanut sate sauce.
6. Using an electric blender or a mortar and pestle, grind and blend all sauce ingredients except oil and water to form a smooth paste.
7. In a pan, heat oil and fry these ingredients until the oil separates.
8. Add a half cup of water and bring to the boil.
9. Reduce heat and simmer for 5 minutes.
10. While sauce is simmering, grill or barbecue the skewered chicken on a low flame, taking care to brown evenly on all sides.
11. Just before serving, arrange the skewered chicken pieces on a platter and pour the peanut sauce over them.
12. Garnish with lime wedges when available, or lemon.
This goes well with rice and salads.

Priya Wickramasinghe
Cardiff

SIMPLE BARBECUED CHICKEN

For 4 people
4 chicken joints
1 tablespoon oil
40 g/1½ oz butter
1 onion, chopped
2 dessertspoons tomato purée
2 level teaspoons barbados sugar
1 teaspoon prepared mustard
1 teaspoon Worcestershire sauce
1 level teaspoon salt
Black pepper
Juice of half a lemon
150 ml/¼ pint water

1. Dry the chicken joints and fry in oil and 25 g/1 oz of the butter until nicely browned. Lift out into a casserole.

2. Add remaining butter to pan and lightly fry onion until soft and golden.
3. Add all remaining ingredients and simmer for 5 minutes. Pour over chicken.
4. Cover casserole and cook in a moderate oven, Gas 4, 350°F, 180°C for 1 hour.

This dish freezes well.

Judith Adshead
Mottram St. Andrew, Cheshire

SPICY CHICKEN JOINTS

For 4 people

4 chicken joints
25 g/1 oz butter
1 tablespoon oil
2 large onions, finely-chopped
1 green pepper, de-seeded and chopped
A clove of garlic, finely-chopped
2 teaspoons dry mustard
2 tablespoons tomato purée*
300 ml/½ pint chicken stock
25 g/1 oz soft brown sugar
3 tablespoons vinegar
1 teaspoon Worcestershire sauce
½ teaspoon salt
1 large sprig fresh tarragon, or ½ teaspoon dried

See how to keep tomato purée fresh, page 45.

1. Skin the chicken joints.
2. In a pan, combine butter and oil and fry chicken joints on all sides until brown.
3. Remove joints to a large casserole.
4. Now lightly fry onion, green pepper and garlic for 3 to 4 minutes.
5. Mix mustard into tomato purée and add stock, sugar, vinegar, Worcestershire sauce and salt. Lastly add the tarragon. Stir until sugar is dissolved.
6. Cover casserole and put it in a moderate oven, Gas 3, 325°F, 160°C, for about 2 hours or until chicken is tender.

TANDOURI CHICKEN

A recipe from the Punjab.
Traditionally a brilliant red, but
colouring is not necessary.
Serves 4 people

A fresh 1·6 kg/3½ lb chicken
1 medium-sized onion, minced
or finely-chopped
3 cloves of garlic, chopped
1 teaspoon fresh ginger,
chopped (*see opposite*)
1 cup natural yoghurt
Rind and juice of 1 lemon
2 tablespoons vinegar
1 tablespoon paprika powder
2 teaspoons garam masala (*see*
opposite)
2 teaspoons coriander powder
1 teaspoon cumin powder
½ teaspoon red food colouring
(optional)

To serve and garnish

2 tablespoons ghee (*see opposite*)
Lettuce leaves
Fresh onion rings
Cucumber slices
Lemon wedges

1. Skin the chicken, then cut it into 2
along breast bone and back bone.
2. Using a sharp knife, make slanting
incisions 2·5 cm/1 inch long in the
chicken on each limb and breast,
taking care not to cut through to the
bone.
3. In a non-metallic large bowl mix all
other ingredients except those listed
for serving and garnish. This will
make a brilliant red marinade.
4. Marinate the chicken in this spicy
yoghurt mixture for between 8 and 24
hours.
5. Turn the chicken occasionally in
the marinade to ensure that all sides
become uniformly soaked.
6. Heat oven to very hot, Gas 8, 450°F,
230°C.
7. Lift chicken out of marinade and
place on a greased wire rack over a
baking tray. Cover with foil.
8. Roast on top shelf of oven for 1
hour. Baste chicken with marinade
mixture once during the cooking.
9. Just before serving, heat ghee, pour
it over the chicken halves and ignite.

10. Serve the chicken on a bed of
lettuce garnished with onion rings,
cucumber slices and lemon wedges.
Serve with Pitta Bread (*see page 139*).

Priya Wickramasinghe
Cardiff

Oriental Recipes

The oriental recipes to be found in this
book have been devised using ingredients
readily available in Britain and the West
and it is to be hoped you will see Mrs
Wickramasinghe making some of the
dishes in the television programmes. A few
explanatory notes follow.

Curry leaves are used fresh if possible.
They are aromatic and slightly pungent
and although not like the bay leaf they are
used in a similar way. Available from
continental and oriental food shops.

Fresh ginger is infinitely preferable to
dried ginger powder. Sometimes called
green ginger, it can be bought in many
supermarkets and greengrocers, besides
the oriental food shops. Look for plump,
smooth roots. Avoid shrivelled pieces. It
freezes well.

Garam Masala, the Indian name for a
basic mixture of curry spices. Many people
prepare their own, grinding the whole
spices specially. It is obtainable ready-
prepared from Indian grocery shops and
some wholefood shops.

Ghee is much used in Indian cookery. It is
simply clarified unsalted butter. It can be
bought in oriental food shops. A cheaper
way is to make it at home. In a heavy-
bottomed pan heat 250 g/8 oz unsalted
butter on a very low heat for about 30
minutes. Do not allow it to smoke or burn.
Remove the floating scum. Strain through
a piece of muslin into a bowl. Allow to cool.
Store in refrigerator. Keeps for months.

Poppadoms are made with a special
blend of lentil flour. Buy them at oriental
food shops. They can either be grilled or
deep fried before serving.

POACHED CHICKEN

A way to prepare chicken when really
moist cooked chicken is required.
Provides also a delicious jellied stock.
(*See Chicken and Ham Pie below.*)

1 chicken
1 litre/1¾ pints water
1 onion, sliced

1 teaspoon mixed dried herbs
Salt and pepper

1. Put whole chicken into a pan which just contains it. *Or*, cut chicken into joints and put in a pan.
2. Add water, onion, herbs and seasoning. Cover pan.
3. Bring to the boil over gentle heat and cook until tender, 1½ to 2 hours.
4. Remove chicken from pan.
5. Boil stock to reduce quantity and so strengthen flavour and jelly properties.

Sybil Norcott
Irlam, Nr. Manchester

CHICKEN AND HAM PIE

A delicious pie to eat hot or cold. Can be made with left-over chicken but it needs to be moist, preferably poached, so that stock sets in a jelly when pie is cold (*see previous recipe*).

175 g/6 oz shortcrust pastry (*see page 104*)
350 g/12 oz cooked chicken, preferably poached
1 small onion, finely-chopped
15 g/½ oz butter
75 g/3 oz fresh breadcrumbs
75 to 125 g/3 to 4 oz cooked ham, minced or finely-chopped
1 teaspoon mixed herbs
Salt and pepper
A little beaten egg
300 ml/½ pint stock from poaching chicken or chicken bone stock

1. Make pastry and chill.
2. Remove skin and bones and cut chicken into pieces. Put them in a 1·2 litre/2 pint pie dish. A pie funnel may be useful.
3. Fry onion gently in butter for 3 minutes. Add to breadcrumbs with ham, herbs, seasoning and a little beaten egg to bind if needed.
4. Form into balls and place in dish with chicken. Pour in stock.
5. Roll out pastry to 1·5 cm/½ inch wider than needed to cover pie. Cut off a strip of this width.

6. Moisten edge of pie dish with water. Lay strip in place, moisten it, then cover pie with pastry, pressing to seal. Flute or fork the edge.
7. Brush with beaten egg or milk and decorate pie with the trimmings.
8. Bake near top of a moderately hot oven, Gas 6, 400°F, 200°C for 20 minutes.

Mrs Aileen Houghton
Kemsing, Nr. Sevenoaks, Kent

CHICKEN SALAD WITH AVOCADO

For 2 to 3 people as a main course, but served in lettuce leaves on small plates would make a starter for 4 people.

175 g/6 oz small macaroni, pasta shapes or noodles
Boiling water
1 teaspoon corn oil
Salt
2 chicken quarters, cooked*
1 tomato
1 avocado pear

*Chicken can be poached (*see previous page*)

Dressing

For this you need a liquidiser.

50 g/2 oz blue cheese
2 tablespoons mayonnaise (*see page 64*)
1 teaspoon lemon juice
A little milk
Salt and pepper

To serve: lettuce leaves

1. The dressing can be made in advance. Put cheese, mayonnaise and lemon juice in a liquidiser, switch on to blend until smooth.
2. As it blends, add milk a little at a time until a pouring consistency is made. Add salt and pepper to taste.
3. Boil macaroni, pasta or noodles in plenty of water with the oil and salt until it is cooked but firm to the bite. Then drain, run cold water through it and chill.

39

4. Meanwhile cut chicken and tomato into small pieces.
5. Skin the avocado, remove stone and dice flesh.
6. Toss all ingredients gently together with dressing and serve on lettuce leaves.

Elizabeth Mickery
Pudsey, West Yorkshire

PHEASANT CASSEROLE

Pheasant may be cooked whole or in joints.

50 g/2 oz seedless raisins
150 ml/¼ pint cider (or home-made white wine)
1 pheasant, about 1.1 kg/2½ lb
450 ml/¾ pint water
A small piece of carrot
1 medium-sized onion
2 sticks of celery
2 medium-sized cooking apples and 1 dessert apple
15 g/½ oz flour
Salt and pepper
A pinch of mixed spice
65 g/2½ oz butter
300 ml/½ pint stock (from giblets)
150 ml/5 fl oz yoghurt or cream

1. Put raisins to soak in cider or wine for 2 hours.
2. Remove giblets from pheasant and make stock by simmering them in the water for ¾ hour with the carrot, a quarter of the onion and a small piece of the celery. Then drain and reserve stock.
3. Chop remaining onion and celery finely. Peel, core and slice cooking apples.
4. Either truss pheasant by tying the legs, or joint it. Dust with flour seasoned with salt, pepper and spice.
5. Melt butter and turn pheasant in it to brown. Then lift it out on to a plate.
6. Fry onion gently until transparent. Then add celery and cooking apple and fry for a further 5 minutes.
7. Stir in any remaining flour and cook for 1 minute.

8. Add cider, raisins and stock and bring to the boil.
9. Put this and the pheasant into a pan which just contains it. Put on a tight-fitting lid and let it just simmer for about 1 to 1½ hours for a whole pheasant, 45 minutes to 1 hour for joints, or until tender. Cooking time will vary according to age of bird.
10. When tender, lift pheasant out into a warmed serving dish and keep it warm.
11. If the sauce is very runny, boil without lid to reduce and thicken. Then add yoghurt or cream, adjust seasoning and reheat but do not boil. Pour into a separate bowl if pheasant is served whole or around the joints in the serving dish.
12. Peel dessert apple, cut out core and slice into fine rings. Fry these lightly in remaining butter and set them on dish around the pheasant.

HARE CASSEROLE WITH MUSHROOMS

1 hare, weight about 1.1 kg/2½ lb, jointed into even-sized pieces

Marinade (*see page 52*)
1 tablespoon redcurrant jelly
75 ml/3 fl oz port or cream sherry
75 ml/3 fl oz wine vinegar
75 ml/3 fl oz mushroom ketchup
1 dessertspoon chopped mixed fresh thyme and marjoram or 1 level teaspoon of each dried
1 medium-sized onion, chopped

To cook hare
225 g/8 oz streaky bacon rashers
50 g/2 oz butter
2 medium-sized onions
50 g/2 oz plain flour
A clove of garlic, crushed
Salt and pepper
Nutmeg
1½ to 1¾ litres/2½ to 3 pints chicken stock
300 ml/½ pint red wine (home-made would be excellent)
225 g/8 oz button mushrooms

1. Melt redcurrant jelly and pour it into a dish. Mix in the other marinade ingredients.
2. Lay the pieces of hare in the marinade and leave for 3 hours.
3. Remove hare from marinade and pat dry. Strain the marinade, discarding onion, but keep liquid to add to gravy.
4. Cut up bacon, discarding rind.
5. Using a large pan, heat the butter, fry bacon gently for a few minutes, then remove to a dish.
6. Add chopped onion and fry gently until transparent. Remove to dish.
7. Sprinkle the flour into the pan and allow it to colour a rich brown.
8. Now put in pieces of hare, turning and shaking the pan to make sure that they are well browned, about 10 minutes. Remove hare.
9. To same pan add garlic, salt and pepper, nutmeg, onion, bacon, stock, wine and all the marinade. Stir well. Return the hare.
10. Put on lid, cook steadily for 1½ hours or until tender. This may be done on top of stove or in a warm oven, Gas 3, 325°F, 160°C.
11. Wash mushrooms and chop roughly.
12. When hare is tender, remove it on to a dish and keep warm. Strain the sauce, putting bacon with hare.
13. Add mushrooms to sauce, cover and simmer for 10 minutes. Then return hare and bacon to sauce and reheat for 10 minutes if necessary.

Serve with plain boiled potatoes and a green vegetable.

RABBIT CASSEROLE WITH DUMPLINGS

Can be done in oven or on top of stove.

700 g/1½ lb rabbit, jointed
1 tablespoon vinegar
Water
25 g/1 oz flour, seasoned with salt and pepper
40 g/1½ oz dripping
2 onions, sliced
2 apples, sliced
A 400 g/14 oz can of tomatoes, or 450 g/1 lb fresh ripe tomatoes, skinned and sliced (see page 72)
450 ml/¾ pint stock
1 tablespoon redcurrant jelly
1 slice of dry bread, without crusts
½ teaspoon made mustard
½ teaspoon mixed herbs

Dumplings*

125 g/4 oz self-raising flour
¼ teaspoon salt
50 g/2 oz grated suet
1 tablespoon freshly-chopped parsley or ½ teaspoon dried mixed herbs
3 to 4 tablespoons water

*See also Sussex Swimmers, page 54.

1. Soak rabbit joints for 1 hour in vinegar and water. Then drain, pat dry and roll them in seasoned flour.
2. Melt dripping in a pan. Fry rabbit for a few minutes, turning pieces over in hot fat to brown a little. Lift joints out into a casserole or large saucepan.
3. Fry onions and apples for just 1 minute. Then put them with rabbit.
4. Add the tomatoes to rabbit.
5. Stir stock into residue in pan. Add redcurrant jelly.
6. Spread mustard on dry bread, sprinkle on the herbs and put it into the stock. Allow to soak, then beat in. Pour over rabbit.
7. Cover the casserole and cook in a moderate oven, Gas 4, 350°F, 180°C, for 1½ hours. If using a saucepan, put on the lid, bring gently to the boil and simmer for 1½ hours.
8. Meanwhile, prepare dumplings. Mix flour, salt, suet and herbs. Mix to a softish dough with water.
9. Turn on to a well-floured board, cut into 8 pieces and roll them into balls.
10. 20 to 25 minutes before rabbit is done drop dumplings into casserole or pan and replace lid. Keep rabbit simmering as dumplings cook. In casserole allow 25 minutes. In saucepan allow 20 minutes.

SOMERSET RABBIT

Enough for 4 but easy to cut down for 1 or 2. Or, as it freezes well, cook quantity given, divide it into portions to suit your household and freeze for future use.

Goes well under a pie crust or cobbler or with dumplings.

1 rabbit
2 tablespoons flour, seasoned with salt and pepper
50 g/2 oz lard or oil
1 onion, chopped
450 g/1 lb mixed root vegetables, scrubbed and cut into chunks
1 tablespoon tomato purée or ketchup
1 teaspoon yeast extract such as Marmite
½ teaspoon mixed herbs
300 ml/½ pint cider
300 ml/½ pint light chicken stock
Salt and pepper

1. Keep the rabbit whole, or, if it will not fit your pan or casserole, just cut it in two between hind legs and rib cage. Dust it over with seasoned flour.
2. Heat lard in a pan and turn rabbit over in it to brown. Lift out of fat on to a plate.
3. Fry onion gently to soften.
4. Put rabbit in a pan or a casserole. Put vegetables on top and add other ingredients. Cover with a lid or foil. *Either* bring to boil and simmer until tender, about 1½ hours, *or* put casserole into a warm oven, Gas 3, 325°F, 160°C, for about 2 hours or until tender.
5. Lift out rabbit, remove all meat from bones and return it to pan. Be careful to remove the small pieces of bone. Re-heat.

Serve as a stew with potatoes and green vegetables, or with pasta shells. Or try one of the following:
As a pie, enough for 6.

Choose a pastry from pages 104 and 105. Allow meat to cool and put it in a dish which it nearly fills so that it supports pastry.
Bake in a hot oven, Gas 7, 425°F, 220°C, for 30 minutes. Check after 15 minutes, reducing temperature to moderately hot, Gas 5, 375°F, 190°C, if it is browning too quickly.
As a cobbler, enough for 6. Delicious with wholewheat flour.

225 g/8 oz self-raising wholewheat* or white flour
A pinch of salt
25 g/1 oz margarine
A bare 150 ml/¼ pint milk

*Use 1½ teaspoons baking powder if you cannot buy self-raising flour.

1. Put rabbit and gravy into a casserole which allows 5 cm/2 inches headroom. Let it cool.
2. Mix flour, salt and baking powder, if used. Rub in margarine and mix to a soft dough with milk.
3. Using a floured board, roll out 2 cm/¾ inch thick. Cut 5 cm/2 inch rounds and lay these overlapping on top of meat.
4. Bake above middle of a hot oven, Gas 7, 425°F, 220°C, for 30 minutes. If using wholewheat flour, check after 15 minutes and reduce temperature to Gas 5, 375°F, 190°C, if browning too quickly.

With dumplings, for 4 people.

175 g/6 oz self-raising flour
½ teaspoon salt
75 g/3 oz shredded suet
About 6 tablespoons water

1. Mix ingredients, using enough water to make a firm dough. Form into small balls and drop into bubbling pan or casserole.
2. Cover and simmer for 15 minutes.

Try also Sussex Swimmers (*see page 54*).

Mrs Angela Mottram
Axbridge, Somerset

Chapter 4

Beef, Lamb, Pork, Ham and Bacon

STEAK WITH BLACK PEPPER AND CREAM SAUCE

For 4 people for a very special occasion

15 g/½ oz crushed black peppers
4 large steaks, either rump, sirloin or fillet
50 g/2 oz butter
1 tablespoon olive oil
1 small onion, chopped
A 142 ml/¼ pint carton of double cream
Salt to taste

1. Press the crushed black pepper into the steaks
2. Fry steaks in the butter and oil for no more than 5 minutes each side.
3. Remove steaks to a hot dish. Fry chopped onion in steak pan for 2 minutes.
4. Add cream, heat but do not boil. Add salt to taste.
5. Pour over steaks and serve without delay.

Judith Adshead
Mottram St. Andrew, Cheshire

RUMP STEAK WITH RICE

For 2 people

275 g/10 oz rump steak
125 g/4 oz brown or white rice
1 large onion, sliced
2 sticks celery, sliced
1 red pepper (optional) cored and sliced
1 to 2 tablespoons wholewheat or plain four
1 teaspoon Salt and Pepper Mix *(see opposite)*
150 ml/¼ pint stock
2 teaspoons Worcestershire sauce
Chopped parsley

1. Cut fat from meat. Cut fat up small, put it in frying pan and fry to extract dripping. You will need 1 tablespoon. Discard the scraps of skin.
If meat is all lean use 25 g/1 oz beef dripping and heat it in frying pan.
2. Follow instructions for Boiled Rice *(see page 86)*.
3. Put onion and celery into frying pan to cook for 5 minutes till softening.
4. Meanwhile, cut steak into strips, 1·2 by 6 cm/½ by 2½ inches. Dust lightly with flour seasoned with Salt and Pepper Mix.
5. Add meat to frying pan and turn it over to seal. Add red pepper. Cook for 7 to 8 minutes.
6. Stir in 3 to 4 tablespoons stock and Worcestershire sauce and let it bubble for 2 minutes, adding a little more stock if it is too thick. Taste and season with more salt and pepper if it is needed.
7. Make a border of rice on a warmed serving dish. Pour meat mixture in centre.
8. Sprinkle on chopped parsley and serve at once.

Serve with green vegetables or green salad.

DOROTHY SLEIGHTHOLME'S SALT AND PEPPER MIX

A mixture of 3 parts salt to 1 part pepper, black for flavour.
Keep in a sprinkler-topped jar.
Useful for flavouring savoury dishes, sauces, gravy, etc.

SEASONED FLOUR

Can be made and stored in a labelled jar. Use for coating fish or meat before grilling, frying, etc.

450 g/1 lb wholewheat flour
50 g/2 oz salt
15 g/½ oz black pepper
15 g/½ oz dry mustard
7 g/¼ oz paprika

This mixture can be divided into separate labelled jars, each incorporating a herb of your choice.

Sybil Norcott
Irlam, Manchester

STROGANOFF

Made with either beef or pork.

Enough for 6 to 8 people, but easy to make less

A 1 kg/2 lb single piece of fillet
of beef or fillet of pork
3 medium-sized onions
225 g/8 oz button mushrooms
About 25 g/1 oz butter
A little chopped fresh parsley

Sauce

25 g/1 oz butter
25 g/1 oz plain flour
1 level tablespoon tomato purée
(*see below*)
¼ level teaspoon nutmeg,
freshly-grated if possible
600 ml/1 pint beef stock
150 ml/5 fl oz yoghurt or soured
cream
Salt and pepper

1. **Start with the sauce.** In quite a
large saucepan melt butter, remove
from heat and stir in flour.
2. Stir in tomato purée and nutmeg,
then gradually stir in stock.
3. Bring to the boil, stirring as sauce
thickens, and simmer for 2 minutes.
4. Stir in yoghurt or soured cream
and season with salt and pepper.
5. **Now for the main part of the
dish.** Cut meat into strips about
5 cm/2 inches long and 1 cm/½ inch wide.
6. Peel and chop onions. Wipe and
finely-slice mushrooms.
7. Heat half of the butter in a large
frying pan and quickly brown the
meat on all sides. Remove from pan
into sauce.
8. Add a little more butter to the pan
if necessary and fry onions slowly
until tender and light brown. Put
these in sauce.
9. In the last of the butter fry
mushrooms for just 1 or 2 minutes. Put
these with meat and onions.
10. Bring the Stroganoff to the boil
and simmer it for 15 minutes.

Serve with boiled potatoes or rice (*see
page 86*).

TO KEEP TOMATO PURÉE FRESH

To keep tomato purée fresh once a tin
has been opened, spoon it into a screw-
topped jar. Smooth top and pour in a
layer of cooking oil. Keep in a cool
place. When it is required, pour off oil,
spoon out what you need, then return
the oil once again.

BEEF CASSEROLE

For 4 to 5 people
Remember to start the night before.
675 g/1½ lb stewing beef

Marinade (*see page 52 for a
note on marinades*)
3 tablespoons oil
1 tablespoon wine or cider
vinegar, or lemon juice
1 wineglass of red wine
1 carrot, sliced in fine rings
1 onion, sliced in rings
1 teaspoon chopped fresh
thyme, or ½ teaspoon dried
1 bay leaf

To cook
40 g/1½ oz lard
350 g/12 oz carrots, cut in
1 cm/½ inch slices
450 g/1 lb tomatoes, skinned (*see
page 72*) and chopped or a
400 g/14 oz tin of tomatoes
Salt and pepper
675 g/1½ lb potatoes, peeled and
thinly-sliced
150 ml/¼ pint beef stock

1. Put marinade ingredients in a pan
and simmer for 15 minutes. Leave to
cool.
2. Trim meat and cut it into 2·5 cm/
1 inch cubes. Put in a basin.
3. Pour cold marinade over meat and
leave overnight in refrigerator or a
cool place.
4. Strain marinade off meat and
reserve it.
5. Brown meat in hot lard and place in
a very deep casserole.
6. Add carrots, tomatoes and
seasoning to casserole.
7. Top with potato slices.
8. Pour over marinade and stock.

9. Cover casserole and cook in a warm oven, Gas 3, 325°F, 160°C, for 2 hours. For the last 15 minutes of cooking time remove lid to let the potatoes brown a little.

BRAISED STEAK WITH VEGETABLES

For 4 or 5 people

A 675 g/1½ lb single piece of lean braising steak cut about 2·5 cm/1 inch thick
675 g/1½ lb mixed vegetables, onions, leeks, carrots, celery, turnip—whatever you prefer
2 teaspoons flour
25 g/1 oz beef dripping
Salt and pepper
150 ml/¼ pint beef stock (*see page 8*)

Marinade (*see page 52*)
2 tablespoons oil
2 tablespoons vinegar
1 small onion, chopped
A clove of garlic chopped (optional)
6 peppercorns

1. Mix the marinade in a flat dish and soak the meat for 3 to 4 hours, turning occasionally.
2. Meanwhile, prepare vegetables and cut into 5 cm/2 inch pieces.
3. Remove meat from marinade, pat dry and dust well with flour.
4. Heat dripping in frying pan, seal meat quickly on both sides. Lift it out on to a plate.
5. Fry vegetables quickly in the frying pan until just golden.
6. Place them in the bottom of a casserole large enough to hold the steak in one piece. Season with salt and pepper. Place steak on top.
7. Remove peppercorns from marinade and pour it with stock into frying pan. Bring to the boil and pour into casserole.
8. Cover tightly to prevent drying up. If casserole has no lid, cover tightly with greaseproof paper and foil.
9. Cook in a warm oven, Gas 3, 325°F, 160°C for 1¼ to 1½ hours.

Can be served with jacket potatoes. Choose small ones, and rub well with butter, bacon dripping or oil. Spear them on skewers and they will cook at the same time as the meat.

SRI LANKAN BEEF CURRY

For 4 people

450 g/1 lb braising beef
2 tablespoons oil
1 medium-sized onion, finely-chopped
3 cloves of garlic, crushed
3 whole cardamoms*
3 whole cloves
A 2·5 cm/1 inch piece of cinnamon stick
50 g/2 oz creamed coconut*
125 ml/4 fl oz hot water
1 teaspoon fresh ginger (*see page 38*) chopped fine
2 teaspoons malt vinegar
1½ teaspoons ground coriander
1½ teaspoons ground cumin
1 teaspoon chilli powder
1 teaspoon salt
¼ teaspoon ground fenugreek
¼ teaspoon turmeric
¼ teaspoon freshly-milled black pepper

*Can be bought at oriental food shops.

1. Cut beef into 2·5 cm/1 inch pieces.
2. Heat oil and fry onions and garlic till just golden.
3. Add the meat and fry over a low heat until quite brown.
4. Grind together in a mortar or electric grinder the cardamom seeds, cloves and cinnamon stick and add to meat.
5. Dissolve the creamed coconut in the hot water and add it with all the other ingredients.
6. Put on the lid and simmer for 1 hour.

Priya Wickramasinghe
Cardiff

CASSEROLED SHIN OF BEEF

This casserole may be made with varying quantities of meat and vegetables according to what you have and how many are to eat it. It is just as good reheated as when it is freshly made, so it is worth making enough for two meals.

2 large onions
2 large carrots
1 stick of celery
1 small parsnip or turnip
A clove of garlic
1 kg/2 lb shin of beef or stewing steak
40 g/1½ oz wholemeal or plain flour
½ teaspoon dried marjoram
½ teaspoon salt
Freshly-grated black pepper
40 g/1½ oz dripping
A wineglass of red wine, or cider or 2 tablespoons vinegar
A 400 g/14 oz tin of tomatoes
Water
Fresh parsley

1. Peel onions and cut them into large pieces. Scrub carrots and cut them into large chunks. Cut up very finely the celery and parsnip or turnip. Crush the garlic.
2. Trim off excess fat and hard gristle from the meat and cut it into easy pieces, about 5 cm/2 inches long, 2·2 cm/½ inch thick. Mix together flour, marjoram, salt and pepper on a plate or in a clean paper bag or polythene bag. Toss the meat in this seasoned flour to coat it well. (*See page 44 for a tip about seasoned flour.*)
3. Heat half of the dripping in a heavy saucepan or a flameproof casserole. (Flameproof means one which can stand direct heat on top of the stove and can also go into the oven.) Add onion and fry till it begins to brown. Then lift it out with a draining spoon on to a plate.
4. Now add remaining dripping and heat till it begins to smoke. Then add the meat, turning it over quickly to brown.
5. Turn down heat and add wine or cider but not the vinegar. Let it bubble for a minute.
6. Now, if you are using a saucepan which cannot go into the oven, turn the contents into a large casserole.
7. Add the onions, garlic, carrots, celery, parsnip or turnip.
8. Add vinegar, if used instead of wine or cider.
9. Now empty the tin of tomatoes on top, refill the tin with cold water and pour in enough just to cover the meat and vegetables.
10. Tie a bunch of parsley together with cotton or string and lay it on top.
11. Cover the casserole and put it in a moderate oven, Gas 4, 350°F, 180°C, for 2½ to 3 hours. After half an hour, when pot will be bubbling nicely, reduce heat to very cool Gas ½, 250°F, 120°C, and let it go on cooking for another 2 hours. If you are using shin of beef a total of 3½ hours is not too long.
12. Remove the bunch of parsley and add freshly-chopped parsley, if you can spare it, just before serving.

STUFFED SKIRT OF BEEF

A very old Gloucestershire recipe, economical and nourishing.

1 kg/2 lb skirt of beef

Stuffing
100 g/4 oz medium oatmeal
50 g/2 oz shredded suet
1 dessertspoon chopped parsley and other herbs to taste
25 g/1 oz finely-chopped onion
Salt and pepper
A little milk

To cook
50 g/2 oz dripping
225 g/8 oz chopped onions
1·2 litres/2 pints brown stock (*see page 8*)
Salt and pepper
125 g/4 oz carrots
125 g/4 oz turnips
50 g/2 oz cornflour
2 tablespoons water

1. Buy the skirt in one piece. Remove skin and with a sharp knife slice a deep pocket in the meat.

2. Combine all stuffing ingredients using enough milk just to bind it.
3. Stuff the pocket in meat and sew up the opening.
4. Melt dripping in a heavy saucepan and brown meat and onions.
5. Add stock and salt and pepper if necessary. Bring to the boil and simmer very gently for 2½ to 3 hours.
6. About 45 minutes before end of cooking time add carrots and turnips, scrubbed and sliced into even-sized pieces.
7. Blend cornflour with water and add to pan at last minute to thicken.
8. Lift out meat and remove sewing thread.
9. Put meat on a hot dish surrounded by carrots and turnips.

Gloucester College of Agriculture, Hartpury

STUFFED BEEFBURGERS

A good way to use up any kind of stuffing.

For 4 people

350 g/12 oz minced beef
Salt and pepper
1 teaspoon Worcestershire sauce
4 heaped teaspoons stuffing
25 g/1 oz flour
1 to 2 tablespoons dripping
1 sliced onion
Half a cup of stock

1. Season mince with salt, pepper and Worcestershire sauce.
2. Divide mince into 8 portions and flatten each one into a thin round.
3. Place stuffing on four of the rounds and cover with remaining four. Pinch edges well together.
4. Dust beefburgers with flour.
5. Meanwhile fry onions in dripping until golden. Make space for the beefburgers and fry them until brown on both sides.
6. Remove browned beefburgers to a plate.
7. Mix in with fried onions any remaining flour. Stir in stock and let it thicken.
8. Replace beefburgers in pan, put on

lid and cook very gently for about 30 minutes.
Serve with creamed potatoes and a green vegetable.

Anne Wallace
Stewarton, Ayrshire

MINCED MEAT CURRY

For 4 people

2 tablespoons oil
1 medium onion, chopped
3 cloves garlic, chopped
2 green chillis, finely chopped
½ teaspoon chopped fresh ginger
2 teaspoons ground coriander
2 teaspoons ground cumin
1 teaspoon garam masala*
¼ teaspoon turmeric
450 g/1 lb lean mince
1 teaspoon tomato purée
50 g/2 oz creamed coconut
125 ml/4 fl oz hot water
1 cup fresh or frozen peas
***Can be bought at wholefood shops and oriental food shops.**

1. Heat oil and fry onions in it until just golden.
2. Add garlic, chillis, fresh ginger and other spices, and fry for a few seconds.
3. Add meat and continue to fry over a low heat.
4. Mix in tomato purée.
5. Dissolve creamed coconut in the water, mix it in, cover pan and allow to simmer for ¾ to 1 hour.
6. Toss in the peas and cook for a further 10 minutes.

Serve with Boiled Rice (*see page 86*), Curried Bhindi (*see page 73*) or Cauliflower Bhaji (*see page 74*) and salad.

Priya Wickramasinghe
Cardiff

SAVOURY BEEF CHARLOTTE

This recipe won first prize in a cooking competition judged by Dorothy Sleightholme and was given to her for this book.

For 3 or 4 people

1 tablespoon oil
1 onion, finely chopped

2 carrots, scrubbed and finely
chopped
225 g/8 oz minced beef
15 g/½ oz plain flour, wholewheat or white
2 level tablespoons tomato
purée*
125 g/4 oz mushrooms, sliced
2 teaspoons chopped fresh
parsley
Salt and Pepper Mix (*see page 44*)
6 large slices bread, wholewheat
is best
50 g/2 oz margarine
1 small beaten egg

Sauce

2 level tablespoons tomato
purée
2 tablespoons vinegar
1 level tablespoon golden syrup
A pinch of dry mustard

*To keep tomato purée fresh, see page 45.

1. Heat oil in a large pan and put in
onions and carrot. Put on lid, turn
heat very low and cook for 10 minutes.
2. Stir in meat, flour and tomato
purée. Cook, stirring to break up meat,
for 5 minutes.
3. Mix in mushrooms, 1 teaspoon of
the parsley and salt and pepper. Cook
for 5 minutes, then remove from heat
to cool a little.
4. Meanwhile, spread margarine on
one side of slices of bread. Cut them to
fit and line sides and bottom of a
greased 1·5 litre/2½ pint oven dish. A
20 cm/8 inch soufflé dish is suitable.
5. Beat egg into cooled meat mixture
and turn into prepared dish. Cover
with a lid or greaseproof paper and
foil.
6. Put dish on a baking tray and into a
moderately hot oven, Gas 5, 375°F,
190°C, for 20 minutes.
7. Blend sauce ingredients together.
Pour over the charlotte and return
dish to oven uncovered for 10 minutes
more.
8. Sprinkle on the rest of the parsley
just before serving.

Mrs Jean Barnard
Harrogate, Yorkshire

MEAT BALLS IN A TANGY TOMATO SAUCE

Plenty for 6 people
Mixture makes about sixteen 50 g/2 oz
balls. Smaller balls can be made for a
fork-meal.

Meat Balls

2 rashers of smoked bacon
450 g/1 lb stewing beef
1 small onion
1 cup fresh wholewheat
breadcrumbs
1 egg
225 g/8 oz sausage-meat
1 level teaspoon salt
½ teaspoon pepper
2 tablespoons flour, seasoned
with salt and pepper
50 g/2 oz lard

Tomato Sauce

1 large onion
A 400 g/14 oz tin of tomatoes
25 g/1 oz lard
5 tablespoons brown sugar
4 tablespoons malt vinegar and
2 tablespoons water
1 tablespoon Worcestershire
sauce
2 teaspoons lemon juice
1 teaspoon dry mustard
Salt and pepper

1. Remove rinds from bacon. Mince
rashers together with beef and onion.
2. To this add breadcrumbs, egg,
sausage-meat, salt and pepper. Mix
thoroughly.
3. Make small balls of the mixture
about 4 cm/1½ inches in diameter and
roll them in seasoned flour.
4. Using a heavy frying pan, heat the
50 g/2 oz lard and fry meat-balls until
well browned all over. Lift out with a
draining spoon on to kitchen paper or
brown paper.
5. Cover casserole and put it in oven
while you quickly make sauce. Set
oven to moderate, Gas 4, 350°F, 180°C.
6. Peel onion and chop finely.
Liquidise tomatoes.

7. Fry onion in lard until soft but not brown.
8. Add all other ingredients. Simmer for 3 minutes.
9. Pour sauce over meatballs.
10. Cover casserole and return to the pre-heated oven for a further 30 minutes. Or, complete cooking on top of stove instead of oven, simmering for 30 minutes.

Don Oldridge
Goole, N. Humberside

POTTED BEEF

8 helpings

1 bacon knuckle
Water
450 g/1 lb shin of beef, cut into large pieces
1 stick of celery, sliced
8 peppercorns
1 bay leaf
A pinch of ground allspice

1. Place bacon knuckle in a large saucepan, cover with cold water. Bring to boil, then discard water.
2. Put beef, celery and rest of ingredients into pan with knuckle and add 1.1 litres/2 pints fresh cold water.
3. Bring to boil, skim off any scum, then lower heat. Cover pan and simmer for 2 to 2½ hours until beef is very tender. Or, pressure cook in 600 ml/1 pint of water for 50 minutes.
4. Strain off stock and reserve. Discard bay leaf and peppercorns. Allow meat to cool.
5. Slice beef finely, removing any fat or gristle.
6. Remove skin from bacon knuckle. Cut bacon into fine cubes.
7. Place meat into an 850 ml/1½ pint mould or bowl. Add stock to almost fill mould. Top up with cold water if necessary. Stir well and cover. Chill and leave to set, overnight if possible.
8. To serve, loosen mould around edges with fingers. Place serving plate on top, invert and shake to release meat.

ROAST STUFFED HEART

Enough for 4 or 5 people
Remember to start the night before.

1 calf's heart, about 1 kg/2 lb in weight
Water
Salt
Vinegar
300 ml/½ pint beef stock
1 level dessertspoon cornflour
2 tablespoons cold water

Stuffing
50 g/2 oz prunes, soaked overnight
50 g/2 oz cooked brown rice (*see page 86*)
50 g/2 oz walnuts, chopped
1 large cooking apple, peeled, cored and chopped
Grated rind of a lemon
25 g/1 oz melted butter
Pepper and salt

1. To prepare heart, cut away the membranes, gristle and veins. Wash thoroughly in cold running water to remove congealed blood. Soak for 4 hours in cold, salted water with 1 tablespoon of vinegar to each 600 ml/1 pint of water.
2. Meanwhile, prepare stuffing. Drain prunes, remove stones and chop flesh.
3. In a bowl, combine all stuffing ingredients.
4. Using a sharp knife enlarge the cavity of the heart and spoon in the stuffing.
5. Tie up like a parcel and place the heart with its stuffing downwards in a roasting tin.
6. Pour over the stock. Cover and bake for 1½ to 2 hours in a moderate oven, Gas 4, 350°F, 180°C, basting frequently.
7. Put the stuffed heart on to a warm dish and keep hot.
8. Pour juices from the tin into a small pan.
9. Slake cornflour in water and stir into juices. Heat gently, stirring as sauce thickens. Serve sauce separately.
Serve with green vegetables.

OXTAIL STEW

It is better to do the first part of the cooking the day before the stew is needed. This ensures that a great deal of the fat can be skimmed off.

1 oxtail
Salt and pepper
225 g/8 oz carrots, diced
225 g/8 oz turnips, diced
225 g/8 oz onions, chopped
2 tablespoons flour
Chopped fresh parsley

1. Trim any surplus fat from the ox-tail and cut it into its separate joints. Put into a bowl, cover with water and leave for 1 hour.
2. Drain and put the pieces in a stewpan. Add seasoning and cover with fresh water. Bring to the boil, reduce heat and simmer for 1½ hours.
3. At this point leave overnight.
4. Next day, skim off fat which has risen to the top.
5. Add chopped vegetables. Simmer again for 1½ hours or until tender.
6. Thicken just before serving. Mix flour to a smooth paste with a little cold water. Add to the stew, stir well and simmer again for a further 10 minutes.
Sprinkle generously with chopped fresh parsley if you have it.

Mrs A. Greenwood
Boroughbridge, Yorkshire

OXTAIL MOULD

1 oxtail
225 g/8 oz bacon in a piece or bacon pieces
1 small onion
4 cloves
Water
Pepper and salt to taste

1. Wash and joint the oxtail.
2. Put in a pan, with the bacon cut in chunks and the onion stuck with the cloves. Cover with water. Put on lid and simmer gently for three hours. *Or*, pressure cook for one hour.
3. Strain off liquid. Remove the onion.
4. Take all meat from the bones and cut it up discarding fat. Cut up bacon quite small.

5. Return the strained liquid and meat to the pan. Season with pepper and salt. Bring to the boil.
6. Pour into a mould and leave to set.
Serve cold with hot creamed potatoes.

HONEYED WELSH LAMB

Oen Cymreig Melog

Good Welsh lamb needs no dressing up and is amongst the best and least adulterated meat that can be bought in Britain. This recipe gives a spicy gloss to the joint and a delicious gravy. It was served to us with medlar jelly (*see page 171*).

A 1·5 to 2 kg/3 to 4 lb joint of lamb, leg or shoulder
Salt and pepper
1 teaspoon ginger
1 dessertspoon dried or 2 sprigs fresh rosemary
2 tablespoons runny honey
About 300 ml/½ pint cider

1. Use a roasting tin in which joint will be a fairly snug fit.
2. Rub salt, pepper and ginger all over joint and put it in tin.
3. Sprinkle rosemary over it and dribble on the honey. Pour cider around it.
4. Allowing 30 minutes per ½ kg/1 lb, roast near top of a moderately hot oven, Gas 6, 400°F, 200°C for the first half hour. Then baste meat and reduce oven heat to moderate, Gas 4, 350°F, 180°C, for remaining cooking time. Baste every 20 minutes and add a little extra cider if necessary.
5. Lift meat on to a warmed dish and make gravy using residue in roasting tin.

Mrs Joyce Powell
Llanddewi Rhydderch W.I., Gwent

MOSSLANDS SADDLE OF LAMB

Enough for 10 people
For a special occasion.

1 saddle of lamb
1 pork fillet

2 tablespoons chopped fresh
parsley or rosemary jelly
Salt and pepper

1. Bone and skin the saddle, or ask the
butcher to do this for you.
2. In place of the bone, lay the pork
fillet.
3. Sprinkle inside meat with parsley
(or spread on the jelly). Season with
salt and pepper.
4. Roll up, tie in place and weigh joint.
5. Roast in a moderate oven, Gas 4,
350°F, 180°C, for 35 minutes per ½ kg/
1 lb.
6. Remove from oven and allow to rest
for 10 minutes before carving.

Sybil Norcott
Irlam, Nr. Manchester

FAST SWEET AND SOUR LAMB CHOPS

For 4 people

4 lamb chops, best end of neck
3 level tablespoons mango
chutney or good home-made
chutney
2 teaspoons made mustard
½ teaspoon mixed herbs
Salt

1. Put chops in a roasting tin with a
cover.
2. Mix sauce ingredients, chopping
mango pieces if they are large.
3. Pour half of the sauce over chops.
Cover.
4. Roast in a moderate oven, Gas 4,
350°F, 180°C for 15 minutes.
5. Turn chops over and pour rest of
sauce over them.
6. Cover and cook 10 to 15 minutes
more until chops are done. If chops are
very thick allow 5 to 10 minutes
longer. If the sauce becomes sticky,
moisten with a little water.

MARINATED LAMB CHOPS

For 4 people
Remember to start the night before.

4 loin or chump chops
A little melted lard

Marinade*

2 tablespoons oil
2 tablespoons lemon juice or
wine vinegar
A clove of garlic, crushed
1 bay leaf
½ teaspoon thyme and ½
teaspoon basil, or 1 teaspoon
chopped fresh mint
½ teaspoon dry mustard
Salt and pepper to taste
For a note on marinades, see below.

1. Mix marinade ingredients
2. Put chops in a flat, shallow dish and
pour over the marinade. Leave in
refrigerator or a cool place overnight.
Turn chops in marinade every now and
then.
3. Next day, drain chops and pat dry.
4. Brush with lard and cook under a
hot grill for about 15 minutes, turning
frequently.

A marinade is a highly seasoned liquid
in which meat, fish or game may be soaked
as a preliminary to cooking. The object is
to impregnate the meat with certain
flavours. It also helps to tenderise. This is
particularly helpful with chops and steaks
to be grilled or fried. Lemon juice, oil,
vinegar, wine and aromatic flavourings
such as bay leaf, parsley, thyme, rosemary,
etc., can be used. The marinade itself is
often used up by incorporating it in the
final sauce. It is not always necessary to
cover the meat—sometimes only enough
marinade is used to moisten the meat,
which can be turned over two or three
times during the waiting period. See
marinated Fried Tarragon Chicken (*page
35*), Marinated Lamb Chops (*above*),
Beef Casserole (*page 45*), Marinated
Smoked Mackerel (*page 13*), and others.

SHEPHERD'S PIE

A 19th century Sussex pie said to have
been a traditional favourite of
shepherds tending the Southdown
sheep.

For 4 people

1 large onion, chopped
4 tablespoons lentils
4 lamb chump chops
1 tablespoon wholewheat flour

½ teaspoon curry powder
Salt and pepper
About 450 g/1 lb small whole peeled potatoes
1 level tablespoon brown sugar
About 600 ml/1 pint stock

1. Cover the bottom of a 1.1 litre/2 pint casserole with onion and lentils.
2. Season the flour with curry powder, salt and pepper. Coat chops and put them on top of lentils.
3. Pack potatoes around and on top of chops.
4. Sprinkle over remaining seasoned flour and the sugar and pour in the stock. Put lid on casserole.
5. Cook in middle of a warm oven, Gas 3, 325°F, 160°C, for 2½ or even 3 hours, removing lid for last 20 minutes to brown potatoes.

Mrs Ruth Brooke & Mrs Sheila Powell
Hove & Portslade, Sussex

MOUSSAKA

A delicious Greek dish.

Enough for 6 people

450 g/1 lb aubergines
1 tablespoon salt
Good cooking oil
2 large onions, thinly-sliced
A clove of garlic, crushed
450 g/1 lb lean lamb, from the shoulder or leg, minced
A 400 g/14 oz tin of tomatoes
2 tablespoons tomato purée
Salt and pepper

Topping
2 eggs
A 142 ml/5 fl oz carton of single cream
50 g/2 oz grated Cheddar cheese
25 g/1 oz grated Parmesan cheese

1. It is necessary to salt aubergines. (This will help them absorb less oil when fried.) Wipe, top and tail, slice into 7 mm/¼ inch thick slices and lay out in a colander, sprinkling with 1 tablespoon salt. Leave for one hour. Press gently and pat dry on kitchen paper.

2. Fry aubergines lightly in 1 or 2 tablespoons hot oil, adding more oil if needed. Lift aubergines out of pan on to kitchen paper or brown paper.
3. Using 1 tablespoon oil, fry onions and garlic until golden.
4. Add lamb and cook for 10 minutes, stirring every now and then.
5. Add tomatoes and purée and mix well. Bring to the boil and simmer with lid on pan for 20 to 25 minutes. Season with salt and pepper.
6. Arrange alternate layers of aubergine and lamb in a 1·1 litre/2 pint soufflé dish or shallow casserole.
7. Cook in a moderate oven, Gas 4, 350°F, 180°C, for 35 to 40 minutes.
8. Meanwhile, prepare topping. Beat eggs and cream together. Stir in grated cheeses.
9. Pour this on top of the moussaka and return it to the oven for a further 15 to 20 minutes until topping is well-risen and golden brown.

LAMB HOT-POT WITH PARSLEY DUMPLINGS

For 4 people

1 medium-sized onion
2 carrots
2 sticks of celery
40 g/1½ oz lard or dripping
8 best end or middle neck lamb chops
1 tablespoon plain flour
A 400 g/14 oz tin of tomatoes
150 ml/¼ pint water
1 level teaspoon rosemary or mixed dried herbs
1 teaspoon salt
Black pepper

Parsley Dumplings (*or try Sussex Swimmers, see over*)
100 g/4 oz self-raising flour
½ level teaspoon salt
40 g/1½ oz shredded suet
1 level tablespoon chopped parsley
A little water

1. Peel and slice onion. Scrub and slice carrots. Wash and slice celery.

2. Melt half the lard in a frying pan. Add onion, carrots and celery and fry for 2 to 3 minutes. Lift out into a 1·5 litre/2½ pint shallow casserole.
3. Coat chops in plain flour.
4. Add remaining lard to pan, then brown the chops quickly on both sides.
5. Arrange chops on vegetables in casserole.
6. Pour excess fat out of pan, put in tomatoes, water, rosemary, salt and pepper. Bring to boil, stirring, and pour over lamb.
7. Cover casserole and cook in centre of a moderate oven, Gas 4, 350°F, 180°C, for 1 to 1½ hours until meat is tender.
8. For the dumplings: sift flour and salt into a bowl. Mix in suet and parsley. Mix to a soft but not sticky dough with water. Form into 8 small balls.
9. Place dumplings on top of hot-pot and cook, uncovered, for a further 15 to 20 minutes, until dumplings are risen and cooked.

Serve immediately.

SUSSEX SWIMMERS

These dumplings used to be served with a good gravy and, like Yorkshire Puddings in Yorkshire, before the meat course. The rule was that those who ate most puddings could have most meat, a canny way to save meat.

Can also be served as a sweet course with golden syrup.

100 g/4 oz self-raising whole-wheat flour*
100 g/4 oz self-raising white flour
100 g/4 oz shredded suet
¼ teaspoon salt
7 to 8 tablespoons milk
Boiling stock or water

*If you cannot buy this use plain wholewheat flour and add 1½ level teaspoons baking powder.

1. Mix dry ingredients and suet.
2. Mix to a stiff dough with milk.
3. Take tablespoons of mixture and form into balls.
4. Have ready a saucepan of boiling stock or water in which the dumplings can be submerged.
5. Slip dumplings into pan and boil for 15 to 20 minutes.
6. Drain well and serve with a very good gravy, or, if for a sweet, golden syrup.

Mrs Ruth Brooke and Mrs Sheila Powell
Hove and Portslade, Sussex

LAMB AND MINT JELLY

Economical

450 g/1 lb scrag end of lamb
850 ml/1½ pints stock, preferably bone-stock (see page 8)
1 carrot, scrubbed and cut small
1 onion, chopped
A bunch of mint, about 25 to 50 g/1 to 2 oz
2 tablespoons water
15 g/½ oz powdered gelatine
1 level teaspoon salt

1. Simmer scrag end in stock for about 30 minutes with carrot, onion and bunch of mint (keeping out 2 or 3 mint leaves for later).
2. Strain off liquid and set aside.
3. Scrape all meat from the bones, separating all the fat, and chop up meat into fairly small pieces.
4. Put 2 tablespoons water in a cup and stand it in a saucepan containing about 4 cm/1½ inches hot water. Heat gently. Sprinkle gelatine into cup and stir until dissolved.
5. Strain gelatine mixture into a bare 600 ml/1 pint of strained stock. Stir and leave until on the point of setting.
6. Add the diced lamb, a few small pieces of cooked carrot, the finely-chopped mint leaves and salt to taste.
7. Pour into a wetted mould to set.

Serve cold turned out on to a plate with salad, or with creamy mashed potatoes and a green vegetable.

BRAISED LAMB HEARTS
For 2 or 3 people

2 lamb's hearts
2 teaspoons salt

Stuffing

1 teaspoon lard or margarine
1 small chopped onion
1 rasher of bacon, de-rind and chop small
4 tablespoons brown breadcrumbs
1 tablespoon finely-chopped suet
1 teaspoon chopped fresh parsley
Grated rind of half a lemon or orange
1 beaten egg, to bind
Salt and pepper

1. Wash hearts well in cold water and cut away veins or gristle.
2. Place hearts in a pan, add salt and cover with water.
3. Bring to the boil and remove any scum. Put on lid and simmer for 1½ hours.
4. Remove hearts and save the liquid.
5. Cut hearts in half or in slices if large. Lay in a casserole or shallow pan.
6. **Meanwhile make the stuffing.** Melt lard or margarine. Fry onion and bacon until cooked. Remove from heat.
7. Add the other ingredients and mix well. Season with salt and pepper to taste.
8. Spread stuffing over the heart slices.
9. Pour 300 ml/½ pint of the reserved liquid around the slices of heart. Cover with lid or foil.
10. Simmer on top of cooker for about 1 hour. Or cook for 1 hour in a moderate oven, Gas 4, 350°F, 180°C. Test meat with a skewer.

Serve with creamed potatoes and a green vegetable.

Mrs A. Greenwood
Boroughbridge, N. Yorkshire

PORK SLICES IN A CAPER SAUCE

For 4 people
4 slices of pork fillet cut about 5 cm/2 inch thick
A little plain flour

1 beaten egg
About 40 g/1½ oz fresh whole-wheat or white breadcrumbs
2 tablespoons oil

Sauce

50 g/2 oz butter or margarine
Half a large onion, chopped
1 anchovy fillet, or 1 teaspoon anchovy essence
2 tablespoons capers, or pickled nasturtium seeds*, or use pickled gherkin
1 tablespoon chopped parsley
1 tablespoon flour
2 tablespoons vinegar
300 ml/½ pint water
Salt and pepper

*French capers, the pickled flower heads of a trailing plant from Southern Europe, are now rather forgotten, although they can still be bought. A good substitute is home-pickled nasturtium seeds (*see page 173*).

1. Smack the pork slices with a rolling pin to flatten.
2. Flour each slice, dip in beaten egg and then in breadcrumbs.
3. Heat oil and gently fry the slices until cooked. Put on a serving dish and keep hot.
4. **Meanwhile make sauce.** Melt half of the butter or margarine and slightly brown onions.
5. Chop anchovy and mash it down with a wooden spoon. Chop capers. Add these with parsley and flour. Cook gently for 3 or 4 minutes.
6. Add vinegar and water gradually, stirring as sauce thickens. Simmer 2 or 3 minutes.
7. Remove pan from heat, stir in rest of butter and pour sauce over pork slices.

PORK CHOPS WITH ORANGE SAUCE

For 4 people, but easy to do for just 1 or 2

4 pork chops
175 g/6 oz brown or white rice (*see Boiled Rice, page 86*)

Orange Sauce

1 level dessertspoon cornflour
1 tablespoon demerara sugar
Finely-grated rind and juice of 2
oranges
1 tablespoon chopped fresh
parsley
Salt and Pepper Mix (*see page 44*)

1. Put chops on to grill and rice on to
boil.
2. Meanwhile, mix together cornflour,
sugar, rind and juice of oranges.
3. When chops are done, put 1
tablespoon of their dripping into a
small saucepan. Mix in prepared sauce
ingredients and stir over gentle heat
until thick. Stir in parsley. Season to
taste.
4. Put rice on a hot dish. Put chops on
top and pour over the sauce.

PORK CHOPS IN MUSHROOM AND CREAM SAUCE

For 4 people

4 pork loin chops
25 g/1 oz butter
1 onion, finely-chopped
25 g/1 oz plain flour
300 ml/½ pint single cream
225 g/8 oz mushrooms, chopped
Salt and pepper
Chopped parsley (optional)

1. Grill chops for about 8 minutes each
side.
2. Meanwhile, fry onion in the butter
till golden brown.
3. Mix in mushrooms and fry for 2
minutes.
4. Add flour and stir to a paste.
5. Add cream and cook *very* gently to
thicken.
6. Season to taste.
7. Pour sauce over chops and garnish
with chopped parsley if desired.

Judith Adshead
Mottram St. Andrew, Cheshire

PORK IN CIDER WITH WALNUT-STUFFED PRUNES

*For 4 to 6 people but easy to cut
down for fewer*
This dish freezes well for about 3
months.
Remember to start the night before.

16 prunes
½ to ¾ kg/1 to 1½ lb diced pork,
from the shoulder
1 heaped tablespoon cornflour
1 onion, chopped
1 tablespoon oil
300 ml/½ pint dry cider
300 ml/½ pint chicken stock
A clove of garlic, crushed
4 cloves or ¼ teaspoon ground
cloves
½ teaspoon marjoram
Salt and pepper
16 walnut halves

1. Start by pouring boiling water over
prunes and leaving to soak and plump
up for at least 12 hours. If using ready
softened prunes, soak in cold water.
2. Toss pork in cornflour.
3. Fry onion gently in oil until
softened.
4. Add meat to pan and stir until
surfaces are brown.
5. Add cider, stock, garlic, marjoram,
salt and pepper.
6. Bring to boil, cover pan and let it
just simmer until meat is tender, about
1½ hours. Or transfer into a covered
casserole and cook in a slow oven, Gas
2, 300°F, 150°C, for about 2 hours.
7. Meanwhile, remove stones carefully
from prunes and stuff with walnuts.
8. 20 minutes before end of cooking
time drop stuffed prunes in with meat.
Serve with rice, pasta or boiled
potatoes and freshly-cooked green
vegetables.

Mrs Angela Mottram
Axbridge, Somerset

SWEET AND SOUR PORK

Deep-fried pork in batter with
vegetables in a sweet and sour sauce.

For 4 people
450 g/1 lb lean pork
75 g/3 oz cornflour
50 g/2 oz plain flour
1 teaspoon salt
1 egg, separated
3 tablespoons cold water
Oil for deep frying

Sweet and sour vegetables
1 green pepper
2 carrots
1 small onion
2 cloves of garlic
2 tablespoons sugar
1 tablespoon soya sauce
3 tablespoons wine or cider
vinegar
1 tablespoon rice wine* or dry
sherry
1 tablespoon oil
½ teaspoon grated fresh ginger
(see page 38)
1 tablespoon cornflour
1 tablespoon water
*Can be bought at Chinese
supermarkets.

1. Trim any fat from pork, cut it into fairly thin slices and cut these into 2·5 cm/1 inch pieces.
2. In a bowl mix the 75 g/3 oz cornflour, plain flour and salt.
3. Lightly mix egg-yolk and water.
4. Make a well in centre of flour and work in the egg-yolk and water to form a smooth batter.
5. Beat egg-white until stiff. Fold it into batter.
6. Heat the oil until it is nearly smoking hot. To test: drop into it a small piece of dry bread; if it immediately rises bubbling to the surface and goes golden in 1 minute, oil is ready.
7. Cooking just a few pieces of pork at a time, dip them into the batter and deep fry until golden brown and crisp, about 3 to 5 minutes.
8. Drain on kitchen paper and keep warm in a low oven until all the pieces are fried.
9. Meanwhile, wash and dry green pepper and cut into bite-sized squares.
10. Scrub carrots, slice lengthwise into fine strips. Cut these into 2·5 cm/1 inch pieces.

11. Chop onion quite small.
12. Finely chop the garlic.
13. In a small bowl, mix together the sugar, soya sauce, vinegar and wine.
14. In a wok or frying pan heat 1 tablespoon of oil until it is just smoking hot. Add carrots, pepper and onion and stir-fry over a medium heat for 2 minutes.
15. Add garlic, ginger and the vinegar mixture. Allow to boil for 1 minute.
16. Slake the cornflour by mixing it with 1 tablespoon of water and then add it to pan and cook for half a minute, stirring until the sauce has thickened and becomes clear.
17. Arrange the pork pieces in a serving dish and pour the sauce over. Serve at once with Boiled Rice (*see page 86*) or noodles.

Priya Wickramasinghe
Cardiff

LIVER AND BACON HOT-POT
450 g/1 lb pig's liver
225 g/8 oz streaky bacon
rashers
2 medium-sized onions or 3
sticks of celery
2 medium-sized, sharp, cooking
apples
2 tablespoons chopped parsley
1 teaspoon chopped fresh
marjoram or ½ teaspoon dried
marjoram
75 g/3 oz soft breadcrumbs
Salt and pepper
About 600 ml/1 pint stock or
water
1. Cut liver into thin slices.
2. Cut bacon rashers into small pieces.
3. Peel and chop onions. Peel, core and chop apples and mix with onion.
4. Place a layer of liver in a greased casserole, cover it with a layer of bacon and a layer of onion and apple.
5. Mix parsley and marjoram into breadcrumbs and sprinkle over onion and apple. Add a shake of salt and pepper.
6. Repeat these layers until dish is full, saving enough breadcrumbs to

cover the final layer of onion and apple.

7. Pour in enough stock or water almost to cover.
8. Put lid on casserole and cook in a warm oven, Gas 3, 325°F, 160°C, for 2 hours.
9. Half an hour before serving, remove lid to let the top brown.

Mrs Becky Blackmore
Exeter, Devon

FAGGOTS

Ffagod Sir Benfro, which means faggots as made in Pembrokeshire.

Enough for 5 or 6 people but easy to cut recipe down

700 g/1½ lb pig's liver
2 large onions
125 g/4 oz fresh brown or white breadcrumbs
75 g/3 oz shredded suet
2 level teaspoons sage
1 teaspoon salt
¼ teaspoon pepper
To serve: green peas and gravy

1. Mince liver and onion into a bowl.
2. Add remaining ingredients and mix thoroughly.
3. Form into balls to fit palm of hand. Traditionally, faggots were wrapped in caul to cook. Nowadays, the best way is to use or make foil cups to hold them in shape. Set these in a small roasting tin and pour boiling water around them.

Or, make a loaf of the mixture. Press into a greased 1 kg/2 lb loaf tin. Set this in a roasting tin and pour boiling water around it to come halfway up sides.
4. Bake in middle of a moderate oven, Gas 4, 350°F, 180°C, for 30 minutes for individual faggots, 1 hour for loaf.

Serve faggots in a bed of peas with a good gravy in a separate jug.

Leave loaf in tin for 10 minutes in a warm place. This gives it time to set and it can then be turned out and will slice quite easily.

Mrs Joyce Porvell
Llanddewi Rhydderch W.I., Gwent

SAUSAGE SAUTÉ

2 tablespoons oil
450 g/1 lb pork sausages
1 medium-sized onion
1 green pepper
225 g/8 oz fresh or tinned tomatoes
1 large cooking apple
Salt and Pepper Mix (*see page 44*)

1. Heat 1 tablespoon of the oil in a large frying pan. Separate the sausages and cook gently for 15 to 20 minutes, turning frequently.
2. Peel and slice onion.
3. Wash and dry green pepper. Cut out core and remove pips. Cut flesh into thin strips.
4. Warm 1 tablespoon oil in another pan. Cook onion and green pepper gently, stirring occasionally, for 5 minutes.
5. Skin the tomatoes (*see page 72*) and chop roughly.
6. Roughly chop the apple.
7. Add tomatoes and apple to onion mixture and continue cooking for 5 minutes, stirring occasionally. Season slightly.
8. Drain sausages and keep hot.
9. Turn out onion mixture into a warmed dish and arrange sausages on top.

Serve with plain boiled potatoes.

SAUSAGE AND KIDNEY HOT-POT

For 4 people
Could be made in electric frying pan.

4 sheep's kidneys
4 large sausages
100 g/4 oz bacon
3 small onions or 3 sticks of celery
100 g/4 oz mushrooms
225 g/8 oz carrots
25 g/1 oz butter
15 g/½ oz flour
300 ml/½ pint stock
1 teaspoon tomato purée, or ketchup
1 tablespoon sherry
Salt and pepper
1 small packet frozen peas

1. Remove skins from kidneys, cut them into 4 pieces and cut out core.
2. Skin the sausages and make each into 2 or 3 small balls.
3. De-rind bacon and cut it into strips.
4. Peel and chop onions or celery. Wipe and slice mushrooms. Scrub carrots and cut into short, very thin strips.
5. Melt butter in pan and fry bacon a little. Add kidneys and sausages and fry them quickly till lightly-browned. Lift out of fat on to a plate.
6. Add onions and mushrooms to pan. Reduce heat and cook slowly for 5 minutes, stirring occasionally.
7. Stir flour into pan and let it cook 1 minute.
8. Stir in stock, tomato purée and sherry and bring to simmering point, stirring as it thickens. Season with salt and pepper.
9. Add carrots, bacon, kidney and sausage balls.
10. Cover pan with a well-fitting lid and simmer gently for ½ hour. 10 minutes before end of cooking time add frozen peas.

Ann E. Craib
King's Park, Glasgow

GAMMON IN CIDER

This Somerset method best suits a large joint such as a half gammon but non-gammon joints such as slipper, forehock and hock can be used. It is boiled then roasted.

If the meat is smoked, soak it first for 12 hours in plenty of cold water. To speed up process, cover pan, bring to boil. Leave until cold. Then discard water, and proceed as follows:

For a large joint
2·4 litres/4 pints water
600 ml/1 pint dry cider
1 chopped onion
6 allspice berries
4 cloves
2 bay leaves

Place joint in a saucepan with the above ingredients, put lid on, bring slowly to the boil and simmer for 10 minutes to the ½ kg/1 lb.

For smaller joints
Reduce liquid in same ratio of 1 part cider to 4 parts water using sufficient to cover meat generously. Reduce onion and spices accordingly. Cook as above.
Then lift out joint, skin it and score fat in a criss-cross pattern.

For basting
Dry cider
2 tablespoons
demerara sugar
1 teaspoon dry mustard } mixed together
1 teaspoon mixed spice

1. Put joint in a baking tin, moisten with cider, sprinkle on some of the dry mix, sufficient to cover surface.
2. Bake near top of a hot oven, Gas 6 to 7, 400 to 425°F, 200 to 220°C, for 10 minutes to the ½ kg/1 lb, basting every 10 to 15 minutes with more cider and dry ingredients. When all is used up, baste from liquor around joint.

For decorating
Sliced oranges
Glacé cherries
Arrange these over joint as it comes out of oven, or if joint is being baked to eat cold, decoration can be done before baking, or part way through for a large joint.

Mrs Angela Mottram
Axbridge, Somerset

FOREHOCK OF BACON

A big joint for a special occasion. Remember to start the night before.

1 forehock of bacon, weighs about 3·25 kg/7 lb before serving
3 level tablespoons demerara sugar
2 sprigs of fresh rosemary or 1 teaspoon dried
Whole cloves

The forehock is to be boned and this is what you do:
1. Soak overnight in cold water.
2. Then working on the underside of the joint, take a small sharp knife and cut off rib bones.

3. Slit meat down to the inner bones and work round them to expose completely. Remove them.

To prepare and cook
4. Sprinkle inside of meat with 2 tablespoons demerara sugar.
5. Then tie up joint with strings at 5 cm/2 inch intervals.
6. Weigh joint and calculate boiling time at 25 minutes per ½ kg/1 lb.
7. Put joint in a pan, cover with water, add rosemary. Bring slowly to the boil. Simmer gently for the calculated time. Leave in the cooking water until cool enough to handle.
8. Skin carefully and score fat in a lattice pattern. Press a clove in each 'box' and sprinkle on the last tablespoon of sugar.
9. Set under a pre-heated grill until brown and bubbly.

Serve cold.

Stock will make excellent soup. Freezes well.

Remember to boil up the bones separately for more stock.

SUSSEX BACON ROLY POLY

This is a lovely, crusty, baked version of the traditional Sussex Roly Poly which used to be wrapped in a cloth and boiled for 3 to 3¼ hours.

Enough for 4 or 5 people, but easy to make less

225 g/8 oz self-raising flour
A pinch of salt
100 g/4 oz shredded suet
7 to 8 tablespoons water
350 g/12 oz lean bacon rashers, cut small
1 onion, finely-chopped
Finely-chopped fresh or dried sage
Black pepper
Beaten egg or milk, to glaze
1. Sift flour and salt into a bowl. Add suet and mix with water to a soft but not sticky dough.
2. Using a floured board, roll out very thin.
3. Cover generously with bacon and onion and add sage and pepper to

taste. Brush edges of pastry with water.
4. Roll up into a long roll, sealing edge and ends. Place on a greased baking tray with join underneath.
5. Decorate with the trimmings made into little leaves. Brush all over with beaten egg or milk.
6. Bake near top of a moderately hot oven, Gas 6, 400°F, 200°C, for 30 to 40 minutes, when it will be crusty and golden.

Mrs Janice Langley
Shoreham-by-Sea, West Sussex

TRADITIONAL SUSSEX BACON PUDDING

For 2 people

125 g/4 oz wholewheat flour
1½ teaspoons baking powder
50 g/2 oz shredded suet
1 onion, finely-chopped
3 to 4 rashers streaky bacon, chopped
1 teaspoon mixed fresh herbs or ½ teaspoon dried
Pepper and a little salt
1 medium to small egg
Milk, if necessary
1. Mix together flour, baking powder, suet, onion, bacon, herbs and seasoning.
2. Mix with egg, adding milk if necessary to make a soft dropping consistency.
3. Grease a 600 ml/1 pint basin and put in a piece of greaseproof paper just to cover bottom.
4. Put pudding mixture into basin. Cover with greaseproof paper and foil, tucked in neatly under the rim.
5. Steam for 1½ hours. If you haven't a steamer, stand basin on a trivet or upturned saucer in a pan of boiling water. Put on lid and boil for 1½ hours, replenishing with boiling water when necessary. Do not let it go off the boil.

Serve with Parsley Sauce (*see page 95*).

Mrs Sheila Powell
Portslade, Sussex

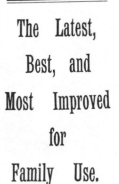

Chapter 5

Salads
and
Vegetables

SALAD DRESSINGS

Some basic dressings and many variations.

French Dressing

Made in a jar in quite a large quantity, will keep in a cool place for several weeks, to be used a little at a time as required. Saves a lot of time.

1 rounded teaspoon French mustard, try Dijon
1 rounded teaspoon cooking or sea salt
½ level teaspoon freshly-ground black pepper
½ level teaspoon sugar (optional)
Juice of 1 lemon (optional)
300 ml/½ pint olive or good salad oil
4 tablespoons wine or cider vinegar

Put all ingredients in a jar with a well-fitting screw top. Shake vigorously to combine.

Try different flavourings but add these to the small amount of dressing required when salad is made. They go stale if kept in the dressing for long:

Crushed garlic or chopped onion; chopped fresh parsley, chives, tarragon, basil, chervil or fennel. Try combinations of one or two. Dried herbs can also be added but take care because most are twice as strong as the fresh ones.

Simple Dressing Without Oil

A mild dressing especially if young children are to eat the salad.

3 tablespoons tarragon vinegar, plain vinegar can be used
2 tablespoons water
½ teaspoon sugar
Salt and pepper to taste
1 large teaspoon chopped fresh mint, parsley, chives, tarragon, fennel or onion

Mix all ingredients thoroughly in a salad bowl and at last minute toss in the salad ingredients

Basic mayonnaise

Made in liquidiser. Keeps in refrigerator for 3 to 4 weeks. Can be thinned down when required with milk or single cream, or more lemon or orange juice, or vinegar.

2 to 4 egg-yolks, according to how extravagant you feel
300 ml/½ pint of good salad oil, olive or sunflower are best
2 dessertspoons lemon or orange juice or wine or cider vinegar
1 rounded teaspoon French mustard, try Dijon
½ level teaspoon cooking or sea salt
¼ level teaspoon freshly-ground black pepper
¼ level teaspoon sugar (optional)

1. Put egg-yolks in liquidiser and switch on for 2 minutes or until thick and creamy.
2. With machine running, add juice or vinegar. Then add oil gradually until 150 ml/¼ pint has been absorbed.
3. Now add all the seasonings, switch on again and gradually add the last of the oil.

Try different flavours but always add them to mayonnaise after it is made: tomato purée, anchovy purée, crushed garlic, chopped chives, capers or cucumber, etc.

Sour Cream and Chive Dressing

Delicious with crunchy salads—e.g., chopped white cabbage, grated carrots, finely-chopped onion.

A 142 ml/5 fl oz carton of soured cream
2 level tablespoons chopped fresh chives
1 tablespoon wine vinegar
1 level tablespoon made mustard
Salt and freshly-ground black pepper
A little milk (optional)

Combine all the ingredients, adding milk to thin it down if necessary.

Cooked Salad Dressing

A good economical dressing of mayonnaise quality but using no oil, therefore not so rich and fattening.

2 teaspoons sugar
½ level teaspoon dry mustard
1 level teaspoon salt
25 g/1 oz margarine
2 tablespoons vinegar
1 tablespoon lemon juice
1 egg

A double saucepan is ideal for this but it can also be made as follows:

1. Put sugar, mustard and salt in a bowl.
2. Cut the margarine into small pieces and add it to the bowl.
3. Add vinegar and lemon juice.
4. Beat egg and strain it into bowl.
5. Stand bowl over a pan of simmering water. Do not let bowl touch water. Let the dressing cook, stirring occasionally with a wooden spoon, until it is thick enough to coat the back of the spoon.
6. Then take bowl off pan and let it cool.

Keeps for a week in a cool place. Keeps for at least two weeks, covered, in a refrigerator.

Margaret Heywood
Mankinholes, Todmorden, Yorkshire

Yoghurt and Tahini Dip

This is a lovely dressing for salads. It may also be used as a dip served with Greek Pitta Bread (*see page 139*). It is used in the recipe for Chicken Kebabs (*see page 33*).

Tahini is made from sesame seed pulp and can be bought at a delicatessen.

3 tablespoons natural yoghurt
1 tablespoon tahini
A clove of garlic, crushed (optional)
Lemon juice
Salt and pepper

Mix yoghurt, tahini and garlic. Beat in lemon juice, salt and pepper to taste.

Serve cold. Will keep in refrigerator for a few days. Stir before serving.

Elizabeth Mickery
Pudsey, West Yorkshire

COOKING WITH DRIED BEANS, PEAS, LENTILS AND GRAINS

Aduki beans: a small red bean, much prized by the Chinese for its goodness. Very useful substitute for mince when cooked with bouquet garni, onion, carrot, tomato purée.
Barley: moist and chewy. Best in soups or roasted for savoury bakes.
Black-eye beans: earthy flavour. Used often in Mexican cooking. Combines very well with red kidney beans.
Brown rice: nutty flavour. Used for risotto, curry, pilaff and sweet puddings.
Buckwheat: a Russian delicacy. Particularly strong nutty flavour; adds meatiness to dishes.
Bulgar wheat: creamy tasting. Quick to use as it needs no cooking when used for salads. Often confused by people with white rice.
Butter beans: rather bland taste.
Chick peas: very popular in Middle Eastern cookery. Nutty in flavour and appearance. Delicious in salads and for making savoury dips.
Field beans: at last something British! Best in soups and stews with root vegetables.
Haricot beans: the traditional baked bean when cooked with treacle and tomatoes.
Lentils: the whole variety: brown, earthy-flavoured; green, more delicate flavour. Hold their shape and make a quick addition to soups and stews. The split red variety purée easily and are excellent for pâtés, rissoles and go well with curry spices.

TO COOK DRIED BEANS, PEAS, LENTILS AND GRAINS

This chart can be followed in conjunction with notes opposite

Bean, Pea, Lentil, Grain	Soak overnight in cold water	Cooking time in fresh cold water	Time needed for hard boil at some stage in cooking	A minimum amount of fresh cold water for 1 cup of beans, etc.
		Minutes	*Minutes*	
Aduki beans	Yes	60–80	10	4 cups
Barley—				
pot or pearl	No	45–50	Nil	3 cups
Black-eye beans	Yes	40–45	10	3 cups
Brown rice				
long grain ⎫	No	20–25	Nil	2 cups
short grain ⎭		20		(*see Boiled Rice page 86*)
Buckwheat	No	20–25	Nil	4 cups
Bulgar wheat	Just soak in boiling water for 5 to 10 minutes, then it is ready for salads			
Butter beans	Yes	40	10	4 cups
Chick peas	Yes	2 hours	10	5 cups
Field beans	Yes	60	10	4 cups
Haricot beans	Yes	45–50	10	3 cups
Lentils—brown ⎫		40–45 ⎫		4 cups ⎫
green ⎬	No	40–45 ⎬	Nil	4 cups ⎬
red ⎭		15–20 ⎭		3 cups ⎭
Lima beans	Yes	40–45	10	3 cups
Millet	No	20–25	Nil	3 cups
Mung beans	No	40–45	Nil	3 cups
Oats	No	25–30	Nil	3 cups
Pinto beans	Yes	60	10	6 cups
Red kidney beans	Yes	45–50	10	4 cups
Soya beans	Yes	2½–3 hours	30	6–7 cups
Split peas— green and yellow ⎭	No	40–45	Nil	3 cups
Wheat	No	60	Nil	5 cups

Lima beans: similar to butter beans but tastier. Good for salads and when combined in creamy dishes and soups.
Millet: a delicate flavoured grain. Easily digested and can be used for sweet and savoury dishes.
Mung beans: best for sprouting.
Oats: sweet creamy-tasting. Main ingredient for muesli.
Pinto beans: rather like speckled eggs. Can be used instead of black-eye or red kidney beans.
Red kidney beans: beautiful distinctive colour. Brightens stews and salads. Popular with chilli spices.
Soya beans: good source of protein. Excellent for absorbing the flavour of all that is cooked with it. Best in soups and casseroles.
Split peas: best for soups. Green type best cooked with mint or rosemary; yellow type go well with spices.
Wheat: very chewy berries. Adds texture to bean dishes. Also when cooked, a good addition to bread.

NOTES ON COOKING DRIED BEANS, PEAS, LENTILS AND GRAINS

Grains only need bringing to the boil and simmering. But the flavour of some is improved if they are lightly toasted in a little oil in the pan in which they are to be boiled. Use ¼ teaspoon oil to the 125 g/¼ lb grain. This applies to buckwheat, millet, rice and barley.
1. Pick over beans, lentils, etc., for sticks and stones then wash before soaking and cooking.
2. Soak beans and peas overnight. This swells them and helps loosen grit and dirt. It also removes excess starch and carbohydrates which cause flatulence. Soak by covering with 8 cm/3 inches of water. Beans, etc., should double in size. This water is then thrown away, the beans washed thoroughly and covered with fresh water.
3. Cook beans, etc., in plenty of water as it is useful stock—125 g/4 oz beans in 850 ml/1½ pints water.
4. All beans and some peas must be fast-boiled for at least 10 minutes. This destroys the anti-nutritional factors on the surface of the beans. Then lightly boil for the remaining time, in a covered pan.
5. Salt is not added during boiling because it tends to harden the outer skin and prevent the bean from becoming soft. The same applies if lemon juice, wine or vinegar is put in at the beginning of cooking. However, adding herbs, spices or vegetables to the cooking water improves the flavour. Adding caraway, aniseed or fennel seed helps counteract flatulence. Fennel is the least dominating. Add ¼ teaspoon to 125 g/ 4 oz beans, etc., during last ½ hour.
6. When cooked, drain liquid and save it for stock. It will keep 3 to 4 days in refrigerator.
7. Cooked beans, etc., drained of ALL liquid to stop fermentation will keep 4 to 5 days in covered containers in refrigerator.
8. Red and brown beans turn the water dark during cooking and will colour any white beans or grains cooked with them. It is best to keep dark beans separate from white during cooking to keep the appearance of each bright and natural.
9. Some people find this type of food indigestible. Dried beans, peas, etc., contain water soluble sugars that the body cannot break down. Some people develop the necessary enzymes to cope with this. Those who have found problems must attack them more thoroughly before cooking. Boil for 3 minutes. Leave to soak in that water for 4 to 5 hours. Drain. Reboil in fresh water for 3 minutes. Leave to soak for 4 to 5 hours. Drain and then cook for use adding 30 minutes on to the recommended times to ensure softness.
10. *Pressure cooking* saves time and fuel and soaking time can be reduced or even eliminated. The anti-nutritional problem (see note 4 above) does not apply because of the higher temperature involved. *Be sure* to follow instructions in your pressure cooker handbook.

MARINADE FOR BEANS

Dried beans are delicious in salads when they have been marinated immediately after cooking.

This is enough for ½ kg/1 lb **cooked** *beans. 225 g/8 oz uncooked beans will weigh about ½ kg/1 lb when cooked.*

175 ml/6 fl oz best salad oil, ideally use a mixture of olive and safflower or sunflower oils
125 ml/4 fl oz cider vinegar
Juice of 1 lemon
A clove of garlic, crushed
1 teaspoon fresh chives, chopped
1 teaspoon marjoram
1 teaspoon oregano
1 teaspoon pepper
½ teaspoon salt

1. Mix everything together.
2. Pour over hot, freshly-cooked, thoroughly-drained beans.
3. Allow beans to remain in marinade until quite cold.
4. Drain marinade into a jar. Beans are ready for use in salads.

Marinade can be used again but will keep only a few days because fresh herbs will go stale. If there is water in it from the beans it will not keep well.

Marinated Bean Salad

Red kidney beans, lima beans and chick peas make a good mixture of contrasting colours, textures and tastes.

1. Cook beans according to directions on previous page.
2. Marinate hot beans as above.
3. Choose favourite salad vegetables, such as radish, celery, green, red or yellow pepper, tomato. Add fresh herbs. No extra dressing is necessary.

Sarah Brown
Scarborough, Yorkshire

BUTTER BEAN AND WATERCRESS SALAD

Enough for 4 small side salads— easy to make less or more

For a more substantial salad, cubes of Cheddar or Gouda cheese may be added.

Salad

125 g/4 oz cooked lima or baby butter beans
A quarter of a cucumber
1 firm small pear, Comice or Beurre Hardy are best
Half a bunch of watercress (about 50 g/2 oz)
Salt and pepper

Dressing: for this you need a liquidiser

2 tablespoons natural yoghurt
25 g/1 oz blue cheese
1 dessertspoon mayonnaise (*see page 64*)
40 g/1½ oz cottage cheese

1. Remember to start the day before by soaking beans overnight and then cooking (*see page 66*).
2. Put dressing ingredients in liquidiser and blend till smooth. This can be done some time ahead.
3. Cut unpeeled cucumber and pear into small cubes.
4. Save a few nice sprigs of watercress to garnish and cut up rest finely.
5. Mix all salad ingredients with dressing. Taste for seasoning.
6. Chill before serving.
7. Garnish with watercress.

Sarah Brown
Scarborough, Yorkshire

BEANSPROUT AND WALNUT SALAD

Enough for 4 to 6 people but easy to make less

2 large crisp apples, unpeeled
3 sticks of celery
225 g/8 oz beansprouts
50 g/2 oz walnuts
50 g/2 oz raisins

Dressing

1 teaspoon lemon juice
200 ml/7 fl oz natural yoghurt

1 tablespoon chopped fresh mint
Pepper and salt

1. Chop apples and celery and mix with beansprouts, walnuts and raisins.
2. Mix dressing ingredients and stir into salad.
3. Chill slightly before serving.

Janet Horsley
Headingley, Yorkshire

BEETROOT AND CELERY SALAD

Equal quantities of cooked beetroot in vinegar and fresh celery, seasoned with a little salt

1. Cut the celery into thin slices and lay it in the dish from which it will be served.
2. Sprinkle with a little salt.
3. Lift the beetroot out of the vinegar, cut it into quarters or neat lumps and lay it on top of the celery.
4. At the last minute pour over a little of the beetroot vinegar.

CAULIFLOWER SALAD

Make as much as you need, but make it fresh each time.

Cauliflower
Carrot
Green pepper
Celery

Dressing

Choose one from pages 64/65

1. Wash cauliflower and break into small sprigs.
2. Scrub carrot and grate it coarsely.
3. Wash green pepper, remove core and seeds and slice flesh finely.
4. Wash and finely slice celery.
5. Combine all with the dressing.

CUCUMBER IN YOGHURT

An oriental version of a well-known and exceptionally refreshing salad.

For 4 people

300 ml/10 fl oz yoghurt
1 cucumber, finely-sliced
1 green chilli, finely-chopped (optional)
$\frac{1}{2}$ teaspoon salt
$\frac{1}{4}$ teaspoon dried ginger—freshly-ground if possible
To garnish: fresh coriander leaves, chopped

Mix all ingredients in a bowl, cover with a well-fitting lid and refrigerate before serving.

Eat this fresh. It does not keep.

Delicious with Cashew Nut Curry (see page 88).

Priya Wickramasinghe
Cardiff

LAYER SALAD

For 4 to 6 people

Layer the following ingredients in a large glass bowl:

100 g/4 oz shredded cabbage
175 g/6 oz grated carrot
75 g/3 oz chopped peanuts
100 g/4 oz chopped celery
2 chopped red apples, unpeeled
75 g/3 oz chopped dates
100 g/4 oz cooked brown rice (see page 86)
25 g/1 oz sesame seeds
1 box mustard and cress, chopped
Garnish with slices of tomato

Janet Horsley
Headingley, Yorkshire

LETTUCE WITH PEANUT DRESSING

For 4 people

1 crisp lettuce, washed and dried
Half a cucumber, sliced

69

Dressing

2 tablespoons oil
¼ teaspoon mustard seed
½ teaspoon salt
¼ teaspoon cumin seed
A pinch of turmeric
1 tablespoon lemon juice
50 g/2 oz peanuts, coarsely-ground

1. Start with dressing. Heat oil and splutter the mustard seeds in it. To do this put seeds in hot oil, put lid on pan, keep pan over medium heat and listen while seeds leap up against lid for a few seconds until the spluttering sound has stopped. Remove pan from heat before lifting lid.
2. Add salt, cumin and turmeric and fry for 5 seconds.
3. Remove from heat and add lemon juice and peanuts. Leave to cool.
4. Just before serving, break up lettuce into small pieces into a salad bowl. Add cucumber and dressing and toss salad thoroughly.

Priya Wickramasinghe
Cardiff

NEW POTATO SALADS

New potatoes, scrubbed
Chopped chives, onion tops or leak tops
4 tablespoons French dressing (*see page 64*)

1. Steam potatoes or cook them in their jackets over low heat in a very little water. Drain. Skin and slice when they have cooled down a bit.
2. Meanwhile, mix dressing ingredients.
3. Toss potato while still hot in the dressing, adding chives, onion or leek tops.

Ideas for more substantial salads

Add any of the following:

Cubes of garlic sausage
Strips of green pepper
Tuna fish, drained and chopped

ONION SALAD

For 4 people

225 g/8 oz onions
2 green chillis, finely-chopped
Juice of 1 lemon
½ teaspoon salt
¼ teaspoon freshly-milled black pepper

1. Slice onions into fine rings.
2. Mix all ingredients and leave for at least 1 hour before serving.

Before serving, finely-sliced tomatoes can be added.

Delicious as an accompaniment to rice dishes.

Priya Wickramasinghe
Cardiff

POTATO SALAD

With capers and mayonnaise. Old potatoes can be used.

450 g/1 lb potatoes cut into 1 cm/½ inch dice
Water
Salt
1 tablespoon chopped capers
3 tablespoons mayonnaise or salad cream (*see page 64*)

1. Put potatoes in a saucepan with salted water just to cover. Bring to the boil, put on lid and cook for 3 to 5 minutes until almost tender.
2. Drain quickly and thoroughly and toss lightly with capers.
3. When cold coat with mayonnaise, mixing gently.

Anne Wallace
Stewarton, Ayrshire

RICE SALAD WITH APPLE DRESSING

A well-balanced meal in itself.

Enough for 4

**350 g/12 oz cooked brown rice
(*see page 66*) or 150 g/5 oz
uncooked
50 g/2 oz cashew nut pieces,
toasted
50 g/2 oz raisins
50 g/2 oz bean sprouts*
Half a red pepper
Lettuce leaves
1 dessert apple**

Dressing

**2 tablespoons apple juice
1 tablespoon sunflower oil
1 tablespoon lemon juice
1 teaspoon shoyu (*see page 80*)
¼ teaspoon ground ginger
Salt and pepper**

1. Cashew nut pieces are cheaper than
whole nuts. They can be toasted under
a moderately-hot grill until crisp and
just turning golden. Toasting makes
them crisp and fresh.
2. Mix together salad ingredients,
except lettuce and apple.
3. Mix dressing ingredients. Beat
well. Mix into salad.
4. Serve on a bed of lettuce, garnished
at last minute with apple slices.

Sarah Brown
Scarborough, Yorkshire

A SALAD OF RED CABBAGE AND MUSHROOMS WITH BROWN RICE

For 3 or 4 people

Keeps for a day or two.

**Juice of 1 small orange
25 g/1 oz sultanas or raisins**

**4 tablespoons French dressing
(*see page 64*)
100 g/4 oz red cabbage
1 small onion
50 g/2 oz mushrooms
100 g/4 oz brown rice
1 tablespoon chopped parsley
2 tablespoons Chinese beansprouts (optional)**

1. Put sultanas or raisins to soak in
the orange juice.
2. Prepare French dressing and divide
it between two small bowls.
3. Finely shred red cabbage and toss it
in one bowl of dressing.
4. Peel and finely chop onion and toss
it with cabbage.
5. Wipe the mushrooms and slice them
thinly. Toss them in the other bowl of
dressing.
6. Leave both bowls for at least one
hour.
7. Meanwhile, cook the rice (*see
Boiled Rice, page 86*).
8. When rice is done, drain off any
liquid. Then spread it out thinly to
cool. If when it is cool it is not nicely
dry, put the dish in a very slow oven,
less than Gas ¼, 225°F, 110°C, for 20
minutes or so to draw the moisture
out.
9. All these preparations may be done
some time in advance, even the day
before it is to be served.
10. Stir each bowl of ingredients then
combine all together in a serving dish
with rice, parsley and bean sprouts.

INDONESIAN TOMATO SALAD

For 4 people

**4 ripe tomatoes
Salt to taste
2 fresh green chillis
3 tablespoons sugar
Juice of 2 lemons**

1. Slice the tomatoes and arrange in a
serving platter. Sprinkle with a little
salt.

2. Slice the green chillis slantwise into elongated rings and arrange over the tomato slices.
3. Sprinkle with sugar and lemon juice and allow to stand for an hour or two before serving.

Priya Wickramasinghe
Cardiff

TO PEEL TOMATOES

Either: Put tomatoes in a bowl, pour boiling water over them and leave for 1 minute. Plunge them into cold water and skin when required.

Or, if only one is needed, spear it on a fork and turn it in the hot air just above a gas flame. Skin will contract and burst and tomato can be easily peeled.

WATERCRESS AND GRAPEFRUIT SALAD
For 4 people

25 g/1 oz lightly-roasted hazelnuts
1 bunch of watercress
1 small lettuce
1 large grapefruit

1. To roast hazelnuts, put them in a shallow tin in a moderate oven, Gas 4, 350°F, 180°C, for 10 minutes. Or put under grill, turning often. Then rub the skins from them and chop coarsely.
2. Wash watercress and lettuce and dry well.
3. Peel grapefruit and remove membrane and pips, working over a bowl so as to retain the juice. Chop flesh into bowl.
4. Break lettuce and watercress into small pieces. Toss it with grapefruit and put it in a salad bowl.
5. Sprinkle hazelnuts over the top.

Janet Horsley
Headingley, Yorkshire

HOME BAKED BEANS
For 4 people

A delicious home-made version of that ever-popular and nourishing tinned commodity, baked beans in tomato sauce. Remember to start the night before.

225 g/8 oz haricot beans, soaked overnight
50 g/2 oz butter or margarine
1 large onion, chopped
A clove of garlic, crushed
A 400 g/14 oz tin of tomatoes
2 teaspoons brown sugar
1 tablespoon chopped fresh parsley
Salt and pepper

1. Cook beans as directed on *page 66*.
2. Melt butter and fry onion and garlic until soft but not brown.
3. Break up tomatoes in the tin and pour into pan.
4. Simmer uncovered for about 10 minutes to reduce tomato juice.
5. Add sugar, parsley, salt and pepper.
6. Pour sauce over the hot beans and keep warm for at least 30 minutes so that beans absorb the flavour.

Sue Maddison
Chislehurst, Kent

RUNNER BEANS AND ALMONDS
For 4 people

15 g/½ oz flaked almonds
40 g/1½ oz butter
275 g/10 oz frozen runner beans or whole green beans
Salt and pepper

Lightly-cooked, drained, fresh (not frozen) beans can be used.

1. Fry the almonds in butter till both are pale golden brown.
2. Add frozen beans, shake them in amongst butter and almonds. Cover pan and simmer gently for 3 minutes.
3. Uncover pan, turn up heat and stir-fry for 1 minute.
4. Season and serve.

Lightly-cooked non-frozen beans are added to pan when almonds are brown. Stir-fry for 1 minute. Season and serve.

Sybil Norcott
Irlam, Nr. Manchester

CURRIED BHINDI

Also known as okra and ladies' fingers.

For 4 people

450 g/1 lb bhindi
1 tablespoon oil
1 small onion, finely-chopped
½ teaspoon ground cumin
½ teaspoon coriander
½ teaspoon chilli powder (optional)
¼ teaspoon ground turmeric
¾ teaspoon salt
150 g/5 oz tinned tomatoes

1. Wash and dry the bhindi. Trim the tops and tails and cut into 2·5 cm/1 inch pieces.
2. In a pan, heat oil and fry onion until it is lightly browned.
3. Add spices and salt and cook for 2 minutes on a low heat.
4. Add bhindi and stir until it is well mixed and coated with spices.
5. Lastly, add tomatoes and bring to the boil. Cover and simmer for about 7 minutes or until the bhindi is cooked.

Serve with Boiled Rice (*see page 86*), Chicken Curry (*see page 35*) and Onion Salad (*see page 70*); or with Puris (*see page 142*) and Cauliflower Bhaji (*see page 74*) as part of a vegetarian meal.

Priya Wickramasinghe
Cardiff

BAKED CARROTS WITH HONEY AND MUSTARD

450 g/1 lb carrots
2 tablespoons water
2 tablespoons oil
2 tablespoons honey
1 teaspoon made mustard, try a whole grain one
Pepper and salt
A few sesame seeds for decorating (optional)

1. Scrub carrots and chop into small sticks.
2. Mix water, oil, honey and mustard.
3. Put carrots in a shallow oven dish, pour over the honey mixture. Sprinkle with pepper and a very little salt.
4. Cover dish (greaseproof paper and foil will do) and bake in a moderately hot oven, Gas 5, 375°F, 190°C, for 50 to 60 minutes until tender.

Serve with a sprinkling of sesame seeds.

Sarah Brown
Scarborough, Yorkshire

BUTTERED CARROTS AND THYME

225 g/8 oz small carrots
15 g/½ oz butter
1 teaspoon chopped fresh thyme

1. Trim carrots and gently scrub clean, leaving skin on. Cut into matchstick strips (known as julienne).
2. Steam carrots for 10 minutes or simmer in a very little water in a tightly-covered pan until nearly tender.
3. Toss in butter, sprinkle with thyme and serve at once.

Janet Horsley
Headingley, Yorkshire

BROCCOLI WITH BUTTER SAUCE

450 g/1 lb broccoli sprigs

Sauce

65 g/2½ oz butter
25 g/1 oz flour

73

300 ml/½ pint boiling water
Salt and pepper
1 egg-yolk
2 teaspoons lemon juice

1. Steam the broccoli until it is just tender, or cook in a very little water in a saucepan with a well-fitting lid.
2. Meanwhile, prepare sauce. Melt a third of the butter in a pan.
3. Stir in flour and cook for 1 minute.
4. Pour in boiling water, whisking all the time until sauce thickens, but do not boil it.
5. Remove pan from heat, beat in egg-yolk and remaining butter.
6. Season to taste and add lemon juice.
7. Pour over cooked broccoli or serve in a separate sauce-boat.

If sauce is not served at once it can be reheated in a double saucepan.

Anne Wallace
Stewarton, Ayrshire

SPICY CABBAGE WITH COCONUT

For 4 people

225 g/½ lb spring greens, cabbage or Chinese leaves, finely-shredded as for coleslaw
½ medium-sized onion, chopped
2 cloves of garlic
½ teaspoon ground cumin
½ teaspoon ground coriander
¼ teaspoon turmeric
1 teaspoon salt
2 tablespoons unsweetened desiccated coconut
2 green chillis, finely-chopped
1 tablespoon water

1. In a bowl mix all the ingredients thoroughly.
2. Using a heavy-bottomed frying pan, stir-fry the cabbage on a low flame for about 5 minutes.

Priya Wickramasinghe
Cardiff

CAULIFLOWER WITH ALMOND SAUCE

1 cauliflower
50 g/2 oz butter
50 g/2 oz flour
125 g/4 oz ground almonds
600 ml/1 pint water or 450 ml/¾ pint water mixed with 150 ml/¼ pint milk
½ teaspoon nutmeg
Salt and pepper

1. Steam cauliflower whole or in florets, or simmer it in as little water as possible in a saucepan with well-fitting lid. Do not overcook. The texture should be almost crisp.
2. Meanwhile, melt butter in a pan, stir in flour and cook for 2 minutes.
3. Mix almonds with water (or water and milk mixture).
4. Pour almond milk over roux, bring to the boil, stirring continuously. Simmer for 3 minutes seasoning with nutmeg, salt and pepper.
5. Pour sauce over hot, well-drained cauliflower and serve immediately.

Sarah Brown
Scarborough, Yorkshire

CAULIFLOWER BHAJI

Bhaji is the Indian name for a vegetable dish.

For 4 people

1 medium-sized cauliflower
2 medium-sized potatoes
2 tablespoons oil
¼ teaspoon mustard seed
3 cloves of garlic, chopped
2 green chillis, chopped
½ teaspoon ground cumin
¼ teaspoon ground coriander
¼ teaspoon turmeric
¼ teaspoon garam masala (*see page 38*)
125 ml/4 fl oz warm water

To garnish: fresh coriander leaves, when available

1. Cut cauliflower into florets and potatoes into matchsticks.

2. Heat oil in a pan and splutter the mustard seeds in it. To do this, put seeds into the hot oil, put lid on pan, keep pan over medium heat and listen while seeds leap up against lid for a few seconds until the spluttering sound has stopped. Remove pan from heat before lifting lid.
3. Add potatoes and fry gently for about 3 minutes.
4. Add the other ingredients, except water, and stir-fry for about 5 minutes.
5. Pour in water and allow to simmer for about 15 minutes until cauliflower and potato are just cooked but not soft.
6. Garnish with freshly-chopped coriander leaves.

To vary the flavour of this dish 1 tablespoon of desiccated coconut may be added during cooking, at paragraph four.

Priya Wickramasinghe
Cardiff

BRAISED CELERY AND BACON

A nice way to serve celery if the oven is on for something else.

For 4 people

1 head of celery
15 g/½ oz butter or margarine
Salt
Black pepper
½ level teaspoon nutmeg
300 ml/½ pint chicken stock
2 or 3 rashers of streaky bacon, without rinds

1. Wash and trim the celery and cut it into 2·5 to 5 cm/1 to 2 inch lengths.
2. Use the butter or margarine to grease an oven dish with a lid.
3. Lay celery in dish and season with a little salt, freshly-grated black pepper and nutmeg.
4. Pour over the stock.
5. Cut bacon into thin strips and fry them a little, then lay the strips over celery.

6. Put lid on dish and cook in a moderate oven, Gas 4, 350°F, 180°C, for 30 minutes.
7. When celery is tender, drain off excess liquor, toss bacon amongst celery and serve.

COURGETTES

A vegetable with a lovely appearance but so delicate a taste that it needs some other flavour with it. Takes only 5 minutes to prepare.

450 g/1 lb courgettes, do not peel
25 g/1 oz butter
Half a clove of garlic, crushed
Salt and black pepper

1. Wash courgettes, trim off the stalks and cut into even-sized very fine rings. This can be done very quickly on the mandolin cutter of a grater.
2. Melt butter and fry garlic for 1 minute.
3. Add courgettes and stir over moderate heat so that garlic butter is well distributed. Season with a little salt and plenty of freshly-ground black pepper.
4. Put on lid, lower heat and let courgettes just heat through for 3 to 4 minutes. Shake pan every now and then.

Serve at once while the green slices are still brilliantly green and not jaded with over-cooking.

ONIONS BAKED IN CIDER

A delicious recipe to serve with meat dishes, especially pork.

450 g/1 lb onions
25 g/1 oz butter
1 level teaspoon sugar
150 ml/¼ pint cider
½ teaspoon salt
Freshly-ground black pepper

1. Slice onions thickly, place in a casserole, dot with the butter. Sprinkle on sugar, salt and pepper.
2. Pour the cider over, and cover casserole tightly. Greaseproof paper and foil will do.
3. Cook in a moderate oven, Gas 4, 350°F, 180°C, for 1¼ hours. Then remove lid and cook a further 15 minutes.

NEW POTATOES

Served in a sweet glaze.

New potatoes
25 g/1 oz butter
25 g/1 oz sugar

1. Boil new potatoes in their jackets until tender.
2. In a clean pan melt butter and sugar and cook gently until golden.
3. Put in potatoes with or without skins. Turn them over in glaze until they are coated and light brown.

Nice with cold ham and a green crisp salad.

SCALLOPED NEW OR OLD POTATOES

Can be made with old potatoes, but choose really waxy ones like Desirée or Dr Mackintosh.

450 g/1 lb new potatoes, scrubbed
125 g/4 oz mushrooms, chopped
15 g/½ oz butter
125 g/4 oz cooked ham, cut in small pieces

Cheese Sauce

50 g/2 oz butter
50 g/2 oz flour
1 teaspoon made mustard
A grating of nutmeg
600 ml/1 pint milk
50 g/2 oz grated cheese

1. Steam potatoes or cook them over low heat in a very little water. Then drain and slice.
2. Meanwhile, chop mushrooms and fry for 1 minute in the 15 g/½ oz butter.
3. Make sauce. Melt butter, stir in flour and cook 1 minute.
4. Stir in mustard and nutmeg. Then add milk gradually, stirring as sauce thickens, and simmer for 3 minutes.
5. Stir in cheese and reheat but do not boil.
6. Arrange slices of potato over-lapping in a buttered, shallow oven dish.
7. Cover with mushrooms and ham.
8. Pour over the cheese sauce.
9. Cook at top of a moderately hot oven, Gas 6, 400°F, 200°C, for 15 minutes.

GLAZED PARSNIPS WITH WALNUTS AND ROSEMARY

450 g/1 lb parsnips
Salt
50 g/2 oz butter
75 g/3 oz broken walnuts
½ teaspoon dried rosemary
Freshly-ground black pepper
Chopped parsley (optional)

1. Scrub parsnips and slice into rings of even thickness.
2. Steam with a little salt or simmer with a good lid on pan in as little water as possible until just tender. Drain.
3. Melt most of butter in saucepan and toss parsnips and walnuts in it until both are lightly-browned.
4. Mix in rosemary and black pepper.
5. Serve with an extra dot of butter or parsley to garnish.

Sarah Brown
Scarborough, Yorkshire

76

SPINACH WITH CREAM

1 to 1·5 kg/2 to 3 lb fresh spinach
25 g/1 oz butter or margarine
3 to 4 tablespoons fresh bread-crumbs
2 to 3 tablespoons single cream
A good grating of whole nutmeg
Pepper and salt

1. Trim, and wash spinach. Put it in a large saucepan with no extra water. Boil for 4 or 5 minutes.
2. Meanwhile heat butter or margarine and fry breadcrumbs till golden, stirring often.
3. Drain spinach, chop, drain again and squeeze out moisture.
4. Mix in cream, nutmeg, pepper and a little salt. Put in a warmed dish and sprinkle piping hot breadcrumbs on top.

Serve at once.

Mrs Joyce Langley
Shoreham-by-Sea, West Sussex

TOMATO AND ONION CASSEROLE

450 g/1 lb onions
Salt and pepper
½ level teaspoon marjoram
450 g/1 lb tomatoes, skinned (see page 72) and sliced
75 g/3 oz breadcrumbs
75 g/3 oz grated cheese
25 g/1 oz melted butter, margarine or bacon fat

1. Peel and slice onions and boil in salted water for about 20 minutes.
2. Drain well and season with pepper and herbs.
3. Put half onion into a greased casserole.
4. Add a layer of half the sliced tomatoes.
5. Next, add a layer of crumbs and grated cheese.
6. Repeat the layers.

7. Pour over the melted butter, margarine or bacon fat.
8. Bake in a hot oven Gas 7, 425°F, 220°C, for 20 minutes.

Sybil Norcott
Irlam, Nr. Manchester

STIR-FRY VEGETABLES WITH BEANSPROUTS

Served with brown rice (see page 86) or wholewheat pasta this makes an appetizing light meal for 4 or 5 people.

2 tablespoons oil, sesame oil is best
1 onion, cut into rings
A clove of garlic, crushed
½ to 1 teaspoon ground ginger
1 green pepper, thinly-sliced
1 large carrot, scrubbed and thinly-sliced
1 leek, sliced
125 g/4 oz small button mushrooms
150 ml/¼ pint water
1 to 2 tablespoons white wine (optional)
1 to 2 teaspoons soya sauce
225 g/8 oz beansprouts

1. Heat oil in a large frying pan with a lid.
2. Fry onion, garlic and ginger until soft but not brown.
3. Add green pepper and fry for 1 minute more.
4. Toss in carrot and fry 3 or 4 minutes more, stirring often.
5. Add leek and mushrooms and stir-fry 3 or 4 minutes more.
6. Stir in water, wine and soya sauce and lay beansprouts on top.
7. Cover pan, bring to boil and simmer very gently for 1 minute before serving.

Janet Horsley
Headingley, Yorkshire

77

AUBERGINES AND TOMATOES

6 firm ripe tomatoes
2 aubergines, fairly large
1 onion, finely-sliced and chopped small
A clove of garlic
½ level teaspoon fresh basil, or a good pinch of dried
1 tablespoon oil
Salt and pepper

1. Put tomatoes in a bowl, cover with boiling water and leave for 30 seconds. Plunge one at a time into cold water and skin.
2. Slice the tomatoes and arrange half of them in a well-greased, shallow oven dish.
3. Wash the aubergines. Trim off stem ends. Cut in half lengthways.
4. Now, with skin side up make lengthways cuts 1 cm/½ inch apart to within 1 cm/½ inch of stem end.
5. Transfer to dish. Space the aubergine fans out in a single layer. Fill the spaces between the fans with slices of tomato.
6. Arrange the rest of the tomatoes, onion, garlic and basil around the fans. Brush all over with oil. Season with salt and pepper.
7. Cover with lid or foil and bake in a very hot oven, Gas 8, 450°F, 230°C, for 10 minutes. Reduce heat to moderate, Gas 4, 350°F, 180°C for another 25 minutes or until the aubergines are tender.

Serve on its own as a snack or as an accompaniment to grilled lamb.

BUTTER BEANS AND MUSHROOMS

Under a crisp cheese topping, this is a light but nourishing dish to eat on its own, with lightly-cooked green beans or just with some crusty French bread and green salad.

Remember to start the night before.

175 g/6 oz butter beans, soaked overnight
225 g/8 oz mushrooms
A little butter
Salt and pepper

White Sauce

25 g/1 oz butter
1 dessertspoon wholewheat flour
150 ml/¼ pint milk
1 tablespoon lemon juice
Salt and pepper

Topping

40 g/1½ oz grated cheese
40 g/1½ oz fresh wholewheat breadcrumbs

1. Having soaked beans overnight in water to cover, drain off water. Put beans in saucepan and cover with fresh water. Boil hard for 10 minutes then reduce heat and simmer until tender, about 40 minutes more. Drain (saving liquid for soups, etc.).
2. Put beans into a well-buttered 1·1 litre/2 pint pie dish. Season well with salt and pepper.
3. Meanwhile, cut stalks from mushrooms and chop them finely, leaving mushroom caps whole.
4. Simmer mushroom caps in a very little water for 2 or 3 minutes to soften a little. Then drain, saving the liquid.
5. For the sauce, melt butter and fry mushroom stalks for 2 minutes.
6. Add flour and cook 1 minute.
7. Add milk and lemon juice to pan, stir as sauce thickens and add enough mushroom liquid to make a smooth pouring sauce. Add salt and pepper to taste. Simmer for 3 minutes.
8. Pour sauce over beans.
9. Lay mushroom caps on top with undersides up.
10. Mix grated cheese and breadcrumbs and sprinkle over mushrooms.
11. Bake near top of a moderate oven, Gas 4, 350°F, 180°C, for 15 minutes to brown the top and heat through.

CHESTNUT HOT-POT

Can be cooked on top of stove or as a casserole in oven. Freezes well.

Enough for 4 people, but this dish improves with keeping and reheating. So 1 or 2 can enjoy it more than once. Baked potatoes and spiced red cabbage go well with it, also wholewheat bread rolls.

50 g/2 oz whole lentils
125 g/4 oz whole dried chest-nuts*
1·1 litres/2 pints water
1 medium-sized onion
225 g/8 oz carrots
2 sticks of celery
1 tablespoon oil
2 tablespoons fresh parsley or 1 tablespoon dried
1 teaspoon sage
½ teaspoon thyme
½ to 1 tablespoon shoyu (*see page 80*)
½ teaspoon mustard powder
Salt and pepper

*Can be bought at good wholefood shops

1. Wash lentils and pick them over for stones.
2. Boil chestnuts and lentils in the water for 40 minutes.
3. Meanwhile, peel onion and scrub carrots and celery and cut into bite-sized pieces.
4. Heat oil and gently fry chopped vegetables for 10 minutes, stirring occasionally so that they do not brown.
5. Combine in one saucepan or casserole the fried vegetables, chest-nuts, lentils and their cooking liquid.
6. Add all remaining ingredients and more liquid, either water or stock, if necessary.
7. Cover pan and simmer for 30 minutes. If using casserole, cook in middle of a moderate oven, Gas 4, 350°F, 180°C, for 45 minutes to 1 hour.

Sarah Brown
Scarborough, Yorkshire

CHESTNUT AND MUSHROOM LOAF

A party dish. Delicious cold as a pâté or served hot in the style of a traditional Sunday lunch.

Enough for 8 to 10 people, but easy to reduce quantities

125 g/4 oz dried chestnuts, whole or kibbled*
1·1 litres/2 pints boiling water
50 g/2 oz butter
1 onion, chopped
2 cloves of garlic, crushed
1 tablespoon chopped fresh parsley
2 teaspoons sage
¼ teaspoon winter savory
½ teaspoon paprika
2 tablespoons wholewheat flour
150 ml/¼ pint stock from cooking chestnuts
150 ml/¼ pint red wine
350 g/12 oz walnuts, ground
50 g/2 oz fresh wholewheat breadcrumbs
4 sticks celery, chopped
1 teaspoon salt
1 tablespoon shoyu (*see page 80*) or Worcestershire sauce
225 g/8 oz mushrooms, sliced
1 beaten egg

*Kibbled is the name given to chestnuts which are sold in small broken pieces.

1. Soak chestnuts in the boiling water for 1 hour.
2. Then cook them in the same water in a covered pan until soft. If whole this will take about 40 minutes; if kibbled, about 20 minutes. Save the cooking water as you drain them. Chop coarsely (not necessary with kibbled chestnuts).
3. Melt butter in a large frying pan and fry onion and garlic gently until transparent.
4. Stir in herbs, paprika and flour and cook 2 minutes.
5. Add the 150 ml/¼ pint stock from chestnuts and wine, stir well. When sauce thickens remove pan from heat.

79

6. Mix together in a bowl chestnuts, ground walnuts, breadcrumbs, celery, salt, shoyu or Worcestershire sauce and mushrooms.
7. Mix in sauce and beaten egg. Check seasoning.
8. Grease a 1 kg/2 lb loaf tin and line it with greased greaseproof paper. Fill with mixture and press down well.
9. Bake in a moderately hot oven, Gas 5, 375°F, 190°C, for 1 hour until firm to the touch. Remove from oven.

When serving hot, leave loaf in tin for 10 minutes before cutting.

Sarah Brown
Scarborough, Yorkshire

SHOYU OR TAMARI

It is a natural fermentation of soya beans and wheat, not dissimilar to commercial soy sauce. Wholefood and vegetarian cooks use it in preference to that and yeast extracts because they find it is a more versatile condiment. It is also highly concentrated food containing valuable vitamins and minerals. It adds depth of flavour, stimulates the appetite and compliments a wide range of foods. It can be used in a number of dishes from seasonings, soups and stews, to dips and dressings.

Although there is no direct substitute, alternatives are yeast extract, soy sauce, tomato purée, mustards and herbs. Also meat extracts or stock cubes if you are not vegetarian.

CIDER WITH ROSEMARY

A well-flavoured casserole of vegetables. The chick peas, wheat grain and cheese provide protein to make this a substantial and nutritionally-balanced main course.

For 4 people

150 g/5 oz cooked chick peas (*see page 66*) **or 50 g/2 oz uncooked**

150 g/5 oz cooked wheat grain (*see page 66*) **or 75 g/3 oz uncooked grain**
About 1 kg/2 lb mixed root vegetables, carrot, swede, turnip, parsnip
1 tablespoon oil
175 g/6 oz fennel, cut in chunks
25 g/1 oz butter
50 g/2 oz wholewheat flour
450 ml/¾ pint cider
450 ml/¾ pint water or stock
1 bay leaf
1 dessertspoon chopped fresh parsley
1 teaspoon rosemary
1 teaspoon sage
1 teaspoon thyme
Salt and pepper

1. Don't forget to soak chick peas and wheat grain overnight before cooking, according to instructions on *page 66*. Save cooking liquid.
2. Cut up root vegetables into even-sized chunky pieces.
3. Heat oil and gently fry fennel for about 5 minutes. This draws out flavour.
4. Add chopped root vegetables and stir well so that all is coated in a very little oil to seal in flavour.
5. Add butter, letting it melt. Stir in flour and let it cook 2 to 3 minutes.
6. Stir in cider and water or stock and bring to the boil.
7. Mix in chick peas, grain and herbs. Bring back to boil, lower heat and simmer for 1 hour. Check seasoning before serving.

Delicious served with baked potatoes and a sprinkling of grated cheese.

Sarah Brown
Scarborough, Yorkshire

CREAMY OAT AND ALMOND CASSEROLE

For 4 to 6 people, but easy to make less

50 g/2 oz whole oats, or barley
50 g/2 oz whole green

continental lentils
225 g/8 oz leeks
225 g/8 oz carrots
125 g/4 oz celery
1 parsnip
1 green pepper
25 g/1 oz butter
½ teaspoon thyme
½ teaspoon mustard

Sauce

50 g/2 oz ground almonds, or
grind whole, unblanched
almonds yourself if you can
300 ml/½ pint stock from
cooking grain and lentils
25 g/1 oz butter
25 g/1 oz wholewheat flour
Salt and pepper

Topping

50 g/2 oz porridge oats
50 g/2 oz wholewheat breadcrumbs
1 tablespoon sunflower seeds

1. Pick over lentils for sticks and
stones. Then rinse with the grain. Put
them together in a pan of fresh water,
about 900 ml/1½ pints, and boil for 45
minutes. Then strain off the liquid and
keep it for use later.
2. Meanwhile, scrub and chop
vegetables finely.
3. Melt 25 g/1 oz butter in a large
frying pan and fry vegetables, stirring
so that they are coated in butter.
4. Pour in about half a cupful of
cooking liquid from grain and lentils.
Cook 10 to 15 minutes until vegetables
are just about tender but not soft.
5. Mix in thyme, mustard and well-
drained grain and lentils. Cook
another 5 minutes.
6. Meanwhile, make sauce. Mix
ground almonds with the stock to form
'milk'.
7. Melt butter in pan, stir in flour,
cook for one minute.
8. Pour in almond milk—stirring
continuously. Bring sauce to boil.
Season.
9. Pour sauce over cooked vegetables.
Turn into a greased oven dish.

10. Mix topping ingredients and
sprinkle over.
11. Bake near top of a moderate oven,
Gas 4, 350°F, 180°C for 20 minutes,
when it will be nicely browned.

Sarah Brown
Scarborough, Yorkshire

MASHED SWEET POTATO

With ham, turkey or chicken

450 g/1 lb sweet potatoes
2 tablespoons milk
50 g/2 oz butter or margarine
300 ml/½ pint béchamel sauce
(see page 95)
Slices of cold meat
2 tablespoons sharp apple purée

1. Cook sweet potatoes with skins on
in water just to cover. Then skin and
mash with milk and half of the butter
or margarine to a creamy consistency.
2. Make up béchamel sauce.
3. Arrange cold meat in a buttered
oven dish.
4. Cover with apple purée and
béchamel sauce.
5. Top with sweet potatoes.
6. Smooth the surface and score in a
pattern. Dot with butter and brown
under the grill.
7. Reheat for 30 minutes in a
moderate oven, Gas 4, 350°F, 180°C.

MUSHROOM AND BUCKWHEAT GOULASH

*Enough for 6 to 8 people, but easy to
reduce for small households*

Contains kidney beans, so remember
to start the day before.

125 g/4 oz uncooked red kidney
beans (or a mixture of these
with pinto and black-eye beans)

1 onion
1 green pepper
2 sticks of celery
2 tablespoons oil
2 teaspoons cinnamon
2 teaspoons paprika
50 g/2 oz unroasted buckwheat
2 tablespoons wholewheat flour
1 to 1·25 litres/1½ to 2 pints
stock, from cooking beans
50 g/2 oz walnuts
50 g/2 oz currants
225 g/8 oz mushrooms
Salt and pepper

1. Soak beans overnight in plenty of cold water (*see pages 66 and 67*).

2. Next day, drain and rinse beans and cook in 1·1 litres/2 pints fresh water. Boil them hard for 10 minutes then simmer for a further 45 minutes.

3. Meanwhile, chop up onion, green pepper and celery into bite-sized pieces.

4. Heat oil and fry onion gently with cinnamon and paprika for 3 minutes.

5. Add green pepper, celery and buckwheat. Stir well so that all the vegetables get a light coating of hot oil, which will seal in the flavour, and the buckwheat has a chance to toast slightly, which will enhance the flavour.

6. Stir in flour. Cook for 2 or 3 minutes.

7. Save the liquid as you drain the cooked beans and pour 1 litre /1½ pints over vegetables.

8. Add beans, walnuts, currants and mushrooms. Bring to the boil, stirring well. Put into a casserole and put on lid.

9. Cook in a warm oven, Gas 3, 325°F, 160°C for 2 or even 3 hours. Check seasoning before serving.

This dish needs slow cooking to bring out the full flavour. The end result is a beautiful dark, rich stew. Goes well with a contrasting vegetable, such as creamed potatoes or leeks.

Sarah Brown
Scarborough, Yorkshire

NEW ENGLAND CASSEROLE

Can be cooked on top of stove or in oven. Very good with Corn Muffins (*see page 147*).

For 6 people

Remember to start the day before.

50 g/2 oz red kidney beans
50 g/2 oz black-eye beans
1·1 litres/2 pints water
1 medium-sized onion
1 green pepper
225 g/8 oz marrow or courgettes
1 aubergine
50 g/2 oz raisins
1 cooking apple (about 175 g/6 oz)
Salt and pepper

Sauce

A 400 g/14 oz can of tomatoes
2 tablespoons cider vinegar
1 tablespoon treacle
1 tablespoon apple juice concentrate
½ tablespoon shoyu (*see page 80*)
Juice of ½ lemon

1. Mix beans together and soak in water overnight.

2. Next day, drain beans, rinse and put in saucepan with 1·1 litres/2 pints fresh cold water. Boil hard for 10 minutes then simmer for 45 minutes more.

3. Meanwhile, mix all sauce ingredients together and simmer for about 20 minutes, or until flavours are well-blended.

4. Chop vegetables into bite-sized pieces.

5. Saving the cooking liquid, drain beans and combine them with vegetables, sauce, raisins and apples. Add some of the bean stock or more tomatoes to moisten if necessary, and salt and pepper according to taste.

6. Cover pan, bring to boil and simmer 20 minutes. *Or*, transfer to a casserole and cook in a moderate oven, Gas 4, 350°F, 180°C for 45 minutes.

If making muffins while casserole is in oven put dish in coolest part.

Sarah Brown
Scarborough, Yorkshire

RED BEAN HOT-POT

A well-flavoured substantial main course.

Enough for 5 people, but easy to make less

Remember to start the night before.

225 g/8 oz red kidney beans
1·1 litres/2 pints water
1 tablespoon oil, olive oil is best
1 onion, sliced
1 green pepper, sliced
225 g/8 oz courgettes
225 g/8 oz mushrooms
225 g/8 oz tomatoes, peeled (*see page 72*) and chopped
2 teaspoons soya sauce
2 teaspoons sage
300 ml/½ pint bean stock
Pepper and salt
450 g/1 lb potatoes, peeled and sliced
25 g/1 oz butter

1. Soak beans overnight.
2. Next day, drain beans and put them in a saucepan with 1·1 litres/2 pints of fresh water. Cover pan and boil beans hard for 10 minutes. Then reduce heat and cook until tender, about 1 to 1½ hours. *Or*, pressure cook for 15 minutes.
3. Saving the cooking liquid, drain beans well.
4. Preheat oven to moderately hot, Gas 6, 400°F, 200°C.
5. Heat oil and fry onion, green pepper, courgettes and mushrooms for 5 minutes.
6. Add tomatoes, cooked beans, soya sauce, sage and 300 ml/½ pint of the bean stock. Add pepper and salt to taste.
7. Put mixture into a greased shallow casserole and lay sliced potatoes on top. Cover with a lid or greaseproof paper and foil.
8. Cook for 45 minutes to 1 hour until potatoes are cooked. Then remove cover, dot potatoes with butter, return to top shelf of oven and cook for 10 minutes more until potatoes are brown on top.

Serve with fresh green vegetables.

Janet Horsley
Author of 'The Bean Cuisine'

RED KIDNEY BEAN RISSOLES

Makes 12 to 14 rissoles

Remember to start the night before.

225 g/8 oz red kidney beans
1·1 litres/2 pints water
2 onions, finely-chopped
50 g/2 oz wholewheat flour
1 tablespoon soya sauce
1 teaspoon dried rosemary or sage
Pepper and salt

For frying: a little oil

1. Soak beans overnight. Drain away the water.
2. Next day, put beans in 1·1 litres/2 pints of fresh cold water. Cover pan and boil hard for 10 minutes, then reduce heat and cook for 1 to 1½ hours until beans are tender. *Or*, pressure cook for 15 minutes.
3. Drain, keep aside half of the beans and mash the rest.
4. Combine all the ingredients, seasoning to taste. Leave aside in a cool place to firm up, about 30 minutes.
5. Shape round rissoles using about 2 tablespoons of mixture for each one. Leave aside in a cool place for 15 minutes to firm up.
6. Heat oil and fry rissoles for 3 to 4 minutes each side until cooked through and lightly-browned and crisp on the outside.

Serve with fried potatoes and a green salad.

Janet Horsley
Headingley, Yorkshire

ENGLISH VEGETABLE COBBLER

For 6 people, but easy to make in quite small quantities

Can be made without cobbler. Really economical.

1 tablespoon oil
2 onions, sliced

225 g/8 oz parsnip
225 g/8 oz swede or white turnip
225 g/8 oz carrot
2 sticks of celery, diced
125 g/4 oz cooked field beans or
carlins or 50 to 75 g/2 to 3 oz
uncooked beans (*see page 66*)
600 ml/1 pint stock, save
cooking water from beans
1 tablespoon parsley
2 teaspoons dried sage
Salt and pepper

Cobbler Topping

125 g/4 oz self-raising brown* or
white flour
A pinch of salt
25 g/1 oz butter or vegetable
margarine
25 g/1 oz grated cheese
About 3 tablespoons milk

*81% extraction rather than pure
wholewheat self-raising flour is
preferable and often easier to
obtain.

1. Heat oil and fry onions until
transparent.

2. Chop root vegetables into bite-sized
pieces and toss in the saucepan with
onions. Add celery. Allow these
vegetables to cook gently for 10
minutes.
3. Add cooked field beans and stock,
herbs and seasoning. Bring to the boil,
cover pan and simmer gently for 20
minutes. Check seasoning.
4. Meanwhile, make topping, just like
a scone. Mix flour and salt.
5. Rub in butter or margarine to form
fine breadcrumbs. Mix in cheese.
6. Mix with enough milk to form a
soft dough.
7. Knead lightly on floured board.
Roll out 7 mm/¼ inch thick. Cut into
circles.
8. Put vegetable and bean mix in an
oven dish.
9. Lay scone circles overlapping on
top.
10. Bake near top of a moderately hot
oven, Gas 6, 400°F, 200°C, for 20
minutes. Topping will rise slightly and
brown. Mixture will bubble underneath.

Nice with baked potatoes.

Chapter 6

Rice, Pasta, Pancakes, Cheese & Egg, Savouries, Snacks and Sandwich Spreads

BOILED RICE

For 4 people

This is the best way of making fluffy white rice to serve with curries and other savoury dishes.

1 cup rice (washed in a sieve under running cold water until the water runs clear)
2 cups water
1 teaspoon salt

1. Put rice, water and salt in a saucepan and bring to the boil.
2. Stir, cover pan, put on a well-fitting lid, reduce heat and simmer for 15 minutes. At the end of that time the rice will have absorbed all the water and be perfectly cooked, but *it is vital* that the lid be kept on for the full 15 minutes.
3. Fluff with a fork and serve.

The above method is suitable for all good rice, Basmati, Patna, Chinese, Japanese and Italian. For part-cooked rice follow manufacturers' instructions on packet.

Brown Rice may also be cooked in exactly the same way but 25 minutes is required for it to absorb the water.

Priya Wickramasinghe
Cardiff

SRI LANKAN YELLOW RICE

This delicately flavoured dish goes well with chicken curries (*see pages 35–38*), Cashew Nut Curry (*see page 88*), Onion Salad (*see page 70*) and poppadoms.

For 4 people

1 cup rice
125 g/4 oz creamed coconut*
2 cups hot water
½ medium-sized onion, finely-chopped.
2 tablespoons ghee (*see page 38*)**, butter or oil**
A few curry leaves (*see page 38*)
3 cloves
3 cardamoms
A 2·5 cm/1 inch piece of

cinnamon stick
1 teaspoon salt
¼ teaspoon saffron or turmeric
8 peppercorns
***Can be bought at wholefood and oriental food shops.**

1. Wash rice in a sieve under running water and leave to drain.
2. Dissolve creamed coconut in the hot water.
3. Fry onion in the oil.
4. Add all the other dry ingredients and fry over a low heat, stirring until the grains of rice become yellow.
5. Add coconut liquid and bring to a rapid boil.
6. Cover with a well-fitting lid, reduce heat and simmer for 15 minutes. Simmer 25 minutes if brown rice is used.

Priya Wickramasinghe
Cardiff

KIDNEYS IN A SAUCE WITH MUSHROOMS

For 2 people

3 lamb's kidneys
25 g/1 oz plain flour
Salt and pepper
25 g/1 oz lard
1 medium-sized onion, chopped
50 g/2 oz mushrooms, thickly-sliced
300 ml/½ pint beef stock, a stock cube will do

1. Remove skins from kidneys, cut them in half and cut out the core. Then chop up.
2. Season the flour with salt and pepper. Toss chopped kidneys in it.
3. Melt lard in a frying pan and gently fry onion.
4. Add kidneys to pan and fry gently for 2 to 3 minutes, turning them over in the fat.
5. Toss mushrooms in with kidneys for 2 or 3 minutes more.
6. Stir remaining flour into pan and let it sizzle for a minute. Gradually stir in stock and bring to the boil. Taste and season if necessary with more salt and pepper.

7. Cover pan and simmer for 10 minutes.
Serve with plain boiled brown or white rice (*see opposite*) and green vegetables.

EGG CURRY

6 eggs
2 teaspoons salt
¼ teaspoon turmeric
3 tablespoons oil
Half a medium-sized onion, chopped
25 g/1 oz creamed coconut*
300 ml/½ pint hot water
2 cloves of garlic, chopped
¼ teaspoon fresh ginger (*see page 38*) chopped
A 5 cm/2 inch piece of cinnamon stick
1 dessertspoon ground coriander
1 teaspoon ground cumin
1 teaspoon chilli powder
¼ teaspoon ground fenugreek
A sprig of curry leaves*, if available
Juice of half a lemon

*Can be bought at oriental and some wholefood shops.

1. Boil eggs for 11 minutes and shell them.
2. Mix salt and turmeric and rub it into eggs. Use a pin and prick them in several places so that they do not burst when fried.
3. Heat 3 tablespoons oil and fry eggs until golden brown, about 2 minutes. Lift eggs out of pan.
4. Fry onions until golden brown.
5. Dissolve creamed coconut in the hot water. Add this to pan with all other ingredients, except eggs and lemon juice. Simmer, stirring occasionally, until sauce is thick.
6. Add eggs and lemon juice and allow to simmer for a further 5 minutes.
Serve with Boiled Rice (*see opposite*), or Sri Lankan Yellow Rice (*see opposite*) and vegetables and salads.

Priya Wickramasinghe
Cardiff

SAUSAGES IN A CURRY SAUCE

For 4 people, but easy to make less for 1 or 2

No need for oven.

700 g/1½ lb sausages
25 g/1 oz dripping
225 g/8 oz brown rice
1 onion, chopped
1 apple, chopped
1 level tablespoon curry powder
1 rounded tablespoon plain flour
A 225 g/8 oz tin of apricot halves
1 green pepper, cut in thin strips
1 dessertspoon mango or good chutney
2 teaspoons lemon juice
Salt and Pepper Mix (*see page 44*)

1. Fry sausages gently in dripping until golden brown. Remove on to a plate, draining all but 1 tablespoon of the fat. (Save this tasty extra fat for something else.)
2. Meanwhile, put rice on to cook, following instructions for Boiled Rice on *page 86*. Keep sausages warm on top of rice pan.
3. Fry onion in sausage pan until softening.
4. Add apple and fry for 2 to 3 minutes.
5. Stir in curry powder, let it sizzle, then stir in flour and cook for 1 minute.
6. Strain juice from apricots into a measure and make up to 300 ml/½ pint with water.
7. Add liquid to pan, stir until boiling.
8. Add green pepper, chutney, lemon juice, salt and pepper. Let sauce simmer for 20 minutes, adding a little more water if it becomes too thick. Add apricots to heat through.
9. Put rice around edge of a serving dish, sausages in the middle, and pour sauce over sausages. Garnish with apricots.

LENTIL RICE

For 4 people

½ cup yellow moong dhal*
½ cup long grained rice, white or
brown
2 tablespoons oil
1 medium-sized onion, sliced
½ teaspoon salt
¼ teaspoon turmeric
2 cups hot water, use same cup
as for lentils and rice
½ teaspoon ground cumin
¼ teaspoon mustard seed
A few curry leaves (*see page 38*)

*Moong dhal is the lentil most
widely used in Asian countries.
When used whole it can be sprouted
and becomes the familiar Chinese
beansprout (*see page 65*). Yellow
moong dhal is the split version with
the green husk removed.

1. Wash the lentils and soak them in
plenty of water for 2 hours. If using
brown rice, soak it also.
2. Wash and drain lentils and rice in a
sieve.
3. Heat oil and fry onion until lightly-
browned.
4. Add rice and lentils and fry over
low heat for about 5 minutes.
5. Add all the other ingredients and
bring to the boil.
6. Cover with a well-fitting lid, reduce
heat and simmer for 15 minutes.

It is nice to eat this with pickles such
as Date Chutney (*see page 174*), or
Tomato Relish (*see page 176*), and
with Poppadoms (*see page 38*).

Priya Wickramasinghe
Cardiff

CASHEW NUT CURRY

A favourite Sri Lankan dish.

For 4 people

225 g/8 oz cashew nuts
900 ml/1½ pints cold water
½ teaspoon bicarbonate of soda
1 tablespoon oil
1 medium-sized onion, finely-
chopped
2 cloves

2 cardamoms
2 pieces of cinnamon stick, each
about 2·5 cm/1 inch long
1½ teaspoons ground coriander
1 teaspoon ground cumin
¼ teaspoon turmeric
1 teaspoon salt
25 g/1 oz creamed coconut
125 ml/4 fl oz hot water

1. Soak the cashew nuts for 8 hours in
cold water to which bicarbonate of
soda has been added. Drain away
water and wash cashew nuts.
2. In a pan, heat oil and fry onions
until lightly-browned.
3. Pound or grind the cloves,
cardamoms and cinnamon sticks.
4. Add them to pan with rest of spices,
salt and cashew nuts and mix
thoroughly.
5. Add creamed coconut dissolved in
the hot water and bring to the boil.
6. Put lid on pan, lower heat and
simmer for 15 minutes.

Serve with Lentil Rice (*see opposite*),
or Sri Lankan Yellow Rice (*see page
86*) and a meat dish such as Chicken
Curry (*see page 35*), or Egg Curry
(*see page 87*). Also Cucumber in
Yoghurt (*see page 69*) and Onion
Salad (*see page 70*).

Priya Wickramasinghe
Cardiff

SPICY RISOTTO

For 4 people

This is an ideal way of using meat left
over from the Sunday joint. When
served with a green salad it provides a
balanced meal.

1 cup Basmati* or long-grain
brown or white rice
2 tablespoons oil
1 medium-sized onion, finely-
chopped
2 medium-sized carrots, grated
Half a green pepper, chopped
225 g/8 oz cooked meat cut into
small pieces (lamb, pork or
chicken)
1 teaspoon salt
½ cup frozen peas
⅛ teaspoon ground cardamom

88

¼ teaspoon ground cinnamon
¼ teaspoon ground cloves
2 cups hot water, use same cup as for rice

*Basmati rice is the best of all the varieties of white rice. It has a distinctive aroma and flavour.

1. Wash the rice in a sieve and allow to drain.
2. Heat oil and fry onion until lightly-browned.
3. Add the rice and fry for about 5 minutes on a low heat, stirring all the time.
4. Add rest of ingredients and bring rapidly to the boil.
5. Reduce heat to a minimum, put on well-fitting lid and cook for 15 minutes. If using brown rice cook 25 minutes.

Priya Wickramasinghe
Cardiff

CANNELLONI

For 4 people

Freezes well, but this should be done before final cooking in oven.

12 cannelloni tubes, the ready-to-bake variety are easiest to use

Filling

1 medium onion, finely-chopped
A clove of garlic, crushed
2 tablespoons oil
175 g/6 oz minced beef
1 tablespoon tomato ketchup
1 tablespoon Worcestershire sauce
1 teaspoon oregano
Salt and pepper
1 tablespoon grated cheese
A 250 g/9 oz tin of spinach
1 beaten egg

Tomato Sauce

1 dessertspoon cornflour
2 tablespoons milk
About 600 g/1 lb 6 oz tomatoes
1 tablespoon tomato ketchup

1 teaspoon sugar
1 level teaspoon oregano
1 level teaspoon sweet basil
Salt and pepper

To cover: 40 g/1½ oz grated cheese

1. Fry onion and garlic in oil until soft but not brown.
2. Stir in the mince and cook about 10 minutes. Turn off heat.
3. Stir in remaining filling ingredients, except egg. Allow to cool.
4. Mix in beaten egg.
5. Fill cannelloni tubes with mixture and place them in a buttered, shallow, oven dish.
6. **For the tomato sauce,** slake cornflour by mixing it with milk till smooth.
7. Put all sauce ingredients with cornflour mixture into a pan. Stir over medium heat until boiling.
8. Reduce heat and cook the sauce for 3 minutes, stirring all the time.
9. Pour sauce over cannelloni, sprinkle with grated cheese.
10. Cook at top of a moderate oven, Gas 4, 350°F, 180°C for 30 minutes.

Elizabeth Mickery
Pudsey, West Yorkshire

CASHEW AND APPLE SAVOURIES

Baked in a tray of 6 Yorkshire pudding tins, allowing one for each person. Served with pasta and a cold creamy piquant sauce.

Enough for 6 generous helpings

225 g/8 oz ground cashew nuts*
1 onion, chopped
A clove of garlic, crushed
50 g/2 oz butter
1 green pepper, chopped
¼ teaspoon each of marjoram, thyme, ground cumin and paprika
50 g/2 oz wholewheat flour
2 tablespoons sweet sherry or madeira

89

150 ml/¼ pint light vegetable stock (water from cooking chestnuts is ideal) or use apple or grape juice
50 to 75 g/2 to 3 oz fresh bread-crumbs, wholewheat if possible
1 large cooking apple, grated skin and all
Salt and pepper
50 to 75 g/2 to 3 oz fancy pasta, wholewheat if possible

To garnish: slices of tomato and lemon

*If you cannot buy ground cashew nuts you can grind your own in an electric coffee grinder.

1. Fry onion and garlic gently in butter until transparent.
2. Add green pepper, herbs and spices and fry a further 3 minutes.
3. Stir in flour and cook for 1 minute.
4. Stir in sherry or madeira and stock or fruit juice. Bring to boil and stir over low heat for 2 minutes.
5. Remove pan from heat. Mix in cashews, breadcrumbs and apple. Season with salt and pepper to taste.
6. Spoon mixture into greased tins.
7. Bake in middle of a moderately hot oven, Gas 5, 375°F, 190°C, for about 20 minutes or until cooked thoroughly and browned on top.
8. Meanwhile, cook pasta in boiling, slightly-salted water until tender.
9. Make the sauce.

Creamy Piquant Sauce
225 g/8 oz cottage cheese
2 tablespoons mayonnaise or cream cheese
2 tablespoons yoghurt
2 tablespoons oil
1 tablespoon cider vinegar
1 tablespoon lemon juice
Herbs to taste—e.g., dillweed, chives or tarragon

Put all ingredients together in a liquidiser and blend until smooth.

Or, if you do not have a liquidiser, press cottage cheese through a sieve, then beat in remaining ingredients.

Sarah Brown
Scarborough, Yorkshire

LASAGNE
For 4 people. Served with salad, enough for 6.

350 g/12 oz lasagne
1·4 kg/3 lb fresh spinach
175 g/6 oz Mozzarella cheese, thinly-sliced*
125 g/4 oz grated Parmesan cheese

*Cheddar cheese can be used

Sauce
40 g/1½ oz butter or margarine
1 finely-chopped onion
A crushed clove of garlic
1 chopped green pepper, core and seeds removed
225 g/8 oz minced beef
Two 400 g/14 oz tins of tomatoes
4 tablespoons tomato purée
1 teaspoon paprika pepper
Pepper and a little salt

1. Put lasagne on to cook in boiling salted water, but put it into water 2 or 3 sheets at a time to prevent it sticking together. Then let it all boil together for about 15 minutes.
2. Wash spinach and simmer it with-out extra water until just tender. Drain and chop.
3. Meanwhile start sauce. Heat butter or margarine in a pan. Fry onion, garlic and green pepper for 5 minutes.
4. Stir in beef and fry until it loses its pinkness.
5. Add remaining sauce ingredients, bring to the boil and simmer for 30 minutes.
6. Line the bottom of a well-greased oven dish with about a third of the lasagne.
7. Cover with half of the cooked spinach, then half of the Mozzarella, then half of the sauce.
8. Sprinkle on about a third of the grated Parmesan cheese.
9. Continue making layers, finishing with a thick layer of Parmesan cheese.
10. Put into a moderate oven, Gas 4, 350°F, 180°C and cook for about 40 minutes.

Judith Adshead
Mottram St. Andrew, Cheshire

LASAGNE WITH VEGETABLES

Enough for 4 to 6 people

A substantial dish, nutritionally well-balanced.

125 to 175 g/4 to 6 oz aduki beans, soaked overnight
125 to 175 g/4 to 6 oz Brussels sprouts
125 g/4 oz cabbage
125 g/4 oz mushrooms
1 leek
1 carrot
½ green pepper
1 onion
A clove of garlic (optional)
1 tablespoon oil
600 ml/1 pint stock saved from cooking aduki beans
2 tablespoons tomato purée
1 teaspoon oregano
1 teaspoon marjoram
Salt and pepper
175 g/6 oz lasagne, wholewheat if you can get it
75 g/3 oz grated cheese

Sauce

20 g/¾ oz butter or vegetable margarine
20 g/¾ oz wholewheat flour
450 ml/¾ pint milk
Salt and pepper

1. Remember to start the night before by soaking aduki beans in cold water (*see page 66*).
2. Drain beans, rinse and bring to boil in at least 1·1 litres/2 pints fresh water. Boil for 40 minutes.
3. Cut up all vegetables, except onion and garlic, into even-sized, quite small pieces.
4. Chop onion finely, crush garlic and fry in oil in a large pan until translucent.
5. Mix in prepared vegetables and cook for 5 minutes, stirring occasionally.
6. Drain aduki beans, saving the water, and add them to vegetables.
7. Mix tomato purée into 600 ml/1 pint of the bean stock and pour this over vegetables and beans.

8. Mix well, adding herbs and salt and pepper to taste. Allow to simmer for 30 minutes, stirring occasionally. Adjust seasoning.
9. Meanwhile, make sauce. Melt butter or margarine over low heat, stir in flour and let it sizzle for 1 minute. Gradually add milk, stirring as it thickens and comes to boil. Cook for 3 minutes.
10. Soak lasagne in hot water for 3 to 5 minutes.
11. Grease an oven dish. Make layers of lasagne, vegetables and sauce, ending with a layer of sauce.
12. Put grated cheese on top.
13. Bake near top of a moderate oven, Gas 4, 350°F, 180°C, for 30 minutes until cheese is golden and bubbling and lasagne is cooked.

Serve with green salad, steamed courgettes or broccoli (*see page 75*).

Freezes well for a week or so.

Sarah Brown
Scarborough, Yorkshire

CREAMY MACARONI AND VEGETABLES

A nice macaroni cheese which is also pleasant to eat cold as a salad.

For 4 people

142 ml/5 fl oz natural yoghurt
50 g/2 oz cottage cheese
50 g/2 oz cream cheese
125 g/4 oz leeks, weighed after preparing
125 g/4 oz macaroni, try wholewheat
2 sticks of celery
Half a green pepper
Half a red pepper
½ teaspoon caraway seeds, or dill weed*
1 dessertspoon shoyu (*see page 80*) or Worcestershire sauce
Salt and pepper
50 g/2 oz grated Cheddar cheese

*If you are not fond of the flavour of caraway or dill you can use instead a mixture of mustard and paprika.

1. Mix together yoghurt, cottage and cream cheeses.
2. Wash leeks well and slice quite finely.
3. Blanch leeks by immersing them in a pan of boiling water. Bring to the boil and then drain.
4. Cook macaroni in boiling salted water until just tender.
5. Chop celery and peppers finely.
6. Combine vegetables, macaroni and yoghurt mixture, add caraway seeds and shoyu and taste for seasoning.
7. Put in an oven dish and cover with grated cheese.
8. Bake near top of a moderate oven, Gas 4, 350°F, 180°C, for 30 minutes.

Sarah Brown
Scarborough, Yorkshire

MIXED FRIED NOODLES, INDONESIAN-STYLE

Made with chicken and prawns.

For 4 people

225 g/8 oz egg noodles
1 to 2 tablespoons vegetable oil
Half a medium-sized onion, finely-chopped
2 cloves of garlic, finely-chopped
125 g/4 oz uncooked chicken flesh, cut into very small pieces
125 g/4 oz prawns, shelled
1 stick celery, finely-chopped
50 g/2 oz Chinese cabbage
½ teaspoon salt
1 tablespoon soya sauce
3 spring onions, sliced
Half a cucumber, finely-sliced
1 tablespoon onion flakes

1. Cook the noodles according to the directions on the packet, making sure not to overcook them. Then drain in a colander until needed.
2. In a wok or large frying pan heat the oil.
3. Add onion, garlic, chicken and prawns and stir-fry over a medium to high heat until the chicken and prawns are cooked, about 3 to 5 minutes.

4. Add the celery and cabbage and stir-fry for a few seconds.
5. Add noodles and salt and mix thoroughly.
6. Lastly, add soya sauce and cook for a further minute or so until the dish is heated through.
7. Serve in 4 shallow bowls and garnish with spring onion, cucumber and fried onion flakes.

Priya Wickramasinghe
Cardiff

A RICH MEAT SAUCE FOR SPAGHETTI

This sauce freezes well.

2 rashers streaky bacon
1 onion
A clove of garlic
1 small pig's kidney
2 tablespoons oil
225 g/8 oz beef mince
1 carrot
1 tablespoon tomato purée
150 to 300 ml/¼ to ½ pint stock
A pinch of mixed herbs
Black pepper
Salt
2 teaspoons wholewheat flour or cornflour
1 tablespoon water

To serve
Wholewheat spaghetti, if you can get it. A little grated cheese, preferably Parmesan.

1. Remove rinds from bacon and cut it very small.
2. Peel and finely chop onion. Crush garlic.
3. Dice the kidney very finely.
4. Heat oil and fry bacon gently.
5. Add onion, garlic, mince and kidney. Cook gently for 5 minutes. Stir occasionally.
6. Grate the carrot and add it with tomato purée, 150 ml/¼ pint stock, herbs, pepper and salt. Bring to the boil.
7. Lower heat, cover pan and simmer for 20 minutes. Stir occasionally to prevent sticking, and add more stock if necessary.

8. Meanwhile, cook spaghetti in plenty of boiling salted water.
9. Thicken meat sauce at last minute, if necessary, by mixing flour and water, stirring in and bringing back to the boil.

Serve the grated cheese separately in a small bowl.

BUCKWHEAT PANCAKES

Makes about 10 pancakes

Keep for a day or two in refrigerator. Freeze well.

425 ml/¾ pint milk
1 large egg
A pinch of salt
75 g/3 oz buckwheat flour
75 g/3 oz wholewheat flour
Oil to grease pan

1. **If you do not have a liquidiser:** put flours and salt in a bowl, make a well in centre and drop in egg. Beat in the milk, gradually incorporating flour. Beat thoroughly. **If you have a liquidiser:** put in milk, eggs and salt and switch on for 15 seconds. Then add flours and switch on again for 30 seconds.
2. Heat a frying pan and lightly grease it. Pour in a little mixture swirling it around to make thin pancakes. Cook till browning a little underneath and drying on top.
3. Toss or flip them over to cook other side.
4. When done, flip on to a cold plate so that they cool quickly. This will prevent them becoming leathery.
5. When cold, stack the pancakes on a plate, layered with greaseproof paper.

Delicious as a sweet with soured cream and maple syrup. In Brittany they are often filled with ham, eggs and onions.

Try also:

Buckwheat Pancakes with Creamy Leek Filling

For 4 people for a special occasion
The filling is delicious to eat on its own.

10 buckwheat pancakes
15 g/½ oz butter

Filling
450 g/1 lb leeks, finely-chopped
25 g/1 oz butter
125 g/4 oz cottage cheese
2 tablespoons mayonnaise
2 tablespoons yoghurt
1 tablespoon single cream
1 tablespoon lemon juice
1 tablespoon oil
¼ teaspoon tarragon
Pepper and salt

1. Prepare leeks.
2. Heat butter and fry leeks for 5 to 8 minutes until just softening but not brown.
3. Put remaining ingredients together in liquidiser and switch on for 30 seconds. If you do not have a liquidiser, push cottage cheese through a sieve, then mix it with remaining ingredients and beat hard till you have a soft cream.
4. Mix this with leeks.
5. Spoon filling on to each pancake, roll up and place in a greased dish, seam side down.
6. Dot with butter.
7. Bake in middle of a moderate oven, Gas 4, 350°F, 180°C, for 15 to 20 minutes until just heated through.

Sarah Brown
Scarborough, Yorkshire

SAVOURY FILLINGS FOR PANCAKES OR VOL-AU-VENTS

Ham

For this you need:

300 ml/½ pint thick basic white sauce (*see over*), **made, if possible, with ham stock— otherwise a chicken or ham stock cube will do**

125 g/4 oz chopped cooked ham
1 dessertspoon cooked peas
½ teaspoon chopped fresh parsley

Mushroom

300 ml/½ pint thick basic white
sauce (*see below*), **using chicken
stock.**
175 g/6 oz chopped, lightly-
cooked mushrooms
1 dessertspoon cooked peas

Prawns

300 ml/½ pint thick basic white
sauce (*see below*), **using stock
made from simmering prawn
shells in a little water, then
making up to 300 ml/½ pint with
milk. Otherwise use all milk.**
125 g/4 oz chopped prawns
1 hard-boiled egg, chopped
1 dessertspoon chopped fresh
parsley

BASIC WHITE SAUCES

40 g/1½ oz butter or margarine
40 g/1½ oz plain flour
Salt and pepper

Thick sauce
300 ml/½ pint milk or stock

Medium thick
450 ml/¾ pint milk or stock

Thin
600 ml/1 pint milk or stock

Several methods

I. Traditional
1. Melt butter in a heavy pan.
2. Add flour and work it into butter,
stirring until it forms a smooth paste
which leaves the sides and base of the
pan clean.
3. Cook for a minimum of 2 minutes,
stirring all the time. This is to start
flour cooking.
4. Pour in milk or stock a little at a
time until all the liquid is
incorporated. Beat vigorously between
each addition of liquid in order to
avoid lumps. Season to taste with salt
and pepper.

II. Shortcut
1. Put three tablespoons of milk or
stock into a screw-topped jar or a shaker.
2. Heat rest of milk or stock in a pan
until almost at boiling point. Add
butter and melt.
3. Add flour to shaker or jar, put on
lid, then pour contents into the pan
and stir well until the sauce thickens
and comes to the boil.

III. All-in
For a thick sauce using 300 ml/½ pint
liquid.
1. Put all ingredients together into a
pan over gentle heat and stir
continuously while sauce thickens and
comes to the boil.
2. Boil for 5 minutes.

Savoury Sauces

Anchovy

Anchovies pounded to a purée and added at last minute to medium-thick or thin white sauce, made with milk or stock as above. Quantity of anchovies to your taste.

Cheese

50 to 75 g/2 to 3 oz grated hard, well-flavoured cheese added at last minute to medium thick or thin sauce, made as above with milk. Reheat but do not boil or cheese may go stringy.

Egg

1 or 2 hard-boiled eggs, chopped small, added at last minute to medium thick or thin sauce made with milk, as above.

Parsley

Medium thick white sauce made with milk or stock as above, adding plenty of chopped fresh parsley at the last minute until sauce is nearly green.

Tomato

Using medium thick or thin white sauce made as above with stock. Remove pan from heat and stir in tomato purée, thyme or basil to taste and a pinch of sugar. Reheat.

Sweet sauces

Coffee

Make up thin sauce as above with half milk and half strong coffee. Add sugar to taste—but no salt and pepper.

Vanilla

Make up thin white sauce as above, using milk. Add a vanilla pod while sauce is simmering. Then remove it, wash and dry and store for further use.

BÉCHAMEL SAUCE

A gently-flavoured classic white sauce.

300 ml/½ pint milk
½ bay leaf
2 peppercorns
1 blade of mace
A piece of carrot, 5 cm/2 inches
¼ of a medium onion
25 g/1 oz butter
25 g/1 oz flour
Salt and pepper

1. Put milk, bay leaf, peppercorns, mace, carrot and onion in a pan. Heat for 10 minutes and strain.
2. Use this milk to make a white sauce. Melt butter, stir in flour and let it sizzle for 1 minute.
3. Gradually add milk, stirring as sauce thickens, and let it cook gently for 3 minutes.

POTATO OMELETTE

This is the Spanish Tortilla.

For 2 or 3 people

For this you need a heavy frying pan about 23 cm/9 inches in diameter.

4 small potatoes, 275 g/10 oz total weight
1 small onion
About 200 ml/7 fl oz good quality oil (it would be olive oil in Spain)
A clove of garlic (optional)
3 large lightly-beaten eggs
Sea salt and freshly-ground black pepper

1. Peel and chop potatoes into 1 cm/½ inch cubes. Rinse and dry.
2. Peel and chop onion finely.
3. Heat the oil and fry the peeled garlic clove for a minute, then remove.
4. Put potato cubes into hot oil and cook gently until soft, turning occasionally.
5. Towards the end of the cooking add onion. Do not let oil get too hot.
6. Remove potatoes and onion and mix gently with eggs.
7. Pour off oil, leaving a light film in pan and heat again. Put in the mixture of eggs, potato and onion and cook gently until the underside is cooked but not too brown and the top is still moist. Season well with sea salt and freshly-ground black pepper.

8. Traditionally the tortilla is turned over at this point. It is inverted on to a large plate, then slid back into the pan, cooked-side uppermost. That is the correct way to do it but a satisfactory method is to put the frying pan and its contents under a hot grill for a couple of minutes. The aim is to serve the tortilla with the centre just a little moist.

Grainne Mulligan
Madrid

OVEN-BAKED OMELETTE

Enough for 4 for a light meal with salad

25 g/1 oz butter
6 eggs
Salt and pepper
50 g/2 oz grated cheese
1 teaspoon chopped fresh parsley or chives (optional)
2 tomatoes, skinned (*see page 72*) and sliced

1. Preheat oven to moderately hot, Gas 6, 400°F, 200°C.
2. Put butter in an ovenproof dish into the oven to melt and get hot.
3. Beat eggs lightly, add grated cheese, seasoning and parsley or chives if used.
4. Put tomatoes in oven dish, pour egg mixture over and bake in centre of oven for about 15 minutes until set.
5. Serve immediately.

Margaret Heywood
Todmorden, Yorkshire

CHEESE AND POTATO SOUFFLÉ

For 2 or 3 people

350 g/12 oz mashed potato
3 eggs, separated
25 g/1 oz margarine, softened
100 g/4 oz grated cheese
2 teaspoons grated onion

2 tablespoons milk
A level teaspoon Salt and Pepper Mix (*see page 44*)

1. Preheat the oven to moderately hot, Gas 5, 375°F, 190°C, and have ready the shelf above the middle.
2. Grease a 1 to 1·5 litre/2 to 2½ pint soufflé dish.
3. Have potato well-mashed in a large bowl.
4. Add egg-yolks, margarine, cheese, onion, milk, salt and pepper and mix all well together.
5. Beat up egg-whites till they are stiff and will stand up in peaks.
6. Using a metal spoon, fold egg-whites into the mixture and pour straight into greased dish. Put in the oven without delay.
7. Bake for 50 minutes. Do not be tempted to open oven door while it is cooking.

Serve immediately.

TOMATO AND CHEESE SOUFFLÉ

15 g/½ oz butter
3 large tomatoes skinned (*see page 72*)
Salt and Pepper Mix (*see page 44*)
50 g/2 oz fresh breadcrumbs
150 ml/¼ pint single cream
¼ teaspoon dry mustard
A pinch of cayenne pepper
100 g/4 oz grated cheese
2 large eggs, separated

1. Preheat oven to moderately hot, Gas 5, 375°F, 190°C.
2. Grease a 15 cm/6 inch soufflé dish with the butter.
3. Slice the skinned tomatoes and lay them in dish. Season with a little salt and pepper.
4. Put breadcrumbs in a bowl and pour cream over them. Leave 5 to 6 minutes to soak.
5. Then add mustard and cayenne to bowl. Beat in cheese and egg-yolks.
6. Whisk egg-whites until stiff but not dry. Fold them in.

7. Pour cheese mixture on top of tomatoes and put dish straight into the pre-heated oven. Bake for 40 to 45 minutes.

Serve as soon as it is ready.

POTATO CHEESE CAKES

Like tiny soufflés, these can be cooked in oven or frying pan.

Enough for 3 people

225 g/8 oz potatoes
2 eggs, separated
175 g/6 oz grated cheese
1 medium-sized onion, grated
1 tablespoon chopped parsley
Try also 1 teaspoon kelp powder
1 tablespoon sunflower seed oil, for frying

1. If baking these, pre-heat oven to moderately hot, Gas 5, 375°F, 190°C.
2. Cook the potatoes in their skins in a little water, cutting them into reasonable-sized pieces. Peel them while hot and mash.
3. Whisk egg-yolks until fluffy and mix in mashed potato, cheese, onion, parsley and kelp powder.
4. Whisk egg-whites until stiff and fold in.
5. Heat oil in frying pan. Put mixture into pan in small mounds and fry quickly till crisp and brown on both sides. If baking, put small mounds on a greased baking tray and bake for 15 minutes, till they are crisp and brown outside and puffy inside.

Eaten with a green salad, these can make a meal in themselves. Nice with home-made tomato sauce (*see Cannelloni, page 89*).

To vary the flavour use chives, paprika, chopped tomato, mixed herbs or a dessertspoon of curry powder.

For extremely light cheese cakes replace potato by 50 g/2 oz wholewheat flour and use two more eggs. Otherwise, make as for potato cheese cakes.

Elizabeth Shears
Author of 'Why Do We Eat'

ONION TART

For 4, but easy to make a smaller tart

Case
12 to 13 cream crackers (175 g/ 6 oz)
50 g/2 oz melted butter or margarine

Filling
2 medium-sized onions
25 g/1 oz butter or margarine
2 lightly-beaten eggs
200 ml/7 fl oz milk
1 teaspoon Salt and Pepper Mix (*see page 44*)
50 g/2 oz grated cheese
A sprinkle of paprika

1. Crush crackers to fine crumbs. Mix in melted butter or margarine and press into bottom and sides of a shallow, 20 cm/8 inch pie plate or quiche dish.
2. Peel and quarter onions and cut thin slices.
3. Cook in butter or margarine until soft but not brown. Put in tart case.
4. Combine eggs, milk, salt and pepper. Pour over onions.
5. Sprinkle grated cheese on top.
6. Bake near top of a moderate oven, Gas 4, 350°F, 180°C, for about 35 minutes, or until set.
7. Sprinkle paprika on top.

Nice hot or cold.

CHEESE CRISPIES

Good with grilled sausages, bacon or liver.

225 g/8 oz grated potato
25 g/1 oz self-raising flour
50 g/2 oz grated cheese
Pepper and salt
1 egg
About 50 g/2 oz lard for frying

1. Grate potato coarsely into a basin, add self-raising flour, cheese and seasoning.
2. Beat egg and mix in.
3. Heat lard in a frying pan until a

light blue smoke rises from it. Then drop in spoonfuls of the mixture.
4. Fry until golden brown on both sides. Then turn down heat until cooked through.
5. Drain on kitchen paper or brown paper.
6. Serve immediately.

Stella Boldy
Sykehouse, N. Humberside

BACON FLODDIES

A way to use up a small amount of cold cooked meat. Turkey or chicken floddies can also be made.

1 large potato peeled
1 medium onion peeled
1 beaten egg
25 g/1 oz self-raising flour
75 g/3 oz bacon, finely-chopped
A pinch of mixed herbs (optional)
Salt and pepper
Oil for frying

1. Grate potato and onion into a basin.
2. Mix in egg.
3. Add flour, chopped bacon, herbs and seasoning and mix well.
4. Heat oil in a heavy-based frying pan.
5. Fry tablespoons of the mixture, turning until golden brown both sides.

Sybil Norcott
Irlam, Nr. Manchester

QUICK PIZZA
No need for the oven.

Enough for 3 or 4 but easy to make less

Base
125 g/4 oz self-raising flour
¼ teaspoon salt
3 tablespoons oil
A little cold water

Filling
25 g/1 oz butter
1 small onion, finely-chopped

225 g/8 oz tinned or fresh tomatoes skinned (*see page 72*) and chopped
1 teaspoon mixed herbs

To finish
125 g/4 oz grated cheese
2 or 3 rashers of streaky bacon cut in strips, or anchovies soaked for 10 minutes in a little milk to remove excess salt, or olives

1. Mix together flour and salt. Stir in 1 tablespoon of the oil and enough water to make a fairly stiff but pliable dough.
2. Using a floured board, roll out to fit a frying pan about 18 cm/7 inches in diameter.
3. Heat rest of oil in the pan and cook dough over moderate heat for about 5 to 6 minutes.
4. Turn it over and cook 4 to 5 minutes on the other side.
5. Meanwhile make filling. Melt butter and fry onion until beginning to soften but not to colour.
6. Add tomatoes and herbs and cook for 1 minute. Drain off excess liquid.
7. Spread tomato mixture on top of cooked base in pan.
8. Sprinkle with cheese.
9. If using **bacon**, arrange the strips on top of cheese and put under a moderate grill for a few minutes. If using **anchovies**, pat dry, arrange on top of cheese and grill. If using **olives**, use them to decorate after cheese has melted under grill.

HAM AND LEEKS WITH CHEESE SAUCE
No need for the oven. The quantity can be varied to suit your household, but there will be *enough sauce for 4 people*.

For each person
1 leek, not too large
1 slice cooked ham

Sauce
40 g/1½ oz butter or margarine

40 g/1½ oz white or wholewheat flour
Salt and Pepper Mix (*see page 44*)
150 ml/¼ pint cooking liquid from leeks
A bare 300 ml/½ pint milk
A grating of nutmeg
50 g/2 oz grated cheese

To finish: 50 g/2 oz grated cheese and 2 tablespoons fresh wholewheat breadcrumbs

1. Trim and wash leeks and cook them in a little boiling water until just beginning to become tender, about 10 minutes. Save the liquid as you drain them.
2. Wrap a slice of ham around each leek and place in a shallow, greased oven dish.
3. Melt butter or margarine, add flour and let it sizzle for 1 minute.
4. Add liquid gradually, stirring as it thickens. Add nutmeg. Bring to the boil and cook for 2 minutes.
5. Add cheese, stir to dissolve and heat but do not boil.
6. Pour sauce over leeks and ham.
7. For the top, mix the second 50 g/2 oz cheese with the breadcrumbs and sprinkle over the sauce.
8. Place dish under a moderately hot grill to heat through and brown a little.

FRIED TRIPE WITH ONIONS

A light meal for 4—enough for 2 or 3 for a main meal

450 g/1 lb tripe
Salt
Milk
Water
2 tablespoons wholewheat flour
Pepper
Deep fat or oil for frying
2 onions, sliced
A small clove of garlic, crushed
25 g/1 oz butter
1 tablespoon cooking oil
A few grains cayenne
1 tablespoon chopped parsley
2 lemons

Slices of wholemeal bread, buttered

1. Although tripe is blanched or partially cooked when bought it may need to be cooked again before being used. If it will cut with a knife it is cooked enough. If not, put it in a pan, add a little salt and cover with mixed milk and water. Put lid on pan and cook until tender.
2. Drain and dry the tripe and cut it into strips.
3. Season the flour and toss in it the strips of tripe. Wholewheat flour gives a nutty flavour and a nice, crisp texture.
4. Deep fry until golden and crisp, 5 to 7 minutes. Drain on kitchen paper and keep hot.
5. Meanwhile, heat butter and oil in a pan. Fry onions and garlic till golden but not brown. Then add parsley and juice of 1 lemon and cook 1 minute more.
6. Turn out on to a warmed dish and put tripe on top.

Serve with quarters of lemon and brown bread and butter. Best just like this, not with extra vegetables.

CHEESE AND WALNUT PÂTÉ

Enough for 8 to 10

Keeps for several days in refrigerator and freezes well.

225 g/8 oz cottage cheese
75 g/3 oz ground walnuts
3 tablespoons butter
75 g/3 oz Cheddar cheese, finely grated
1 teaspoon caraway seeds, nice but not essential
1 to 2 teaspoons wholegrain mustard
Salt and black pepper
5 to 6 tablespoons fresh wholewheat breadcrumbs

To garnish: lettuce leaves, cress, tomato slices, walnut halves

1. If you like a fine-textured pâté, first sieve the cottage cheese.

2. Walnuts may be ground in an electric coffee grinder.
3. Cream butter and cottage cheese.
4. Add grated cheese, walnuts, caraway seeds and seasonings. Mix well.
5. Mix in breadcrumbs.
6. Press pâté into a nice dish or into ramekins. Or serve with an ice cream scoop on individual plates garnished with lettuce, cress, tomato slices and extra walnut halves.

Sarah Brown
Scarborough, Yorkshire

SPICED HAM AND EGG SALAD

Enough for 8, but easy to make less

Can be made with a boiled bacon joint or with sliced boiled ham or pork shoulder.

12 hard-boiled eggs
350 g/12 oz long grain brown or white rice
A small piece of saffron
150 ml/¼ pint mayonnaise (*see page 64*)
450 g/lb boiled ham or bacon

Dressing

3 tablespoons olive oil, or good salad oil
2 tablespoons wine or cider vinegar
2 tablespoons tomato ketchup
2 tablespoons mango chutney
A dash of tabasco
Salt and pepper

To garnish: watercress

1. Cook rice with saffron following instructions for Boiled Rice *on page 86*.
2. Mix mayonnaise with rice and spread it on a large serving plate to cool.
3. Cut eggs in half and arrange them on rice.
4. Shred ham finely and place it on top of eggs.
5. Thoroughly mix dressing ingredients, cutting mango chutney pieces very small. *Or*, put all these

ingredients into a liquidiser and switch on for 1 minute.
6. Pour dressing over ham and eggs. Garnish with watercress.

Judith Adshead
Mottram St. Andrew, Cheshire

SAVOURY PEANUT LOAF

Nice hot or cold. If hot, serve with a well-flavoured tomato sauce, see Cannelloni (*page 89*) or Meat Balls in Tangy Tomato Sauce (*page 49*). Good for picnics and packed lunches.

175 g/6 oz peanuts, finely-chopped or ground
125 g/4 oz carrot, grated
125 g/4 oz celery, finely-chopped
75 g/3 oz fresh wholewheat breadcrumbs
2 beaten eggs
2 tablespoons milk
2 teaspoons tomato purée
2 teaspoons mixed herbs
Pepper and salt

To finish: 50 g/2 oz butter

1. Pre-heat oven to moderate, Gas 4, 350°F, 180°C.
2. Mix ingredients, adding pepper and salt to taste.
3. Line the bottom of a greased ½ kg/1 lb loaf tin with greaseproof paper.
4. Spoon mixture into tin and press it down lightly. Dot with butter.
5. Bake near top of oven for 30 to 35 minutes.
6. Leave to cool for 5 minutes before turning out of tin.

Janet Horsley
Headingley, Yorkshire

SANDWICH SPREADS

Tuna and Walnut

A 100 g/3½ oz tin of tuna, drained and chopped
25 g/1 oz walnuts, chopped
A 5 cm/2 inch piece of cucumber, chopped small
2 dessertspoons salad cream
2 dessertspoons chutney

1 level teaspoon dry mustard
Pepper and salt

Combine all ingredients and season to taste. If too thick to spread add a little more salad cream or chutney.

Roe Paste

225 g/8 oz cooked cod's roe
50 g/2 oz melted butter
Pepper and salt
A dash of vinegar

1. Skin the roe and mash it.
2. Add melted butter and pepper, salt and vinegar to taste.

3. Beat well or use a liquidiser to blend.

Liver Spread

125 to 175 g/4 to 6 oz lightly-cooked lamb's liver
1 large spring onion, chopped
25 to 50 g/1 to 2 oz melted butter
Pepper and salt

Put all ingredients in a liquidiser and blend for 2 or 3 minutes.

See also Potted Meat from Clear Beef Soup (*page 9*).

Chapter 7

Pies
and
Pastries

PASTRY

A few tips

1. All pastry is less likely to shrink during cooking if it is allowed to rest in a cool place or refrigerator for 10 to 15 minutes before rolling out, and again immediately before baking. Cover it with greaseproof paper, polythene or cling-film.

2. When recipes indicate a certain quantity of home-baked pastry is required it means that you make up pastry using that quantity of flour— e.g., for 225 g /8 oz short-crust you make up pastry based on 225 g/8 oz flour.

3. Quantity of pastry required for different-sized flans. It is usually rolled out to 7 mm/¼ inch thick:

15 cm/6 inch
18 cm/7 inch } 125 g/4 oz flour

20 cm/8 inch
23 cm/9 inch } 150 g/6 oz flour

25 cm/10 inch   225 g/8 oz flour

4. To prepare a flan case for baking 'blind' requires:

(a) a circle of pastry 5 cm/2 inches wider than diameter of flan tin, ring or dish.

(b) not to stretch pastry when fitting it into tin.

(c) to prick base all over with a fork.

(d) a circle of foil to fit into bottom and sides of flan.

(e) dried peas or beans to fill and hold pastry in shape during baking (ceramic 'beans' can now be bought).

5. To bake a flan case with hard-to-handle, rich shortcrust pastry. Lay pastry on the *outside* of an upturned flan or cake tin. Prick base and bake as usual.

6. To bake flan cases blind:

(a) White shortcrust: hot oven, Gas 7, 425°F, 220°C, 10 to 12 minutes. Remove beans, foil, reduce temperature to moderate, Gas 4, 350°F, 180°C, and bake for a further 7 to 8 minutes.

(b) Cheese pastry, either white or wholewheat, also wholewheat short-crust and sweet wholewheat: moderately hot, Gas 6, 400°F, 200°C, for 15 minutes. Remove beans and foil and return to oven for 10 minutes more.

(c) Rich sweet shortcrust: moderately hot, Gas 5, 375°F, 190°C, for 10 minutes. Remove beans and foil and return to oven for a further 10 to 15 minutes. If you have your pastry on the outside of the tin, allow it 20 to 25 minutes complete baking time.

7. To avoid a soggy bottom in a flan which has a moist filling:

(a) If flan case is ready-baked, paint inside with beaten egg and allow to dry before putting in filling.

(b) If flan case is uncooked, pre-heat a baking sheet at the highest possible oven temperature. Put flan into oven on to this, then turn heat down immediately to the baking temperature required.

8. Half-cooked flan cases. These are useful when a flan filling needs lower heat than temperature required to seal pastry. Prepare as if baking blind and bake near top of a moderately hot oven, Gas 6, 400°F, 200°C, for 10 to 12 minutes. Remove from oven, cool, then fill and bake to suit filling.

Shortcrust, white or wholewheat

225 g/8 oz plain white or whole-wheat flour or a mixture
½ level teaspoon salt
50 g/2 oz hard margarine (add 25 g/1 oz for wholewheat pastry)
50 g/2 oz lard or hard vegetable fat
2 tablespoons cold water (3 for wholewheat) use a measure

Sieve or mix flour and salt in a bowl. Cut fats into small pieces, put them into bowl and rub between fingers until mixture is like fine breadcrumbs. Add water and, using a round-ended knife, stir until mixture begins to bind. Then use your hand to knead lightly and quickly until dough is formed.

Rich sweet shortcrust

Ideal for rich dessert flans and tartlet cases. Almost as rich as shortbread and needs careful handling. See tip 5 *opposite.*

225 g/8 oz plain white flour*
A pinch of salt
150 g/5 oz butter or margarine, softened
25g/1 oz sugar
1 egg-yolk
A squeeze of lemon juice
2 or 3 tablespoons cold water
*There is no benefit in making this with wholewheat flour. The previous recipe is rich enough especially if some of the fat is replaced with butter and 1 teaspoon sugar is added.

Sieve flour and salt into a bowl. Rub in butter or margarine as lightly as possible. Add sugar. Mix together egg-yolk, lemon juice and 2 tablespoons water. Stir it into flour with a round-ended knife. Then use your hand to knead lightly to a firm dough, adding 1 or 2 teaspoons more water only if necessary.

Cheese pastry

Delicious for savoury flans, meat pies, sausage rolls, etc.

225 g/8 oz plain white or whole-wheat flour
½ level teaspoon salt
½ level teaspoon dry mustard
A pinch of cayenne pepper
75 g/3 oz hard margarine or vegetable fat
75 g/3 oz well-flavoured cheese, finely-grated
1 egg-yolk
2 tablespoons water (3 for wholewheat pastry) use a measure

Sieve or mix flour, salt, mustard and cayenne pepper. Rub in margarine with fingertips until mixture is like breadcrumbs. Mix in cheese. Mix egg-yolk with water and stir it with a round-ended knife. Then knead lightly until smooth and a firm dough is formed.

RICH PIE PASTRY

For savoury pies. Can be used where a more difficult hot water crust is normally used. The following

ingredients make enough pastry to line and cover a ½ kg/1 lb loaf tin.

275 g/10 oz plain flour, or half white and half wholewheat
1 teaspoon salt
140 g/4½ oz lard
1 beaten egg
About 65 ml/2½ fluid oz water

1. Sieve or mix flour and salt in a bowl. Rub in lard.
2. Keep 1 teaspoon of the beaten egg for glazing. Mix the rest with water and use it to bind flour and lard into a soft elastic dough. If using whole-wheat flour it may take a bit more water.
3. Leave dough to rest for at least 1 hour before rolling out.

Anne Wallace
Stewarton, Ayrshire

GROUND ALMOND FLAKY PASTRY

275 g/10 oz plain flour
125 g/4 oz ground almonds
50 g/2 oz ground rice
Pinch of salt
350 g/12 oz butter
1 tablespoon lemon juice
6 tablespoons iced water

1. Sift flour, ground almonds, ground rice and salt into a bowl.
2. Rub one quarter of the butter into flour mixture and mix to a pliable but not sticky dough with lemon juice and iced water as required.
3. Cover and put aside in a cool place to rest for 10 to 15 minutes.
4. Soften remaining butter with a knife and divide into thirds.
5. Using a floured board, roll out pastry 3 times as long as wide, about 7 mm/¼ inch thick.
6. Using one third of the butter, place in dabs over the top two-thirds of pastry.
7. Fold bottom third up, and top third down. Seal edges lightly with rolling pin. Turn, leaving pressed edges at top and bottom and at right-hand side. Wrap in greaseproof paper and put to

rest in the refrigerator or in a cold place for 10 minutes.

8. Repeat rollings with second and then third portions of butter. Then wrap and leave in a cold place for 1 hour, or overnight. If leaving it overnight, wrap a damp cloth around greaseproof covering to make quite sure it is still soft and has no crust when you need to use it.

This pastry will keep in refrigerator for 2 or 3 days. Freezes well.

Mrs Angela Mottram
Axbridge, Somerset

PUFF PASTRY

Usually bought ready made, frozen. This is nevertheless satisfying to make but a long, slow job with frequent use of the refrigerator to chill the pastry at various stages. It is used for very special pastries like vol-au-vents. *See page 93* for a variety of fillings.

225 g/8 oz plain white flour
A pinch of salt
225 g/8 oz unsalted butter
A squeeze of lemon juice
Cold water to mix

1. Sift flour and salt into a bowl and rub in 50 g/2 oz of the butter.
2. Add lemon juice and a little water to make a stiffish dough.
3. Place on a wooden board and knead until smooth.
4. Allow the butter to soften until it is pliable enough to form into a neat brick about 2 cm/¾ inch thick.
5. Roll out dough into a rectangle 30 by 15 cm/12 by 6 inches. Place butter on one half and fold the rest over to enclose it completely. Seal edges. Wrap in a polythene bag and chill for 10 minutes.
6. Put pastry on board with the fold to the left. Roll it out lightly to a long strip about 45 by 15 cm/18 by 6 inches. Fold into 3. Seal edges by pressing lightly with rolling pin. Replace in polythene bag and chill for 10 minutes.
7. Repeat rolling, folding, sealing and chilling so that this process has been done about 7 times in all. For the final chill in refrigerator allow 30 minutes.

Pastry is then ready for use. Or it can be frozen.

8. Roll out 7 mm/¼ inch thick for use. When shaped, chill again for 30 minutes before baking.

ROUGH PUFF PASTRY

As the name implies, an economical and a quickly-made puff pastry. Excellent for Christmas mince pies, sausage rolls and used also in Cheese Strudel Slices (*see page 17*).

225 g/8 oz strong plain flour
A pinch of salt
75 g/3 oz firm margarine
75 g/3 oz firm lard
½ teaspoon lemon juice
About 125 ml/¼ pint water

1. Sieve flour and salt into a basin.
2. Cut fats into 1 cm/½ inch cubes. Mix lightly into flour, but do not break up.
3. Mix to a dough with lemon juice and water. It usually takes the full amount. Form dough into a brick-shape and chill for 10 minutes.
4. On a well-floured board, lightly roll out pastry 7 mm/¼ inch thick, 3 times as long as wide. Fold bottom third up and top third down. Press edges lightly with rolling pin to seal. Wrap in greaseproof paper, polythene or cling-film and chill for 10 minutes.
5. Put pastry on board, folded edges to right and left. Repeat rolling, folding, sealing and chilling 3 times more.

Chill for 30 minutes before using. Freezes well at this stage.

CHOUX PASTRY

This pastry is made in an unusual way. It is almost always associated with éclairs and profiteroles, but it also makes an excellent container for savoury fillings (*see page 93 for some fillings for pancakes or vol-au-vents*). They can be served hot or cold.

65 g/2½ oz flour
A pinch of salt
50 g/2 oz butter
100 ml/4 fl oz water
2 well-beaten eggs

1. Sift the flour and salt on to a piece of paper (this is a help when adding the flour to the hot water and butter).
2. Cut up butter into small pieces and put this with the water into a saucepan. Bring this mixture to the boil. When the butter has melted shoot in the flour and remove pan from heat. Beat well with a wooden spoon until there are no lumps left.
3. Now beat in half of the beaten egg with care and when well mixed add the second egg a bit at a time.
4. At this point the mixture should be slack enough to pipe easily, but firm enough to retain its shape. Put lid on pan and let it cool a little.
5. Put mixture into a forcing bag with a 1 cm/½ inch plain nozzle. Pipe either small rounds or sausage shapes on a well-greased tin or on a baking sheet lined with non-stick paper.
6. Bake in a moderately hot oven, Gas 6, 400°F, 200°C, for 20 to 25 minutes or until crisp, golden and puffy.
7. Cool on a wire rack. They are now ready to be filled.

SARAH BROWN'S WHOLEWHEAT PASTRY

An unorthodox approach to pastry-making but one that answers complaints that wholewheat pastry is unmanageable and hard. It is meant to be wet as you make it. This way it will roll out easily and thinly.

225 g/8 oz wholewheat flour
75 g/3 oz mixed hard fats, solid vegetable fat and butter are suitable
15 g/½ oz soft brown sugar
A pinch of salt
A pinch of baking powder
100 ml/4 fl oz water
1 teaspoon oil

1. Rub fats into flour.
2. Mix in sugar, salt and baking powder.
3. Add water and oil and mix to a dough, which should be fairly wet.

If it seems too wet leave it for a few minutes for flour to absorb some of moisture. Otherwise simply squeeze out excess water.
4. Roll out as required on a floured board.

Keeps a week in refrigerator if well-wrapped.

To bake blind

1. Using a floured board, roll out very thinly and line the tin. Prick bottom all over with a fork.
2. Bake near top of a moderately hot oven, Gas 6, 400°F, 200°C, for 12 minutes.

CHEESE AND ONION PIE

A simple-to-make pie which can be made with either wholewheat or white shortcrust pastry (*see page 104*). The strong flavoured Canadian Cheddar gives the filling a bite.

Enough for 4 or 5 people

350 g/12 oz shortcrust pastry

Filling
2 large onions, minced or finely-chopped
225 g/8 oz Canadian Cheddar cheese, grated
Pepper
2 tablespoons milk
25 g/1 oz butter

1. Line a 25 cm/10 inch pie tin or flan ring on a baking sheet with two thirds of the pastry. Roll out the rest for the lid.
2. Mix onions and cheese, season to taste and add a little milk to keep pie moist.
3. Put filling into pastry base, dot top with small pieces of butter.
4. Brush edges of pie with water, fit on lid, press to seal. Brush top with milk to glaze. Make two or three slits to let out steam.
5. Bake in centre of a hot oven, Gas 7, 425°F, 220°C, for 30 to 35 minutes. If

using wholewheat pastry, bake just above middle of a moderately hot oven, Gas 6, 400°F, 200°C.

Best served just warm or cold.

Can be frozen either before baking, in which case do not glaze, or after cooking when quite cold.

Mrs Iris Dargavel
Llanellen, Gwent

COLD SAVOURY FLAN

For 4 people

For this you need a 20 cm/8 inch flan case baked blind. Cheese or whole-wheat pastry is nice for this filling (*see pages 104/105*).

3 eggs
25 g/1 oz butter
2 tablespoons thin cream or top-of-the-milk
75 to 125 g/3 to 4 oz lean cooked ham or bacon, chopped small
2 tablespoons mayonnaise
125 g/4 oz frozen mixed vegetables, cooked and cooled
Black pepper and a little salt

To garnish: tomato or cucumber slices

1. Scramble eggs with butter and cream.
2. Add chopped ham, mayonnaise, vegetables and seasoning.
3. Fill flan case and decorate with slices of tomato and or cucumber.

COURGETTE TART

For this you need a 20 or 23 cm/8 or 9 inch pastry case baked blind. Choose a pastry on page 104 and follow instructions given for baking blind (*see page 104*).

350 g/12 oz courgettes
15 g/½ oz butter
1 small onion, chopped
1 teaspoon chopped fresh tarragon or ½ teaspoon dried
2 large eggs

142 ml/5 fl oz soured cream
3 heaped tablespoons grated Parmesan cheese
Salt and pepper

1. Wash courgettes and trim off stalks, but do not peel. Cube them. Do not slice.
2. Melt butter, add courgettes, onion and tarragon. Put on lid and cook over a low heat, shaking pan occasionally, until courgettes are barely done. Leave to cool.
3. Beat together eggs and cream. Stir in Parmesan.
4. Fold this sauce into courgettes. Add pepper and a little salt to taste.
5. Pour into pastry case.
6. Bake above middle of a moderate oven, Gas 4, 350°F, 180°C, for 30 to 40 minutes.

HAM, EGG AND ONION FLAN

150 g/5 oz wholewheat or white shortcrust pastry (*see page 104*)

Filling

25 g/1 oz ham fat or lard
1 small onion, finely-chopped
125 g/4 oz cooked ham
2 beaten eggs
300 ml/½ pint milk
Pepper and a little salt
50 g/2 oz grated Cheddar cheese

1. Using a floured board, roll out pastry to fit a 20 cm/8 inch flan tin, or a ring set on a baking tray, or a flan dish.
2. For the filling. Heat fat and fry onion gently to soften.
3. Put onion and ham in flan.
4. Mix eggs, milk and seasoning and strain into flan.
5. Sprinkle cheese on top.
6. Bake near top of a moderately hot oven, Gas 6, 400°F, 200°C, for 20 minutes. Then reduce heat to moderate, Gas 4, 350°F, 180°C, for another 10 minutes.

LEEK FLAN

Tarten Gennin in Wales.
An excellent, rich and well-flavoured
flan. Easy to make half the given
quantity.

Pastry

A 25 cm/10 inch ready-baked
flan case, of either wholewheat
or white shortcrust pastry (*see
page 104*)
Or, two 15 cm/6 inches in
diameter

Filling

6 large leeks
25 g/1 oz butter
150 g/5 oz bacon, chopped
4 well-beaten eggs
300 ml/½ pint milk or cream
Pepper and salt
75 g/3 oz grated cheese
(optional)

1. Wash leeks and cut both white and
green into 2·5 cm/1 inch pieces.
2. Heat butter in a saucepan and cook
leeks over very low heat with lid on
pan until they are soft.
3. Spread leeks in pastry case.
Arrange bacon on top.
4. Beat eggs with milk or cream,
adding pepper and a little salt. Pour
into flan case.
5. Sprinkle cheese over and put at
once in the middle or lower part of a
moderate oven, Gas 4, 350°F, 180°C, for
35 minutes.

If making 15 cm/6 inch flans bake for
25 to 30 minutes.

Serve hot or cold.

Mrs Eileen Trumper
Llanvair Kilgeddin, Gwent

MINCED BACON AND PORK PIE

Makes about 6 portions

275 g/10 oz rich pie pastry (*see
page 105*)

Filling

175 g/6 oz cheapest bacon

175 g/6 oz minced pork
luncheon meat
Pepper and salt
2 eggs
75 ml/2½ oz milk

This quantity is enough for a loaf
shape or round pie with a lid.

1. Roll out two thirds of the pastry
and line a ½ kg/1 lb loaf tin, an 18 cm/
7 inch pie plate or flan ring set on a
baking sheet.
2. Mince bacon, mix it with pork and
season with pepper if necessary.
3. Put it into pastry-lined tin.
4. Beat eggs, adding milk and a little
salt, and pour over meat, saving 1 or 2
teaspoons to glaze the pie.
5. Roll out the pastry lid, damp edges,
place it over filling and seal all round.
6. Use trimmings to decorate and
brush over with remaining egg and
milk to glaze. Do not make holes in top
yet or filling may boil over and spoil
top.
7. Bake near top of a moderately hot
oven, Gas 6, 400°F, 200°C for 1 hour,
moving pie down to middle when it
has begun to brown.
8. Remove pie from oven and pierce
lid in one or two places to let out
steam.

Serve hot or cold.

Anne Wallace,
Stewarton, Ayrshire

SAVOURY SAUSAGE PIE

*Quantities given makes two 15 cm/6
inch pies, so it is easy to make just
one.*

Freezes well.

Mrs Odell had this recipe given her
many years ago by a 90-year-old
Worcester woman who remembered
the filling being minced up pork pieces
left after the pig was killed. It was
known as 'Bits and Pieces'.

350 g/12 oz shortcrust pastry,
white or wholewheat or a
mixture (*see page 104*)

Filling

450 g /1 lb pork sausagemeat

125 g/4 oz bacon bits, fat pork
or streaky bacon
1 medium-sized cooking apple
1 tablespoon chopped fresh
parsley
2 beaten eggs
Pepper and salt

An optional addition: 1 hard-
boiled egg for each pie, but if
you are going to freeze pies it is
best to leave this out.

1. Using a floured board, roll out
225 g/8 oz of the pastry to fit two
15 cm/6 inch flan rings or dishes,
saving the rest for the lids.
2. **Now for the filling.** Mash up
sausagemeat in a large bowl.
3. Mince bacon or pork.
4. Grate the apple.
5. Mix all filling ingredients together,
except hard-boiled egg, seasoning with
pepper and a little salt if necessary.
Save a dessertspoon of beaten egg to
glaze pie tops.
6. Divide filling between the two
flans. Arrange a quartered hard-boiled
egg in each if desired, covering them
carefully with sausage mixture.
7. Roll out lids. Moisten edges, secure
them in place and pinch edges to seal.
Use trimmings to decorate.
8. Prick tops in several places with a
fork. Mix a dessertspoon of milk with
remaining beaten egg and brush tops
of pies to glaze.
9. Bake for 45 minutes in all at top of a
moderately hot oven, Gas 5, 375°F,
190°C, for 30 minutes, then if
browning too quickly reduce heat to
moderate, Gas 4, 350°F, 180°C, for the
last 15 minutes.

Mrs Olive Odell
Hartlebury, Worcestershire

CORNISH PASTY

We sampled this pasty with members
of the Women's Institute in Truro and
it was excellent—but the variations
are as many in Cornwall as elsewhere.

**100 g/4 oz shortcrust pastry
using the flour of your choice**
(*see page 104*)

Filling
125 g/4 oz skirt of beef
1 potato
1 small onion
A small piece of swede
Salt and pepper
A little milk
A small piece of butter

1. Make up pastry and leave it in a
cool place to rest.
2. Cut meat into strips and then slice
finely (but do not mince).
3. Slice vegetables finely and mix
together.
4. Roll out pastry into a round, about
23 cm/9 inches in diameter.
5. Place mixed vegetables on one half
of pastry and season to taste. Put meat
on top of vegetables and season again.
6. Damp edges of pastry with milk and
fold it over into a pasty. Seal edges.
7. Crimp the sealed edges. Brush
pastry with milk. Cut two slits in top
of pasty.
8. Bake in a hot oven, Gas 7, 425°F,
220°C, for 20 minutes or until pastry
starts to brown. Then reduce heat to
moderately hot, Gas 5, 375°F, 190°C,
and bake for a further 30 minutes.

About 10 minutes before cooking time
is completed, remove pasty from the
oven and put butter in the slits in
pastry. Replace in oven to finish
cooking.

Mrs Jean Wootton
Cornwall Women's Institute

DEEP-FRIED PASTIES

175 g/6 oz white shortcrust
pastry (*see page 104*)
Fat for deep-frying

Filling
225 g/8 oz cooked meat, beef,
chicken, bacon or ham, minced
2 teaspoons Worcestershire
sauce
1 teaspoon Salt and Pepper Mix
(*see page 44*)

1. Using a floured board, roll out
pastry, 7 mm/¼ inch thick. Cut 10 cm/
4 inch rounds.

2. Mix together minced meat, sauce, salt and pepper.
3. Place a dessertspoonful on each round of pastry. Damp edges, fold into pasties and seal edges.
4. Heat fat, 340°F, 170°C is the correct temperature. Otherwise you can test heat by dropping in a 1 cm/½ inch cube of bread. The bread should turn golden in 30 seconds. If it turns brown the fat is too hot, allow to cool a little. If fat is not hot enough the bread will not colour.
5. Cook for 4 to 5 minutes until golden. Drain on brown paper or kitchen paper. Eat piping hot.

Fillings can be varied: add 50 g/2 oz chopped mushrooms if you don't have sufficient meat. Also try minced pork with a little onion, a small apple and 2 to 3 teaspoons sage and onion stuffing or a pinch of dried sage.

DEVONSHIRE PORK PASTIES

Makes about 6 or 7 pasties

Especially good made with whole-wheat pastry and eaten cold with salad.

350 g/12 oz white or whole-wheat shortcrust pastry (*see page 104*)
350 g/12 oz cooked pork
1 small onion or 1 stick of celery
1 teaspoon Worcestershire sauce
Salt and pepper

1. Make up pastry and leave it to rest in a cool place while preparing filling.
2. Cut up pork into 1 cm/½ inch cubes.
3. Grate onion or chop celery very finely.
4. Mix pork and onion with Worcestershire sauce, adding salt and pepper to taste.
5. Using a floured board, roll out pastry about 7 mm/¼ inch thick and cut rounds about 15 cm/6 inches across, saucer size.
6. Place equal amounts of filling in centre of each pastry round.

7. Damp edges of pastry and bring edges together to make a join across top. Press lightly to seal and flute edges with fingers and thumb. Make 2 slits alongside the join.
8. Bake above middle of a moderately hot oven, Gas 6, 400°F, 200°C, for 30 minutes until firm and just golden.

Mrs Becky Blackmore
Exeter, Devon

SUSSEX CHURDLES

Delicious pasties with a crisp cheese topping.

Makes 6

225 g/8 oz shortcrust pastry

Filling

100 g/4 oz lamb's liver
100 g/4 oz bacon
1 medium-sized onion
25 g/1 oz lard
50 g/2 oz mushrooms*
½ dessertspoon chopped fresh parsley
¼ teaspoon dried rosemary (optional)
Salt and pepper

Topping

1 tablespoon grated cheese
1 tablespoon wholewheat bread-crumbs
Beaten egg to glaze
*Mushrooms can be replaced with tomatoes or apple if preferred

1. Skin liver and cut up small. Cut up bacon and chop onion finely.
2. Fry these together in the lard for 5 minutes.
3. Add mushrooms, herbs and seasoning and cook 2 or 3 minutes more.
4. Using a floured board, roll out pastry about 7 mm/¼ inch thick. Cut rounds about 15 cm/6 inches in diameter.
5. Divide filling between rounds of pastry.
6. Damp edges of pastry.
7. Make pasties leaving the centre open.
8. Mix cheese and breadcrumbs and put a little topping in each pasty.

9. Brush pastry with beaten egg.
10. Bake on a greased baking sheet in a moderately hot oven, Gas 5, 375°F, 180°C, for 30 minutes.

Serve hot with vegetables. Delicious with redcurrant jelly.

Mrs Janice Langley
Shoreham-by-Sea, West Sussex

VOL-AU-VENTS

Large

225 g/8 oz puff pastry (*see page 106*)
Beaten egg

1. Using a floured board, roll out pastry 2 cm/¾ inch thick into an oval or a round.
2. Put pastry on to a baking sheet. Using a sharp knife or cutter and keeping at least 1 cm/½ inch in from edge of pastry, cut another oval or round, but cut only half-way through the pastry. This inner piece will form the lid of the vol-au-vent.
3. Brush top with beaten egg and leave to rest for 30 minutes.
4. Bake above middle of a hot oven, Gas 7, 425°F, 220°C, for 8 to 10 minutes until well-risen and golden brown. Then reduce heat to moderately hot, Gas 6, 400°F, 200°C, and cook for a further 25 to 30 minutes.
5. Remove from oven on to a wire cooling rack. Lift off the lid and press down the pastry beneath so that there is room for the filling.

Small vol-au-vents are rolled out 1 cm/½ inch thick. Cut and glaze as above. Bake at above temperatures, reducing heat after 8 minutes and continuing at the lower temperature for a further 8 to 10 minutes.

ALMOND TART

Shortcrust pastry made up with 100 g/4 oz flour (*see page 104*)

Filling

75 g/3 oz butter or soft margarine

75 g/3 oz sugar
1 beaten egg
50 g/2 oz cake crumbs
25 g/1 oz ground almonds
A few drops almond essence
Raspberry jam
A few split almonds

1. Roll out pastry on a floured board and fit it into an 18 cm/7 inch flan ring.
2. Now mix the filling. Cream butter and sugar together and then beat in the egg.
3. Fold in cake crumbs and ground almonds and add the almond essence.
4. Spread jam inside flan case then fill it with mixture. Make sure filling spreads nicely to sides of flan case.
5. Scatter split almonds over the top.
6. Bake in a moderately hot oven, Gas 5, 375°F, 190°C, for 30 to 40 minutes. Look in oven after 20 minutes and reduce heat to Gas 4, 350°F, 180°C, if browning too quickly.

DUTCH APPLE PIE

A much travelled recipe. It reached our contributor from Canada.

For this you need 225 g/8 oz unbaked pastry (*see page 104*) rolled out to fit a 25 cm/10 inch flan tin or ring

Filling

225 g/8 oz cooking apples, peeled and cored
2 tablespoons plain flour
¼ teaspoon salt
175 g/6 oz sugar
1 beaten egg
A 150 g/5 oz carton natural yoghurt
¼ teaspoon nutmeg
1 or 2 drops vanilla essence

Spicy Topping

65 g/2½ oz flour
40 g/1½ oz butter
50 g/2 oz sugar
1 teaspoon cinnamon

1. Dice apple.
2. Mix other filling ingredients well.
3. Stir in apple and fill flan.

4. Bake near top of a moderately hot oven, Gas 6, 400°F, 200°C, for 15 minutes. Then reduce heat to moderate, Gas 4, 350°F, 180°C, for about 30 minutes more until filling is firm and golden.
5. Meanwhile, prepare topping. Rub butter into flour, and mix in sugar and cinnamon.
6. Sprinkle topping on pie and bake 10 minutes more.

June Lambton
Goole, N. Humberside

FUDGE TART

First published in a book of family recipes 'In a Bisley Kitchen', collected over 100 years.

For this you need a ready-baked shallow 15 cm/6 inch pastry case (*see page 104*)

Filling
50 g/2 oz butter
50 g/2 oz light soft brown sugar
200 ml/⅓ pint sweetened condensed milk
25 g/1 oz roughly-chopped walnuts
25 g/1 oz seedless raisins
25 g/1 oz glacé cherries, chopped

1. Melt butter in pan. Add sugar and condensed milk. Stir over low heat until sugar is dissolved and mixture boils. Boil for 5 minutes stirring all the time.
2. Take pan off heat. Stir in walnuts, raisins and cherries.
3. Pour mixture into pastry case and leave to cool.

Mrs A. Bucknell
Bisley, Gloucestershire

MINCEMEAT AND ALMOND DELIGHT

For 6 people

Pastry
150 g/5 oz self-raising flour—if using plain wholewheat flour add ¼ level teaspoon baking powder

50 g/2 oz butter
25 g/1 oz lard
1 egg yolk
½ teaspoon lemon juice

Filling
50 g/2 oz butter
50 g/2 oz castor or soft brown sugar
2 lightly-beaten eggs
50 g/2 oz ground almonds
A few drops almond essence
4 heaped tablespoons mincemeat
2 bananas, thinly sliced

1. Put flour in a bowl (with baking powder if wholewheat flour is used). Rub in butter and lard.
2. Add egg-yolk and lemon juice and mix to a firm dough.
3. Roll out pastry on a floured board to fit a 20 cm/8 inch flan tin or pie plate.
4. Filling. Cream butter and sugar.
5. Stir in eggs, ground almonds and essence and mix well.
6. Fill pastry case with alternate layers of mincemeat and bananas. Then spread almond mixture on top, taking care that it covers fruit right to pastry edge.
7. Bake in middle of a hot oven, Gas 7, 425°F, 220°C, for half an hour, when it will be firm on top and nicely browned. If using wholewheat pastry, reduce heat after 15 minutes to moderately hot, Gas 5, 375°F, 190°C, and cook for another 15 to 20 minutes.

Mrs Becky Blackmore
Exeter, Devon

PECAN AND RAISIN FLAN

A rich pudding.

Pastry
225 g/8 oz rich sweet shortcrust pastry (*see page 104*)

Filling
125 g/4 oz seedless raisins
120 ml/4 fl oz water
1 tablespoon cornflour

Grated rind and juice of 1
orange
Grated rind and juice of ½ lemon
50 g/2 oz soft brown sugar
50 g/2 oz pecans or walnuts,
chopped to size of raisins

To decorate

A 142 ml/5 fl oz carton of double
cream
1 tablespoon rum

1. Using a floured board, roll out
pastry 7 mm/¼ inch thick and line a
20 cm/8 inch flan dish or a flan ring on
a baking sheet. Prick base with a fork.
Chill it for 10 minutes.
2. Cut a piece of foil big enough to line
base and sides of flan case. Fill with
baking beans.
3. Bake near top of a moderately hot
oven, Gas 5, 375°F, 190°C, for 10 to 15
minutes. Remove beans and foil at 10
minutes and return flan to oven to
crisp up base. If pastry is already very
brown, reduce temperature to warm,
Gas 3, 325°F, 160°C, for final few
minutes. (Save beans and foil for
another occasion.)
4. Take flan out of oven, remove from
dish or ring on to a wire rack to cool.
(Return it to dish or ring for support
while filling.)
5. Put raisins in water and simmer for
10 minutes.
6. Mix cornflour to a paste with 1
tablespoon of the juice and add sugar.
7. Stir cornflour mixture and rind
into raisin mix and cook until thick. If
too thick add more juice, but
consistency should be like jam. Allow
to cool.
8. To this cooled mixture add chopped
pecans. Pour into cold flan case.
9. Whip cream and add rum. Whip
again.
10. Fill a piping bag and, using a star
nozzle, decorate surface of flan.

TOFFEE CREAM TART

First make an 18 cm/7 inch
shortcrust flan case and bake it
blind (see page 104)

Filling

150 ml/¼ pint milk
65 g/2½ oz margarine or butter
40 g/1½ oz white or soft brown
sugar
25 g/1 oz plain flour
75 g/3 oz golden syrup

For special occasions decorate with
grated chocolate and whipped cream.

1. Heat the milk but do not boil it.
2. Melt margarine and sugar in a
small pan and stir in flour.
3. Whisk in the hot milk. Stir as it
thickens and reaches boiling point.
Cook for 2 or 3 minutes, stirring.
4. Remove from heat, add syrup and
whisk again.
5. Spread filling in flan case.

Mrs A. E. Phillips
Selsey, Sussex

YORKSHIRE CURD TART

Sometimes called Cheesecake, but not
quite the same. This recipe uses home-
produced curd.

To make curd

1·2 litres/2 pints milk (Channel
Islands milk is best*)
1 teaspoon Epsom salts
*Ordinary pasteurized milk can
be used but skimmed,
homogenised, sterilised and
'long-life' milks are not suitable.

1. Bring milk to boiling point.
Remove from heat and stir in Epsom
salts.
2. Leave for a few hours or overnight
for curds to form. Strain.

To make tart

175 g/6 oz shortcrust pastry (see
page 104)
225 g/8 oz curd
25 g/1 oz butter or margarine
25 g/1 oz washed currants
1 large beaten egg
1 tablespoon castor sugar
1 tablespoon golden syrup
1 tablespoon rum

1. Roll out pastry and line an 18 cm/7
inch flan ring placed on a greased
baking sheet.

2. Combine all other ingredients and fill the pastry case.
3. Bake above middle of a moderately hot oven, Gas 6, 400°F, 200°C, for 30 minutes until pastry is cooked and the filling firm and golden.

DATE PASTY

Crisp, short pastry with a thick filling.

300 g/11 oz dates, chopped
300 ml/½ pint water

Pastry

125 g/4 oz fine wholewheat flour
125 g/4 oz fine wholewheat semolina
150 g/5 oz butter
5 to 6 teaspoons cold water

To glaze: beaten egg or milk

1. Simmer dates in the water for 10 to 15 minutes until soft. Leave to cool.
2. Pre-heat a moderately hot oven, Gas 5, 375°F, 190°C.
3. To make the pastry, mix dry ingredients in a bowl and rub in butter.
4. Add enough water to make a soft dough.
5. Cut dough into 2 pieces and, using a board well dusted with semolina, roll out each piece to a 23 cm/9 inch square.
6. Lift one piece of pastry on to a lightly-oiled baking tray. Spread cooked dates to within 1·2 cm/½ inch of the edges.
7. Moisten edges with a little water, put on top piece of pastry, pressing edges to seal. Trim off any surplus pastry.
8. Brush with beaten egg or milk. Prick through top layer of pastry several times with a fork.
9. Bake near top of oven for 20 to 25 minutes.
10. Leave pastry on baking tray for 15 to 20 minutes to cool. Then cut into squares and lift them on to a cooling wire to go quite cold.

Janet Horsley
Headingley, Yorkshire

DELUXE MINCEMEAT PUFFS

For this you need ground almond flaky pastry—make up quantity given on *page 105*

Filling

225 g/8 oz chopped eating apple, weighed after peeling and coring
225 g/8 oz currants
225 g/8 oz seedless raisins
150 g/5 oz chopped candied orange peel, mixed peel will do but orange is nicer
275 g/10 oz flaked or chopped blanched almonds
Half a nutmeg, grated
4 to 6 tablespoons brandy

Mix all filling ingredients together and leave to soak and infuse for at least 1 hour.

To make the mincemeat puffs

1 beaten egg
Demerara sugar

1. Roll out cold pastry to about 3·5 mm/ ⅛ inch thick. Cut into 10 cm/4 inch squares.
2. Place 1 tablespoon of filling on each square.
3. Fold over diagonally, sealing join with beaten egg.
4. Brush top with egg, sprinkle with demerara sugar and place on baking trays.
5. Bake above middle of a hot oven, Gas 7, 425°F, 220°C, for 12 to 15 minutes until risen, golden brown and firm. Puffs at centre of tray may need another 2 to 3 minutes if pastry is still pale underneath.

Delicious served with Rich Brandy Butter (*see page 123*) or a simple Brandy Sauce (*see page 123*).

Instead of individual puffs, a large roly-poly can be made. Roll out pastry as above, spread over it all the filling and roll up, sealing edges with beaten egg. Brush with beaten egg and sprinkle with demerara sugar. Bake for 30 minutes as above, then reduce temperature to moderately hot, Gas 5, 375°F, 190°C, for a further 15 minutes until well-risen, brown and set. Centre of roly-poly will remain quite soft inside.

Mrs Angela Mottram
Axbridge, Somerset

HOW D'YOU DO CAKE

For this you need 350 g/12 oz shortcrust pastry (see page 104), made up with self-raising flour

Filling

350 g/12 oz currants
50 g/2 oz mixed peel
1 tablespoon golden syrup
1 tablespoon demerara or soft brown sugar
1 level teaspoon nutmeg or cinnamon
A pinch of ground cloves. Or, instead of these spices, 1 level teaspoon mixed spice

To glaze: 1 dessertspoon golden syrup warmed with 1 dessertspoon sugar

1. Divide pastry into 2 pieces, one to line tin, the other for top. Shape these into rectangular blocks. Put in a cool place or refrigerator to rest for 20 minutes.
2. Using a floured board, roll out pastry about 7 mm/¼ inch thick and line a Swiss roll tin, about 28 by 18 cm/11 by 7 inches.
3. Warm filling ingredients together in a pan so that they mix easily. Spread filling over pastry in tin.
4. Damp edges of pastry and cover filling with second piece, pressing to seal.
5. Brush with the glaze. Prick top all over with a fork.
6. Bake in a hot oven, Gas 7, 425°F, 220°C, for 25 minutes when it will be shining and golden.
7. Allow to cool in tin and then cut into slices.

Mrs Jill Marshall
Hythe, Kent

KIDDERMINSTER PLUM CAKES
Makes 12 cakes

For this you need a 375 g/13 oz packet of puff pastry, just thawed. Or make up your own using recipe *on page 106*. There will be some pastry over if you use home-made.

Filling

4 glacé cherries
225 g/8 oz mixed dried fruit
50 g/2 oz plain flour
50 g/2 oz soft brown sugar
50 g/2 oz soft margarine
1 egg
½ level teaspoon mixed spice

To finish: water, granulated sugar.

1. Start with filling. Roughly chop cherries and put them in a bowl.
2. Add remaining filling ingredients and beat with a wooden spoon for about 3 minutes to mix thoroughly.
3. Roll out pastry on a lightly-floured board to 3·5 mm/⅛ inch thick.
4. Cut twelve rounds 10 cm/4 inches across; a saucer may be useful to cut round.
5. Place 2 teaspoons of filling in centre of each round. Brush edges with water.
6. Gather pastry together over filling and seal well.
7. Turn each plum cake over and roll out lightly to form a round about 7·5 cm/3 inches across.
8. To finish, brush tops of cakes with water and invert on to a saucer of granulated sugar to give a thick sugary coating on top.
9. Put cakes on a baking sheet and, using a sharp knife, make 3 cuts on top of each,
10. Bake on shelf just above centre of a moderately hot oven, Gas 6, 400°F, 200°C, for 20 minutes when cake will be golden brown.
11. Remove from oven and slide cakes on to a wire rack to cool.

Mrs Cynthia Cooksey
Cofton Hackett, Worcestershire

PARADISE BARS

Makes 20 pieces

175 g/6 oz white or wholewheat shortcrust pastry (*see page 104*)

Filling

75 g/3 oz margarine
75 g/3 oz castor sugar
1 beaten egg
75 g/3 oz currants, washed and dried
50 g/2 oz chopped glacé cherries
65 g/2½ oz ground rice
50 g/2 oz ground almonds
3 drops of vanilla essence

1. Using a floured board, roll out pastry 7 mm/¼ inch thick and line bottom and sides of a Swiss roll tin, 27 by 18 cm/11 by 7 inches.
2. Cream margarine and sugar. Mix in egg and other ingredients gradually.
3. Smooth filling over pastry base.
4. Bake above middle of a moderate oven, Gas 4, 350°F, 180°C, for about 40 minutes.
5. Leave to cool in tin.

6. Then turn out, cut into four and then into bars.

SUSSEX PLUM HEAVIES

Adapted from an old recipe in 'Sussex Cooking'. The original called for 3 lb flour.

225 g/8 oz self-raising flour
A pinch of salt
175 g/6 oz butter or butter and margarine mixed
75 g/3 oz currants
1 tablespoon castor sugar
About 2 tablespoons cold water
A little milk

1. Put flour and salt into a bowl.
2. Divide fat into 3 even amounts. Rub one third into flour.
3. Add currants and sugar and mix to a firm dough with water.
4. Using a floured board, roll out to an oblong three times as long as it is wide.
5. Using second lot of fat, put little pieces on to the top two thirds of pastry. Fold up bottom third and fold down top third. Turn pastry so that folds are at sides.
6. Roll out again, use remaining fat and fold as before. If pastry has got hot and sticky leave in a cool place or refrigerator for 15 minutes to firm up.
7. Roll into a 20 cm/8 inch round cake, score top and brush with milk. Place on a greased baking sheet.

8. Bake in middle of a moderately hot oven, Gas 6, 400°F, 200°C, for 30 minutes.
9. Slide off on to a wire rack to cool. These freeze well.

Mrs Janice Langley
Shoreham-by-Sea, West Sussex

SUSSEX TARTLETS

100 g/4 oz shortcrust pastry, white or wholewheat (*see page 104*)

Filling
1 large or 2 small cooking apples, peeled and cored
2 lightly-beaten eggs
Grated rind and juice of 1 lemon
50 g/2 oz castor sugar
A pinch of cinnamon

1. Using a floured board, roll out pastry 7 mm/¼ inch thick and line 18 tartlet tins.
2. Grate apple and put it in a bowl.
3. Mix in eggs, lemon, sugar and cinnamon.
4. Spoon filling into pastry cases.
5. Bake near top of a moderately hot oven, Gas 5, 375°F, 190°C, for 15 to 20 minutes.
6. Allow to cool in tins for 10 minutes and then remove on to a wire rack.

Mrs Ruth Brooke and Mrs Sheila Powell
Hove and Portslade, Sussex

Chapter 8

Puddings, Hot and Cold

APPLE AND FIG CRUMBLE

For 3 or 4 people

Crumble

50 g/2 oz wholewheat flour
40 g/1½ oz porridge oats
15 g/½ oz desiccated coconut
50 g/2 oz melted butter, or 2 tablespoons vegetable oil
Several drops of vanilla essence

Filling

125 g/4 oz figs, chopped
150 ml/¼ pint water
225 g/8 oz cooking apples, peeled, cored and sliced

1. Pre-heat oven to moderately hot, Gas 5, 375°F, 190°C.
2. Mix crumble ingredients well together.
3. Put figs in a pan with water and simmer for 5 minutes.
4. Mix apple and figs in an oven dish and pour over remaining fig juice.
5. Sprinkle crumble on top and bake near top of oven for 25 to 30 minutes.

Janet Horsley
Headingley, Yorkshire

DORSET APPLE CAKE

Enough for 6 people

250 g/8 oz self-raising flour
A pinch of salt
125 g/4 oz margarine, butter, lard or dripping or a mixture of these fats
350 g/12 oz sour cooking apples
125 g/4 oz sugar
1½ to 2½ tablespoons milk
Demerara sugar for sprinkling

1. Sift flour and salt into a bowl and rub in fat.
2. Peel, core and roughly chop up apples.
3. Mix in apple and sugar, adding enough milk to form a soft but not sticky dough.

4. Dust with flour, shape into an oval about 20 by 15 cm/8 by 6 inches and place on a greased baking sheet.
5. Bake in centre of a moderate oven Gas 4, 350°F, 180°C, for about 50 minutes until the cake is lightly browned and slightly firm when pressed in centre. Cake will spread during baking.
6. Eat hot, straight from oven, sprinkled with demerara sugar.

Very nice buttered or with Lancashire cheese. Also nice cold.

Miss Betty Butt
Woodsford, Dorset

GOLDEN APPLE BETTY

For 4 people, easy to make for 1 or more people

175 g/6 oz wholewheat or white bread
125 g/4 oz butter
1 level teaspoon cinnamon
125 g/4 oz plus 1 tablespoon light soft brown sugar
450 g/1 lb cooking apples

1. Use a little of the butter to grease a 1·2 litre/2 pint shallow oven dish.
2. Slice bread thickly, remove crusts and cut each piece into 4 triangles.
3. Put remaining butter in a large frying pan and melt over a low heat. Stir in cinnamon and 125 g/4 oz of the sugar. Add bread and turn the pieces over carefully until melted butter and sugar are absorbed.
4. Place one-third of bread mixture in base of dish.
5. Peel and core apples and cut into thick slices. Arrange these in dish. Sprinkle over remaining tablespoon of sugar.
6. Cover with remaining bread mixture.
7. Place dish on a baking sheet in centre of a warm oven, Gas 3, 325°F, 160°C, and bake for 1 to 1¼ hours until bread is crisp on top.

Serve hot with custard or cream.

120

MALVERN APPLE PUDDING

Malvern is apple-growing country. Although this dish is made with Russet apples, small sweet eating apples can be used.

Enough for 6, but it is easy to make half quantity

Freezes well.

125 g/4 oz butter
125 g/4 oz sugar
2 beaten eggs
125 g/4 oz plain or self-raising flour
A pinch of salt
2 smallish Russet apples (about 225 g/8 oz, peeled and cored)
Grated rind of 1 lemon
50 g/2 oz currants
2 to 3 tablespoons brandy*

It is nearly as nice with sherry, or ½ teaspoon brandy flavouring with 2 tablespoons milk, or even with apple juice.

1. Cream butter and sugar.
2. Add beaten eggs.
3. Fold in flour and salt.
4. Peel, core and chop apples and mix with lemon rind, currants and brandy.
5. Grease a 1·1 litre/2 pint pudding basin. If making half quantity a 450 ml/¾ pint basin suits. Put a small square of greased, greaseproof paper to cover bottom of basin to help when pudding is turned out.
6. Put mixture in basin and cover with greaseproof paper and foil, or tie a double layer of greaseproof paper firmly in place with string.
7. Steam pudding for 1½ to 2 hours. If making half quantity 1 hour will be enough.

If you haven't a steamer, stand basin on a trivet or upturned saucer in a saucepan with a lid. Pour in boiling water to come halfway up sides of basin. Cover pan and boil, replenishing with more boiling water if necessary.

8. Turn pudding out on to a warmed dish and serve it with custard or brandy or sherry sauce (*see page 123*).

If freezing, do so as soon as pudding is cold, covering with fresh paper and foil. To reheat, thaw first, then steam or boil in basin for ½ hour.

Mrs Cynthia Cooksey
Cofton Hackett, Worcestershire

SPICY APPLE BARS

Makes 6 pieces

175 g/6 oz plain flour
½ level teaspoon salt
75 g/3 oz margarine
75 g/3 oz light soft brown sugar

Topping
1 tablespoon soft brown sugar
1 level teaspoon cinnamon
2 small or 1 large cooking apple
25 g/1 oz butter

1. Sift flour and salt and rub in margarine until it is like breadcrumbs.
2. Stir in soft brown sugar.
3. Spread this mixture loosely in a greased shallow baking tin, about 18 cm/7 inches square.
4. Now start the topping. Mix together sugar and cinnamon.
5. Peel, core and slice the apples into neat pieces. Lightly press them into mixture in tin.
6. Sprinkle the sugar and cinnamon on top. Dot with butter.
7. Bake in a moderately hot oven, Gas 6, 400°F, 200°C, for 35 to 40 minutes.
8. Cut into 6 bars and serve hot or cold with cream, ice-cream or custard.

Freezes and re-heats well.

Mrs M. K. Smith
Dartford, Kent

BANANA FRITTERS

For 6 people

50 g/2 oz plain flour
A pinch of salt
2 teaspoons icing sugar
4 tablespoons lukewarm water
2 teaspoons melted butter
White of 1 egg
3 or 4 bananas
Oil for deep frying

1. Sift flour and salt into a bowl.
2. Add sugar and mix with water and butter to a thick, smooth batter.
3. Whisk egg-white until stiff.
4. Fold into batter.
5. Quarter the bananas, cutting each lengthways and then across.
6. Heat the oil until it is nearly smoking hot. Test by dropping in a small piece of bread. If it rises bubbling to surface and turns golden in 30 seconds oil is ready to cook fritters.
7. Dip each piece of banana in the batter and fry until golden brown.
8. Drain on kitchen paper and serve hot with a jam sauce.

Pineapple Fritters

Same as for Banana Fritters except use pineapple rings in place of banana quarters.

Priya Wickramasinghe
Cardiff

CARROT SWEET

**450 g/1 lb carrots, finely-grated
50 g/2 oz whole cashew nuts or blanched almonds, whole or chopped a little
150 g/5 oz sugar
650 ml/1¼ pints milk
75 g/3 oz butter or ghee** (see page 38)
6 cardamoms

1. Put carrots, nuts, sugar and milk in a pan. Stir over low heat to dissolve sugar. Then cook very gently, stirring occasionally, until carrot has absorbed all the liquid.
2. In another pan melt butter. Stir in the carrot mixture and cook for a few minutes.
3. Crush seeds from cardamom pods and mix in.
4. Pile mixture into a nice dish and serve at room temperature.

Priya Wickramasinghe
Cardiff

CHICHESTER PUDDING
For 4 people

A very light bread pudding, almost like a soufflé.

**4 slices of white bread, preferably real bread
15 g/½ oz butter
2 eggs, separated
2 tablespoons castor sugar
250 ml/9 fl oz milk
Grated rind and juice of 1 large lemon**

1. Preheat oven to moderate, Gas 4, 350°F, 180°C.
2. Cut crusts off bread and make it into coarse crumbs. Use the grater.
3. Use butter to grease a 600 ml/1 pint soufflé or oven dish.
4. Beat egg-yolks with sugar and milk.
5. Add crumbs, lemon juice and rind.
6. Whisk egg-whites quite stiff and fold them in.
7. Turn mixture into prepared dish and put straight into pre-heated oven, near top. Bake 35 to 40 minutes until pudding is set, well-risen and golden.

Serve at once or, like a soufflé, it will fall.

Mrs Sheila Powell
Portslade, Sussex

CHRISTMAS PUDDING

An excellent pudding, full of fruit. Can be made just a few weeks before Christmas but keeps for 6 months.

A pudding made in a 1·1 litre/2 pint basin will provide 10 to 12 helpings

There is enough mixture for a 1·1 litre/2 pint basin plus a 300 ml/½ pint basin, or an 850 ml/1½ pint basin and a 600 ml/1 pint basin. Smaller puddings can be cooked with larger ones and removed from steamer slightly sooner.

225 g/8 oz raisins	washed
225 g/8 oz sultanas	and
225 g/8 oz currants	dried

225 g/8 oz fresh breadcrumbs,
wholewheat or white
50 g/2 oz almonds, blanched and
finely-chopped
1 apple
Grated rind and juice of 1 lemon
4 small beaten eggs
250 g/9 oz moist brown sugar,
try muscovado
225 g/8 oz shredded suet
50 g/2 oz cut mixed peel
50 g/2 oz plain flour, wholewheat or white
1 rounded teaspoon mixed spice
3 tablespoons sherry or brandy

1. Grease basins and place in the
bottom of each a circle of greaseproof
paper or foil. This will make sure
puddings are turned out easily.
2. In a very large bowl, mix all
ingredients thoroughly. Make sure
you get some help with the stirring.
3. Fill basins to 1 cm/½ inch below the
rim. Do not ram the mixture down too
hard.
4. Cover basins with a piece of greaseproof paper, pleated along middle, and
then with a piece of pleated foil. Tuck
foil securely under rim of basin.
5. Steam the puddings 4 hours for 1·1
litre/2 pint basins and 2 hours for
600 ml/1 pint basins. The longer the
steaming, the darker the pudding.
If you do not have a steamer, stand
basins on a trivet in a large pan of
boiling water, put on the lid and boil.
Do not let water go off the boil and
remember to replenish with more
boiling water from time to time.
A pressure cooker will reduce cooking
time considerably. Follow instructions
in the handbook.
6. Remove puddings from steamer,
take off paper and foil covers and leave
to cool under a clean towel. When
quite cold re-cover with fresh greaseproof paper and foil and store in a cool
cupboard until required.
7. On Christmas Day, steam puddings
2 hours for a 1·1 litre/2 pint basin and
1 hour for a 600 ml/1 pint basin. Or
pressure cook to save time and fuel.
Serve with Rum Sauce or Rich
Brandy Butter (*see opposite*).

RUM SAUCE
For Christmas Pudding.

600 ml/1 pint milk
40 g/1½ oz cornflour
40 g/1½ oz sugar
2 tablespoons rum, or more if
desired

1. Blend cornflour with 2 or 3
tablespoons of the cold milk.
2. Heat rest of milk and, when near
boiling point, pour a little over
cornflour mixture. Stir and return it
all again to the pan.
3. Bring to the boil and simmer for a
few minutes, stirring all the time.
4. Add rum and keep sauce hot in a
jug.

Brandy or sherry sauce can be
made in exactly the same way.

RICH BRANDY
BUTTER

50 g/2 oz butter
100 g/4 oz icing sugar
1 egg
50 g/2 oz ground almonds
1 dessertspoon brandy
150 ml/¼ pint double cream

1. Use soft but not melted butter.
2. Cream butter with icing sugar.
3. Beat in the egg and ground
almonds.
4. Whip cream until it holds soft
peaks, then beat in brandy. Fold into
the creamed mixture.
5. Refrigerate for at least an hour
before use, but preferably overnight.
Serve to accompany the Christmas
pudding.

The mixture can be frozen well in
advance or refrigerated for up to four
days beforehand.

JAMAICAN
OMELETTE
Enough for 3

3 eggs, separated
50 g/2 oz demerara sugar

Grated rind and juice of 1
lemon
A pinch of salt
1 dessertspoon apricot jam
1 banana
3 tablespoons rum
40 g/1½ oz butter

1. Put egg-yolks, 15 g/½ oz of the sugar
and 1 teaspoon lemon rind in a basin.
Whisk lightly.
2. In another bowl whisk egg-whites
and salt.
3. **For the filling.** Warm jam. Mash
banana and mix with jam. Add rest of
lemon rind and 1 tablespoon of the
rum. Heat gently.
4. **For the sauce.** Melt 25 g/1 oz of
the butter and the remaining sugar in
a small pan and let it cook for a few
seconds.
5. Stir in 1 teaspoon lemon juice and
the last 2 tablespoons of rum.
6. **Now to complete the
omelette.** Melt remaining 15 g/½ oz
butter in omelette pan.
7. Fold egg mixtures together and
pour into hot butter in pan. Cook until
golden underneath.
8. Place under a low grill for a minute
to firm top and toast it until slightly
golden.
9. Lift omelette out on to a warmed
dish. Place on it the banana mixture
and fold it over.
10. Pour the hot sauce over and serve
at once.

PINEAPPLE PUDDING

An oven is not required for this
pudding. It is cooked on top of stove
and under grill. Can be made with
stewed rhubarb or plums.

50 g/2 oz margarine
100 g/4 oz plain white flour
425 ml/¾ pint milk
25 g/1 oz sugar
A 450 g/16 oz tin of pineapple
pieces
2 egg-yolks

Meringue
2 egg-whites
75 g/3 oz castor sugar

1. Heat grill just to warm and put a
deep 1·1 litre/2 pint dish under to
warm.
2. Melt margarine in a large pan.
Remove from heat and stir in flour.
Cook for 2 minutes, stirring all the
time.
3. Remove pan from heat and stir in
milk gradually. Now heat gently until
it thickens, stirring all the time.
Simmer for 3 minutes.
4. Mix in sugar and 150 ml/¼ pint of
juice drained from pineapple.
5. Mix in egg-yolks and cook, stirring
for 2 or 3 minutes more. It should
bubble but not boil.
6. Lastly, mix in pineapple pieces and
pour into the warmed dish. Put it back
under grill to keep warm.
7. Whisk egg-whites until they stand
up in peaks. Add sugar and whisk
again.
8. Spread this meringue over pudding
and put dish back under grill. Keep
heat low. Grill for 15 minutes until top
is a lovely golden brown.

This meringue is not crisp, but soft
like marshmallow.

Mrs Patricia Chantry
Hook, Nr. Goole, N. Humberside

PLUM CARAMEL PUDDING

A delicious bread pudding which can
be made in any quantity to suit your
household.

Plums
Butter or margarine
Brown sugar
Slices of stale bread, whole-
wheat, brown or white

1. Wash plums and cut in halves,
removing stones.
2. Thickly grease sides and bottom of a
pie dish and sprinkle all over with
sugar.
3. Line dish with pieces of stale bread.

4. Place a layer of plums over bread cut side uppermost. Sprinkle with sugar. Cover with another layer of bread, and a second layer of plums and sugar.

5. Finish top with slices of buttered bread, butter-side uppermost.

6. Cover with greaseproof paper and bake in middle of a moderate oven, Gas 3 to 4, 325° to 350°F, 160° to 180°C. Remove paper after 30 minutes.

7. Turn pudding out on to a warmed dish.

Serve with cream or custard.

Mrs Cynthia Cooksey
Cofton Hackett, Worcestershire

WHITE LADIES PUDDING

This recipe is named after a village near Worcester called White Ladies Aston where a convent of Cistercian nuns lived in the 12th century. They wore white habits.

Enough for 6 people, but easy to reduce to one third or two thirds for 2 or 4 people

Can be baked in oven or steamed on top of stove.

6 medium-thick slices of white bread
75 g/3 oz butter
125 g/4 oz desiccated coconut
600 ml/1 pint milk
A pinch of salt
Vanilla essence
3 eggs
75 g/3 oz sugar

1. Remove crusts from bread. Butter it thickly and cut into squares or triangles.

2. Use remaining butter to grease a 1·5 litre/2½ pint pie dish. Sprinkle it with the coconut. Then arrange bread in dish.

3. Heat milk till it feels comfortably hot when tested with little finger. Add salt and a few drops of vanilla essence.

4. Beat eggs with sugar. Pour in milk, stirring to dissolve sugar, and strain into pie dish. Leave to soak for 30 minutes.

5. Stand dish in a roasting tin, pour hot water around it to come halfway up.

6. Bake in middle of a warm oven, Gas 3, 325°F, 160°C, for about 1½ hours until pudding is set.

Or the pudding can be steamed if you prefer not to use oven.

7. Turn pudding out on to a warmed dish. Delicious hot or cold.

To cook on top of stove
Using ingredients scaled down to 2 eggs, pudding will fit a 1·1 litre/2 pint pudding basin. Cover top with grease-proof paper and foil. Steam for 1½ hours. If you do not have a steamer, stand basin on a trivet in a large saucepan. Pour in boiling water to come halfway up sides of basin. Cover pan and boil for 1½ hours, replenishing with more boiling water if necessary.

Mrs Jeanne Round
Cookley, Worcestershire

ALMOND JELLIES

A Chinese confection to eat on their own or with fruit salad, tinned fruits, coffee, etc.

10 g/¼ oz agar agar*
1·5 litres/2½ pints cold water
450 ml/15 fl oz milk
350 g/12 oz sugar
2¼ teaspoons concentrated almond essence

*Agar agar is a type of seaweed and unlike gelatine has setting properties that do not need refrigeration. It is colourless and flavourless and sets to a superb solid texture which can be easily cut into cubes. It is available from Chinese supermarkets and some wholefood and health food shops.

1. Using a pair of scissors, snip the strips of agar agar into 2·5 cm/1 inch pieces.

2. In a large bowl, soak agar agar in the water for about 8 hours.

3. In a pan, bring agar agar and water to the boil. Simmer until dissolved.

4. Add rest of ingredients, stirring to dissolve sugar, then boil for a further 10 minutes.

5. Remove from heat and pour into shallow oiled dishes or baking tins to a depth of about 2·5 cm/1 inch.
6. When set, cut into cubes and pile on to individual serving dishes.
Eat while fresh.

Priya Wickramasinghe
Cardiff

COLD FRUIT SOUFFLÉ

Can be made with blackberries, blackcurrants, cranberries, plums, raspberries or strawberries.

Enough for 10 people but it is easy to make a smaller quantity scaling ingredients down to 1 or 2 eggs

900 g/2 lb fruit, fresh or frozen
Water
About 50 g/2 oz sugar
40 g/1½ oz gelatine (3 sachets)
3 large egg-whites

To decorate: chopped nuts, whipped cream for piping (optional)

This can be served in a 1·75 litre/3 pint glass dish or in a specially prepared 1·1 litre/2 pint straight-sided dish. This measures 15 cm/6 inches across and 7·5 cm/3 inches deep.

To prepare a traditional soufflé dish with a paper collar:

1. Cut from a roll of greaseproof paper a single piece measuring 56 cm/22 inches long and 39 cm/15 inches wide.
2. Now fold this lengthways so that you have three thicknesses, 56 cm/22 inches long and 13 cm/5 inches wide.
3. Wind this strip around the outside of the dish and fix it as tightly as you can. Elastic bands are best to hold it in place. It needs to fit very well especially at rim edge.

Now for the soufflé

1. Wash fruit and put it in a saucepan with water barely to cover. Simmer until soft. If using frozen fruit take care to defrost it and add very little water.

2. Push cooked fruit through a nylon sieve, scraping purée from underneath as you do it.
3. Measure purée and, if necessary, top up with water to 1·25 litre/2¼ pints. Return purée to pan.
4. Add sugar according to taste. Stir until it is dissolved. Pour into a large bowl.
5. Put 3 tablespoons water into a cup and sprinkle on the gelatine. Place cup in a small pan of warm water. Heat gently. Stir until gelatine has dissolved, about 2 or 3 minutes.
6. Now strain gelatine mixture into fruit purée, stir well and leave to set in a cool place, or refrigerator.
7. When fruit is set but still wobbly, take a fork and mix it all up again.
8. In a clean, grease-free bowl, whisk egg-whites until stiff. Fold them into fruit.
9. Pour into prepared dish. If you have used a soufflé dish with paper collar, the soufflé will be about 3 cm/1¼ inches above top of dish. Put it carefully in refrigerator to set, allowing 2 or 3 hours.
10. To serve, peel paper gently away using the blunt edge of a knife. Decorate risen edge by gently pressing on chopped nuts. Top can be decorated with a border of chopped nuts or piped rosettes of whipped cream. Otherwise, a jug of pouring cream is nice.

CHRISTMAS JELLY

Made in a pudding basin so that the jelly looks like a Christmas pudding.

450 g/1 lb black grapes
1½ packets of dark jelly (blackcurrant or blackberry)
150 ml/¼ pint port or sherry
Water
50 g/2 oz raisins
50 g/2 oz chopped blanched almonds*

*****To blanch almonds: put them in a basin, pour over boiling water to cover. Leave until cool enough to handle when almonds will squeeze easily out of their skins.**

1. Cut each grape in half and remove seeds.

2. Make up the jelly according to packet instructions but using the 150 ml/¼ pint of port or sherry so that in all you have 850 ml/1½ pints of liquid jelly.
3. Wet a 1·75 litre/3 pint pudding basin with cold water. Pour the liquid jelly into wet basin.
4. Add to this the grapes, raisins and nuts. Stir occasionally until set.
5. Turn out and decorate with a sprig of holly.

Serve with single cream.

CHOCOLATE CREAM PIE

For at least 6 people

Base

75 g/3 oz butter
75 g/3 oz crushed cornflakes
50 g/2 oz soft brown sugar
25 g/1 oz crushed All Bran

Filling

90 g/3½ oz plain cooking chocolate
1 tablespoon water
5 ml/1 teaspoon gelatine
1 egg
25 g/1 oz sugar
150 ml/¼ pint double or whipping cream

1. Start with base. Melt butter, mix it with cornflakes, sugar and All Bran.
2. Press mixture into a 20 cm/8 inch pie plate.
3. Bake above middle of a moderately hot oven, Gas 5, 375°F, 190°C, for 10 minutes. Remove from oven and leave to cool.
4. Now the filling. Grate 15 g/½ oz of the chocolate and keep it for decorating. Break up the rest of it into a small bowl and stand it over a pan of simmering water to melt.
5. Put water in a cup, sprinkle in gelatine and stand cup in a pan of hot water until dissolved.
6. Beat egg and sugar. Add melted chocolate and then gelatine.

7. Whip cream till it will stand in soft peaks. Put 2 tablespoonfuls in a piping bag with fluted nozzle and keep in refrigerator till required. If you haven't a piping bag you can still save 2 tablespoons cream for decorating in a different way.
8. Fold rest of cream into chocolate mixture and pour into cooled case. Put pie in a cool place or refrigerator to set.
9. When set, sprinkle with grated chocolate and decorate with rosettes of piped cream. If you haven't a piping bag, carefully spread cream over surface of pie, fork it and sprinkle with grated chocolate.

Anne Wallace
Stewarton, Ayrshire

ORANGE CREAM CHEESE CAKE

For this you need a loose-bottomed 20 cm/8 inch flan tin or a ring set on a baking sheet.

Flan case

100 g/4 oz digestive biscuits
50 g/2 oz butter

Filling

70 g/2½ oz sugar
75 ml/3 fl oz concentrated orange juice, the frozen variety gives a good strong flavour
275 g/10 oz cream cheese

To decorate: finely-grated orange rind

1. Start with the flan case. Crush the biscuits. To do this lay biscuits flat in a single layer inside a large polythene bag and press with a rolling pin.
2. Melt butter gently. Add crushed biscuits and turn them over and over until well integrated with butter.
3. Now the filling. Stir sugar and orange juice together until dissolved.
4. Mix in cream cheese very gradually until it is all incorporated.
5. Pour this mixture over the biscuit base and press down gently. Level and smooth the top.

127

6. Return to refrigerator to set.
7. When needed, sit the flan case on an upturned basin. The ring will drop away leaving you to slide the cheese-cake on to a flat plate. Or, if using a flan ring, carefully slide cheesecake and ring on to a flat plate, then lift off ring.

Serve with single cream in a jug.

CHOCOLATE SUPRÊME

Enough for 6 people but you can make half quantity

Freezes well up to 3 months.

Very rich. Best made the day before it is needed so that flavour matures.

125 g/4 oz best quality plain eating chocolate
4 eggs, separated
90 g/3½ oz butter, cut in small pieces
1 tablespoon brandy or very dry sherry
2 level dessertspoons icing sugar, sieved
3 tablespoons double cream

To decorate: toasted flaked almonds, or piped double cream

1. Break up chocolate into a bowl. Stand bowl over a pan of simmering water. Do not let water boil and do not let bowl touch water. Chocolate must melt without getting too hot.
2. Add egg-yolks to melted chocolate and mix gently. Do not beat at any stage in this recipe.
3. Remove bowl from pan. Add the small pieces of butter and stir gently until dissolved.
4. Now add brandy or sherry and sieved icing sugar. Stir until dissolved.
5. Lastly, add cream and stir again.
6. In another bowl, whisk egg-whites until thick and fluffy and fold into chocolate mixture.
7. Pour into tiny glasses, cover with foil or cling film and keep in refrigerator until needed.

8. Just before serving, decorate with a sprinkling of toasted almonds or a whirl of double cream.

CHOCOLATE ORANGE MOUSSE

Makes 6 individual helpings

175 g/6 oz plain cooking chocolate
1 orange
15 g/½ oz butter
3 eggs, separated
150 ml/¼ pint whipped cream (optional)
1 teaspoon castor sugar
Chopped walnuts to decorate

1. Break up chocolate into quite a large basin. Set it to melt over a pan of simmering water. Do not let water touch bowl.
2. Grate zest from orange. Squeeze out juice.
3. Remove bowl of chocolate from pan, stir in butter, orange zest and juice. Mix well.
4. Beat in egg-yolks one at a time.
5. Mix in whipped cream.
6. Whisk egg-whites firmly and then whisk in sugar.
7. Fold egg-whites into chocolate mixture.
8. Serve in small sundae glasses. Decorate with a sprinkling of chopped walnuts when cool.

COCOA COFFEE MOUSSE

For 4 to 6 people

2 eggs
75 g/3 oz castor sugar
1 teaspoon vanilla essence
4 level teaspoons cocoa
1 level teaspoon instant coffee
300 ml/½ pint milk
3 tablespoons hot water
15 g/½ oz gelatine, 1 sachet
150 ml/5 fl oz double cream
Flaked almonds

1. Separate eggs. Put whites in a clean grease-free basin.

2. In another bowl, put yolks, castor sugar and vanilla essence. Beat until light and creamy.
3. In a saucepan, blend cocoa and coffee with a little of the measured milk. Add remaining milk and bring to boil. Remove from heat and let it cool for a minute.
4. Stir into egg-yolk mixture and pour back into pan.
5. Return to heat, bring to the boil and boil for 1 minute, stirring. Remove from heat and pour back into the bowl.
6. Measure 3 tablespoons of hot water into a small bowl, sprinkle on gelatine. Stir a little just to mix. Leave for 5 minutes to soften.
7. Stir gelatine into chocolate mixture. Leave in a cool place until just on setting point.
8. Whip cream until just thick. Keep 2 tablespoons aside until later for decoration.
9. Whisk egg-whites until stiff but not dry.
10. Using a metal spoon, carefully fold cream and egg-whites into chocolate mixture. Pour into a fluted mould or a nice serving dish. Put in refrigerator to set, allow at least 30 minutes.
11. If using a mould, dip it into a bowl of hand-hot water and turn mousse out on to a serving plate.
12. Put remaining whipped cream in a piping bag with a star nozzle. Pipe on stars to decorate and arrange flaked almonds to look pretty.

Chill until ready to serve.

RASPBERRY MOUSSE

This can be frozen and is delicious to eat frozen or just chilled.

A 170 g/6 oz can of evaporated milk
A 369 g/13 oz can of raspberries, or equal quantity of frozen raspberries
1 raspberry jelly

To decorate (optional): 150 ml/¼ pint whipped cream

1. Put evaporated milk into the refrigerator for about 1 hour so that it is thoroughly chilled when needed.
2. Drain liquid from can of raspberries into a measuring jug and make up with water to 300 ml/½ pint. Bring to the boil.
3. Make jelly with this hot liquid. If using frozen raspberries just use water for the jelly. Leave till cool and just beginning to set.
4. Whisk evaporated milk until thick.
5. Whisk jelly, add the milk and continue to whisk. It should double its bulk.
6. Fold in raspberries.
7. Leave to set. It will set almost immediately with frozen raspberries.
8. Decorate by piping with whipped cream.

Sybil Norcott
Irlam, Nr. Manchester

DEVONSHIRE JUNKET

This can be made from pasteurized or farm-bottled milk, but homogenised, sterilised and UHT milk are not suitable. Delicious made with Channel Island milk.

600 ml/1 pint milk
1 tablespoon sugar
2 teaspoons brandy or rum
1 teaspoon essence of rennet
Cinnamon
Grated nutmeg

1. Put milk in a pan with sugar and warm gently till only blood heat, 98°F, 30°C. Stir to dissolve sugar.
2. Remove pan from heat, stir in brandy or rum and pour into a nice dish. Without delay, stir in rennet and put dish aside to set at room temperature. It takes about 1½ to 2 hours.
3. When junket is set, sprinkle cinnamon and nutmeg on top. It can then be chilled.

Serve with sugar to taste and Devonshire cream if you can (*see over*).

Mrs Elizabeth Selby
Exeter, Devon

129

DEVONSHIRE CREAM

It takes 1 gallon of rich, creamy milk to produce 350 to 450 g/¾ to 1 lb of clotted cream, but the result is delicious. Channel Island milk gives the best result.

1. Put fresh milk in a shallow bowl and leave it at room temperature (55°F, 13°C) for 12 to 24 hours until cream rises to the top.
2. Stand bowl over a pan of boiling water till a crust forms on top of milk. Do not let water touch bowl. This will take about 1 hour.
3. Leave bowl in a cool place till next day.
4. Carefully skim off thick creamy top. Underneath is scalded milk suitable for sauces, soups and puddings.

Mrs Elizabeth Selby
Westleigh, Tiverton, Devon

FLOATING ISLANDS

For 4 people

600 ml/1 pint milk
2 eggs, separated
50 g/2 oz castor sugar plus 2 level teaspoons
1 level tablespoon cornflour
Vanilla essence
A very little water

To decorate: grated chocolate or chocolate vermicelli

1. Pour milk into a saucepan, heat to simmering point.
2. Whisk 1 egg-white until stiff, add 25 g/1 oz of the sugar.Whisk again until stiff. Fold in another 25 g/1 oz sugar.
3. Divide egg-white into 4 and spoon each portion on to milk. Poach until set, about 4 to 5 minutes. Lift on to greaseproof paper with a draining spoon.
4. Blend cornflour, egg-yolks, 2 teaspoons sugar and a few drops of vanilla essence with just enough water to slake cornflour.
5. Sowly stir in the milk in which meringue was poached. Return to pan, stir as it thickens but do not let it quite boil.

6. Cool a little. Pour into 4 glass dishes and place 1 egg island on top of each.
7. Sprinkle on a little grated chocolate or vermicelli.

FRESH PEACHES (OR PEARS) IN A FUDGE SAUCE

For 4 people but easy to make less

Tinned fruit can be used but the contrast of fresh fruit and fudge sauce is particularly delicious.

4 ripe peaches or pears
A little butter

Sauce
225 g/8 oz light soft brown sugar
15 g/½ oz butter
2 tablespoons milk

1. Start with sauce. Put sugar, butter and milk in a heavy pan. Stir over low heat to dissolve sugar.
2. Bring to boil and boil to soft ball stage, 235°F, 114°C. This stage is reached when dribbles of sauce dropped in some cold water set to a soft ball, not crisp. Stir frequently.
3. Peel, stone and halve the peaches. For pears, use soft ripe fruit, peel, quarter and core.
4. Place fruit cut side down in a buttered heat-proof dish.
5. Pour hot sauce over the fruit. Cool and serve really chilled.

FRESH FRUIT WITH ORANGE CREAM

For 4 people

1 small punnet raspberries or strawberries, or 2 large bananas*
A 150 g/5 fl oz carton of double cream
1 dessertspoon castor sugar
1 large orange
½ lemon

1. Divide raspberries or strawberries between 4 small bowls or sundae glasses. If using bananas, follow instructions below to keep them from going brown, then slice and divide between 4 bowls.
2. Beat cream and sugar until thick.
3. Grate zest only from orange and half lemon. Squeeze juice from half lemon.
4. Peel orange and roughly chop flesh, catching the juice.
5. Fold orange, juices and zest into the cream.
6. Spoon cream mixture on top of the fruit in the bowls.
7. Chill before serving.

Elizabeth Mickery
Pudsey, West Yorkshire

*To keep sliced bananas from going brown

Put unpeeled bananas in cold water for 5 to 10 minutes. They may then be peeled, sliced and kept for at least 4 hours without going brown.

Miss M. Owen
Elworth, Cheshire

LEMON DELIGHT

Another recipe from the West Sussex Federation of Women's Institutes' book 'Come Cooking Again'. A truly delightful sweet, set off by the egg-custard which accompanies it.

450 ml/¾ pint water
25 g/1 oz cornflour
150 g/5 oz sugar
Grated rind and strained juice of 2 lemons
2 egg-whites

Custard

2 egg-yolks
1 tablespoon sugar
300 ml/½ pint milk

1. Bring to the boil all but 2 tablespoons of the water. Remove from heat.
2. Mix cornflour with remaining water, stir it into boiled water, return to heat. Stir as it thickens and boil for 1 minute.

3. Stir in sugar until dissolved. Allow to cool a little and add lemon rind and juice.
4. Whisk egg-whites until really firm. Fold into mixture. Pour into a dish, leave to set in a cool place or refrigerator.
5. Make custard by mixing egg-yolks, sugar and milk. Pour into a saucepan and heat gently, stirring as it thickens. Do not let it boil.

Mrs Janice Langley
Shoreham-by-Sea, West Sussex

LEMON SOLID

An old family recipe.

Rind and juice of 2 lemons
175 g/6 oz castor sugar
600 ml/1 pint milk
15 g/½ oz gelatine

1. Finely grate rind from the lemons and squeeze the juice.
2. Put lemon rind into a basin with sugar and half of the milk.
3. Heat remaining milk with the gelatine, stirring continuously until gelatine is dissolved. Be very careful not to boil it.
4. Mix heated milk with cold milk mixture, stirring to dissolve sugar.
5. Add lemon juice. Don't be alarmed if milk appears to curdle.
6. Pour into a wet jelly mould and leave to set in a cold larder for about 12 hours or 5 hours in refrigerator.
7. Turn pudding out of mould. It should have separated with a clear jelly at top and 'curds' at bottom.

Mrs Marion Wightman
Piddletrenthide, Dorset

MANGO MOUSSE

For 6 people

2 tablespoons water
2 heaped teaspoons gelatine
340 ml/12 fl oz tinned evaporated milk, chilled in refrigerator
2 tablespoons sugar

A 454 g/16 oz tin of 'Kissan' mango pulp*

*Can be bought from oriental food shops.

1. Measure water into a cup. Sprinkle in gelatine. Stand cup in hot water to dissolve gelatine, stirring once to combine.
2. Whisk the chilled evaporated milk. Gradually add sugar. Whisk in the gelatine.
3. Fold in the mango pulp and set in a covered mould in refrigerator for 3 hours.

This dish may be decorated with whipped cream and mango slices.

Priya Wickramasinghe
Cardiff

PORT AND PRUNES

A party dessert for 15 people but easy to make less

Can be made with less expensive wine than port.

Remember to start the day before, or even sooner, as it improves with keeping. A liquidiser is useful.

450 g/1 lb dried prunes
175 to 225 ml/6 to 8 fl oz ruby port, sweet sherry or mature home-made dessert wine
284 ml/½ pint double cream
50 g/2 oz castor sugar

1. The day before, soak prunes in water to cover.
2. Next day simmer prunes gently until very soft. Leave to cool. Drain.
3. Remove stones and liquidise prunes with 175 ml/6 fl oz port to produce a very thick purée. Add more port if necessary.
4. Whisk cream with sugar until it is as thick as purée.
5. Fold purée into cream and spoon into tiny glasses.

Serve with crisp biscuits such as Shortcake Biscuits (*see page 158*) or Shortbread Biscuits (*see page 157*).

A SYLLABUB FROM KENT

For 4 people

2 egg-whites
50 to 75 g/2 to 3 oz castor sugar
Juice of ½ large lemon
150 ml/¼ pint white wine
150 ml/¼ pint double cream, whipped till thick

1. Beat egg-whites until stiff and frothy.
2. Beat in sugar
3. Add lemon juice and wine.
4. Beat in the thickly-whipped cream.
5. Pour the thick curdy mixture into little glass dishes and put in a cool place or refrigerator for 4 to 5 hours so that flavours blend.

Mrs Jill Marshall
Hythe, Kent

ICE-CREAM

A delicious variation on Anne Wallace's recipe printed in *Farmhouse Kitchen II*, giving a subtle caramel flavour and a creamy appearance.

2 eggs, separated
50 g/2 oz light soft brown sugar
142 ml/5 fl oz double cream

1. Whisk egg-whites until stiff, add sugar and whisk again.
2. Whip cream till stiff.
3. Whisk egg-yolks.
4. Combine all three and whisk together.
5. Pour straight into a plastic food box or margarine carton, put on lid and freeze.

Two ideas for bought ice-cream

Ice-cream Snowball
2 tablespoons sultanas
1 tablespoon currants
1 tablespoon rum, sherry or orange juice
1 litre/1¾ pint firm vanilla ice-cream, not the whipped or 'soft' variety
125 g/4 oz glacé cherries, cut small

1 tablespoon chopped walnuts
To decorate: 1 teaspoon of the chopped cherries, angelica, marzipan, *or*, whipped double cream for piping

1. Soak sultanas and currants in rum, sherry or orange-juice for 2 hours. Then drain.
2. Allow ice-cream to soften slightly.
3. Reserve 1 teaspoon of the chopped cherries for decorating. Then mix all ingredients together.
4. Pack this mixture into two round pudding basins. (Heat-proof pyrex basins are ideal.) Make sure mixture comes to the very brim of the basins. Any that is left can be frozen separately.
5. Press the two bowls together to form a ball, and freeze until solid.
6. Prepare decorations, cherries and angelica. Or marzipan to look like holly. Or whipped cream in a piping bag.
7. Just before serving, carefully remove basins with the aid of hot damp cloths or a bowl of warm water. Set the snowball on a chilled dish and decorate with the 'holly', or pipe rosettes of cream all over.

Once decorated, the snowball could be returned to freezer, but remember to take it out about 10 minutes before serving so that cream is not too icy.

Ice-cream Surprises

For this you need 10 small washed yoghurt cartons.

1 litre/1¾ pint firm vanilla or strawberry ice-cream, not whipped or 'soft' variety
About 1 dozen small meringues
1 dozen grapes
225 g/8 oz toasted* desiccated coconut

*To toast coconut: spread it in grill pan and toast under moderate heat, stirring often until it is evenly-golden. Take care, it burns easily.

1. Allow ice-cream to soften a little. Then fill each carton about ¾ full. Return to freezer.
2. Meanwhile, crumble the meringues and remove pips from grapes.

3. When cartons of ice-cream have frozen hard, take them out one at a time. Scoop out a cavity in the middle of each and fill with one grape and crumbled meringue. Seal up again with a dollop of ice-cream and return to freezer.
4. When frozen again, remove ice-cream from cartons and roll each one in toasted coconut, shaping a rough ball at same time. Either wrap each ball in foil and return to freezer, or open-freeze on a tray and pack in a polythene bag until required.

FUDGE SAUCE

For plain ice-cream.

50 g/2 oz butter
50 g/2 oz granulated sugar
75 g/3 oz soft brown sugar
150 g/5 oz golden syrup

Combine ingredients in a pan and stir over low heat until all the sugar grains have dissolved.

MELBA SAUCE

For puddings or ice-cream.

This sauce freezes well.

Raspberries, fresh or frozen
Icing sugar

1. Sieve uncooked raspberries to make a purée.
2. Sift icing sugar and beat it into purée, one teaspoon at a time, until sauce is sufficiently sweet.

Anne Wallace
Stewarton, Ayrshire

QUICK CHOCOLATE SAUCE

50 g/2 oz sugar
65 ml/2¼ fl oz water
50 g/2 oz dark cooking chocolate
A small nut of butter

1. Dissolve sugar in water over low heat. Then boil for 3 minutes.
2. Add chocolate broken in pieces, stir until it is melted and simmer sauce for 1 minute.
3. Stir in butter.

Serve hot or cold.

Anne Wallace
Stewarton, Ayrshire

MINT PARFAIT

150 g/5 oz castor sugar
150 ml/¼ pint water
2 egg-whites
A pinch of salt
45 ml/3 tablespoons Crême de Menthe
275 ml/½ pint double cream, whipped to soft-peaks

Toppings

Grated chocolate or sugared mint leaves* or Quick Chocolate Sauce (see above)

1. Dissolve sugar in water over a low heat. Do not let it boil until sugar is dissolved. Then, using a sugar thermometer if you have one, boil to 238°F, 110°C. If you have not got a thermometer, the syrup is boiled when a little forms a very soft ball when tested in a cup of cold water.
2. Whisk egg-whites with salt until stiff but not dry. While still whisking, pour on boiling syrup in a steady stream and keep on whisking until it has cooled.
3. Mix in Crême de Menthe, then fold in cream.
4. Put into a covered plastic box and freeze.

Serve scoops of the parfait sprinkled with grated plain chocolate, or a topping of your choice.

*Sugared mint leaves

Paint fresh mint leaves with lightly-beaten egg-white. Coat well with castor sugar. Allow to dry in a warm room.

Anne Wallace
Stewarton, Ayrshire

ORANGE AND LEMON ICE

A generous 150 ml/5 fl oz water
200 g/7 oz granulated sugar
Grated rind of 1 lemon
Strained juice of 2 oranges and 2 lemons

1. Put water in a pan and bring to the boil. Reduce heat. Add sugar and stir to dissolve.
2. Bring to boil. Add lemon rind and leave to cool and infuse for 2 hours.
3. Add fruit juice. Stir well.
4. Pour into a shallow container and put into freezer.
5. When almost frozen—i.e., soft in middle and hard around edges, turn it out into a bowl and whisk very well. It will whisk up into almost a froth of snow.
6. Rinse and dry the container and pour in the mixture. Cover lightly with a lid or foil and freeze until required.
7. To serve, scoop into glass dishes or fill hollowed out orange or lemon shells.

PEANUT BRITTLE GÂTEAU

For this you need 1 fatless sponge, about 20 cm/8 inches across and 6 to 7 cm/2½ to 3 inches deep (see page 150)

125 g/4 oz peanut brittle
A 142 ml/5 fl oz carton double cream
120 ml/4 fl oz rum
120 ml/4 fl oz water

1. Crush peanut brittle. The best way to do this is to put it inside 2 polythene bags and knock it with a hammer. Do not crush it too fine because the beauty of this gâteau is the crunchy texture of the brittle with the soft rum and cream centre.
2. Whip cream until thick.
3. Mix rum and water.
4. Cut sponge into 2 layers. Lay bottom half on a serving plate, pour about half of the rum and water mix

over the sponge. Then spread about half of the whipped cream over this.
5. Lay top half of sponge over the cream and drench this with the rest of the rum and water.
6. Cover top and sides with cream.
7. Sprinkle and pat the crushed peanut brittle over the top and sides of the gâteau. Chill and serve.

GRACE'S CHOCOLATE FANCY

For this you need 1 chocolate fatless sponge, about 20 cm/8 inches across and about 7·5 cm/3 inches deep (*see page 150*)
A 110 g/4 oz jar of maraschino cherries in syrup
120 ml/4 fl oz sherry
120 ml/4 fl oz water
300 ml/½ pint double cream, whipped
2 tablespoons of chocolate mousse, or a 105 ml/3·7 fl oz carton of bought mousse

Chocolate curls decoration
50 g/2 oz top-quality plain eating chocolate
2 teaspoons salad oil

1. First start preparing chocolate for decorating. Heat a small empty bowl in a moderate oven, Gas 4, 350°F, 180°C. Take it out and put into it the chocolate broken into small pieces.

2. Add oil and stir gently until dissolved.
3. Spread this mixture very thinly over a hard surface and leave to set in a cool place. Ideally a marble slab should be used but you can use a formica surface, such as a large formica chopping board.
4. Now drain syrup from cherries and mix it with sherry and water.
5. Cut each cherry in two.
6. Slice sponge into 3 layers. Place bottom layer on a large serving plate.
7. Use one third of sherry mixture to pour over bottom layer of sponge. Spread with 2 tablespoons of the whipped cream and 1 tablespoon chocolate mousse. Top this with half of the cherries.
8. Put middle slice of sponge in position and repeat the above process with sherry mixture, cream, mousse and cherries.
9. Put on top layer of sponge. Pour over remaining sherry mixture. Press sponge down gently.
10. Now cover sides and top with rest of cream. Set gâteau aside to firm up in a cool place or refrigerator.
11. Make chocolate curls. Draw a sharp knife, held at an angle, across the board making curls of chocolate. Drop curls and broken bits of chocolate all over the gâteau. Chill and serve.

Can be frozen.

Chapter 9

Yeast Cookery, Teabreads and Scones

SHORT TIME BREAD

White

15 g/½ oz fresh yeast, 7 g/¼ oz
dried
A 25 mg Vitamin C tablet (buy
from chemist, also called
ascorbic acid)
¼ teaspoon sugar
About 150 ml/¼ pint warm water
225 g/8 oz strong plain flour
½ teaspoon salt
15 g/½ oz margarine

Wholewheat or Brown

Use 225 g/8 oz wholewheat
flour, or half wholewheat and
half white

1. Blend together the yeast, crushed
Vitamin C tablet and half of the
water. If using dried yeast, add sugar
also and wait until it froths up before
using.
2. Sieve flour and salt, rub in
margarine.
3. Pour yeast liquid into dry
ingredients and mix well.
4. Add sufficient warm water to make
a soft, beatable dough.
5. Beat dough until the bowl is clean.
6. Turn out on to a lightly-floured
board and knead until smooth, 10
minutes.
7. Rest dough for five minutes,
covered lightly.
8. Shape into bread buns or cottage
loaf, twist or plait and put on a
greased baking tray. Cover with a
damp cloth or greased polythene, and
leave in a warm place to rise until
doubled in size.
9. Bake near top of a hot oven, Gas 7,
425°F, 220°C.

Bread buns take 10 to 12 minutes.
Loaves take 25 to 30 minutes.

Pizza

The above quantity of dough will
make 4 pizza bases 18 to 20 cm/7 to 8
inches in diameter.

Filling

For 1 pizza, 2 people

½ to 1 tin anchovy fillets
50 g/2 oz chopped bacon

1 teaspoon oil or melted butter
25 g/1 oz grated cheese
25 g/1 oz sliced mushrooms
2 sliced tomatoes
A large pinch of basil
Black olives (optional) or
pickled prunes (*see page 173*)

To garnish: chopped parsley

1. If you find the flavour of anchovies
rather too strong, drain them and soak
in milk for about half an hour.
2. Fry bacon lightly.
3. Roll out a piece of dough to 7 mm/
¼ inch thick and 18 to 20 cm/7 to 8
inches in diameter.
4. Place it on a well-greased tin.
Brush it over with oil or butter.
5. Sprinkle top of dough with cheese,
mushrooms and bacon. Finish with
tomatoes and basil.
6. Arrange drained anchovies in a
lattice design on top. Place olives in
the spaces.
7. Cover lightly and leave aside to
rise, or until the pizza dough has
doubled in size or puffed up well.
8. Bake near top of a hot oven, Gas 7,
425°F, 220°C, for 20 to 30 minutes,
reducing heat to moderately hot, Gas
5, 375°F, 190°C, after 15 minutes if
browning too quickly.
9. Garnish with chopped parsley.

Wholewheat Tomato Pizza

For 4 people

25 g/1 oz margarine or 1
tablespoon oil
450 g/1 lb onions, chopped
2 cloves of garlic, crushed
Two 400 g/14 oz tins of tomatoes
¼ teaspoon oregano
Salt and freshly-ground black
pepper
A pinch of sugar
75 g/3 oz finely-grated cheese

To garnish: 2 or 3 mushrooms,
or fine slices of green and red
pepper

1. Heat margarine or oil and fry onion
and garlic until softening.
2. Add tomatoes, oregano, salt, pepper
and sugar and cook gently for about 20
minutes until thick.

3. Meanwhile, roll out enough dough to fit a greased Swiss roll tin. Prick all over with a fork. Cover with a cloth and let it rise until puffy.
4. Bake the pizza base near top of a hot oven, Gas 7, 425°F, 220°C, for 5 minutes. Then remove from oven and reduce heat to moderate, Gas 4, 350°F, 180°C.
5. Spread tomato mixture over the hot pizza base. Sprinkle cheese on top and decorate with mushroom slices or rings of pepper.
6. Return to oven near top and bake for 20 minutes until cheese is melted and browning.

Sweet Pears and Cheese Pizza

Eaten hot or cold.

For 3 or 4 people

3 dessert pears
Rind and juice of ½ lemon
50 g/2 oz Lancashire, Cheshire or Mozzarella cheese, grated
25 g/1 oz plain cooking chocolate, grated
50 g/2 oz chopped walnuts
25 g/1 oz butter

1. Peel and core pears and cut into slices, about 3 slices to each quarter. Dip into lemon juice to prevent browning.
2. Roll out dough about 7 mm/¼ inch thick and 18 to 20 cm/7 to 8 inches in diameter.
3. Arrange slices of pear on the dough leaving a 1 cm/½ inch border all round.
4. Scatter on the lemon rind. Cover pears with cheese, sprinkle on chocolate and chopped walnuts. Dot with butter.
5. Cover lightly and leave aside in a warm place to rise.
6. Bake near top of a very hot oven for 5 minutes, Gas 8, 450°F, 230°C, then lower temperature to Gas 7, 425°F, 220°C and bake for about 15 minutes more, or until pizza dough is brown.

PITTA BREAD

2 teaspoons dried yeast
A pinch of sugar

300 ml/½ pint warm water
1 teaspoon salt
1½ tablespoons oil
400 g/14 oz strong plain flour, sifted

1. In a large mixing bowl, dissolve yeast and sugar in 3 tablespoons of the warm water. Let it stand for 10 minutes in a warm place until frothy on top.
2. Add rest of water, salt and oil.
3. Stir 100 g/4 oz flour at a time into yeast mixture, forming a sticky dough. If it is too sticky to work when all flour is used, add a little more flour.
4. Transfer dough to lightly-floured board and knead until smooth, about 10 minutes.
5. Shape dough into a ball and coat lightly with oil. Return it to bowl. Cover and let it rise in a warm place until doubled in bulk, about 1½ hours.
6. Punch dough down and form 6 or 7 balls. On a lightly-floured board, roll or press out the dough with the hands into 15 cm/6 inch circles that are 7 mm/¼ inch thick. Dust lightly with flour.
7. Put on to lightly-oiled baking sheets, cover and allow to rise again for 15 minutes.
8. Preheat oven to very hot, Gas 8, 450°F, 230°C.
9. Bake for 8 to 10 minutes. Wrap the bread in foil immediately after removing from oven to preserve moistness.

Serve hot or reheated under grill.

Freeze well. Reheat from frozen under grill.

Elizabeth Mickery
Pudsey, Yorkshire

KENTISH HUFFKINS

These are plain, white, flat yeast cakes, traditionally baked with a dimple in the middle.

Makes 10

15 g/½ oz fresh yeast or 1½ tea-spoons dried yeast
1 teaspoon castor sugar

300 ml/½ pint warm milk and water mixed
450 g/1 lb strong plain white flour
½ teaspoon salt
25 g/1 oz lard

1. Mix yeast and sugar into warmed milk and water. If using dried yeast, whisk it in with a fork so that granules dissolve without clogging together. Leave in a warm place for 5 minutes until yeast is active and frothy.
2. Mix flour and salt in a bowl. Rub in lard.
3. Add yeast mixture. Mix to a pliable dough and turn out on to a floured board.
4. Knead well until dough is no longer sticky, and is smooth and shiny, about 10 minutes.
5. Lightly grease bowl and put in the dough. Cover with a cloth or greased polythene. Keep in a warm place, away from draughts, so that dough will rise (or 'prove') until doubled in size.
6. Turn on to a floured board. Knead lightly to let out air and to make dough pliable again.
7. Divide this dough into 10 equal pieces.
8. Shape into flat oval cakes about 1·2 cm/½ inch thick. It is best to do this by forming a roll first and then flattening to an oval with rolling pin.
9. Place well apart on greased baking trays and press a floured finger into the centre of each cake. Cover trays and leave to 'prove' until doubled in size.
10. Bake near top of a very hot oven, Gas 8, 450°F, 230°C, for 15 to 20 minutes.
11. Transfer to a wire rack.

Eat hot or cold, split and buttered.

Mrs Jill Marshall
Hythe, Kent

CURRANT LOAF

15 g/½ oz fresh yeast or 7 g/¼ oz dried
300 ml/½ pint warm milk
25 g/1 oz castor sugar
450 g/1 lb strong plain white flour
1 teaspoon salt
1 level teaspoon cinnamon
25 g/1 oz margarine
125 g/4 oz washed and dried currants
Beaten egg

1. Blend the yeast into the warm milk. If using dried yeast, add 1 teaspoon of the sugar and wait until it froths up before using.
2. Sift together flour, salt and cinnamon.
3. Add sugar and rub in fat.
4. Stir in yeast and milk and mix to a soft dough.
5. Turn on to a floured board and knead until smooth.
6. Cover and leave to rise until doubled in size, about 1 hour.
7. Work the currants into the risen dough until evenly distributed.
8. Form into loaf shape and place in a greased 1 kg/2 lb loaf tin.
9. Brush the loaf with beaten egg. Cover and leave to 'prove' again, about 1 hour, until well-risen and puffy.
10. Bake near top of a moderately hot oven, Gas 6, 400°F, 200°C, until golden brown, about 50 minutes.
11. Cool on a wire rack.

Freezes well.

SWEDISH TEA RING

225 g/8 oz strong plain flour
¼ teaspoon salt
50 g/2 oz margarine
40 g/1½ oz sugar
15 g/½ oz fresh yeast or 7 g/¼ oz dried
150 ml/¼ pint warm milk and water mixed
1 beaten egg

Marzipan filling

40 g/1½ oz ground almonds
40 g/1½ oz castor sugar
Beaten egg

Decoration

A little glacé icing
4 glacé cherries, chopped
Angelica, chopped
25 g/1 oz chopped walnuts

1. Sieve flour and salt, rub in margarine, add sugar, except for one level teaspoonful.
2. In a small jug work together the yeast and the level teaspoon of sugar until it is liquid. Add a little of the warm milk and water mixture to the jug. If using dried yeast, combine yeast, sugar and enough liquid to dissolve and leave jug in a warm place to froth up.
3. Make a well in the centre of the flour and pour in the yeast liquid. If using fresh yeast, leave it to become frothy, about 10 to 15 minutes. If using dried yeast, it is better to wait until you are certain it is active before adding to flour.
4. Add beaten egg and enough of the liquid to make a soft dough.
5. Turn out and knead well until the dough is smooth and elastic, about 10 minutes. Leave aside in a warm place to rise for about 1 hour until doubled in size.
6. Roll out dough to a rectangle 30 by 10 cm/12 by 4 inches.
7. Make up almond paste by mixing ground almonds and castor sugar with just enough egg to bind. Form it into a roll about 30 cm/12 inches long.
8. Lay the roll of paste on the dough and roll up.
9. Form it into a ring on a greased baking tray and leave aside, covered lightly, to rise again until doubled in size.
10. Bake above middle of a hot oven, Gas 7, 425°F, 220°C, for 20 to 25 minutes.
11. Remove it on to a wire rack to cool.
12. When cold, spread with a little glacé icing and scatter chopped cherries, angelica and nuts on top while icing is wet.

LOAF CAKE
Teisen Dorth
A Glamorgan recipe for a rich fruit loaf. Can be made with white or wholewheat flour or a mixture of wholewheat and white. With wholewheat the loaf will not be as light as with white.

15 g/½ oz fresh yeast, or 2 teaspoons dried yeast
300 ml/½ pint lukewarm milk
450 g/1 lb plain flour
A pinch of salt
¼ teaspoon mixed spice
65 g/2½ oz butter or lard
65 g/2½ oz soft brown sugar
150 g/5 oz sultanas
150 g/5 oz currants
65 g/2½ oz raisins
25 g/1 oz candied peel
1 beaten egg

1. Mix yeast with a little of the warm milk and leave in a warm place for 5 minutes. If using dried yeast, add a teaspoon of the sugar also, wait until it is active and frothy before using.
2. Put flour, salt and spice into a bowl and rub in fat.
3. Mix in rest of dry ingredients.
4. Make a well in centre, add yeast mixture, well-beaten egg and enough warm milk to make a soft dough. Mix and then knead in basin for 5 minutes.
5. Grease the mixing bowl. Put dough in it, cover with greased polythene or a damp cloth and leave it in a really warm place to rise for about 1½ hours, until it has doubled in size.
6. Knead dough again to knock out the bubbles.
7. Shape and place in a well-greased 1 kg/2 lb loaf tin. Cover again and leave 20 minutes in a really warm place to rise again. Dough should rise well above top of tin.
8. Bake just above middle of a hot oven, Gas 7, 425°F, 220°C, for 20 minutes. Then reduce heat to warm, Gas 3, 325°F, 160°C, for 45 minutes more.
9. Turn loaf out on to a wire rack immediately to cool.
Freezes well.

Mrs Doreen Owen
Llanwenarth Citra W.I., Gwent

FRIED INDIAN WHOLEWHEAT FLOUR BREAD

These are known as puris. They are usually eaten with vegetables, or at the start of a meal, and are a great favourite among children and adults alike.

This quantity makes 12 or 13

They go well with Cauliflower Bhaji (*see page 74*), Curried Bhindi (*see page 73*) and Onion Salad (*see page 70*).

175 g/6 oz wholewheat flour
175 g/6 oz plain white flour
1½ teaspoons salt
2 teaspoons oil
150 to 175 ml/5 to 6 fl oz tepid water
Oil for deep frying

1. In a bowl mix flours, salt, 2 teaspoons oil and sufficient water to form a soft pliable dough.
2. Knead the dough thoroughly and leave covered at room temperature for about 1 hour.
3. Roll out one third of the dough at a time into a large pancake, less than 7 mm/¼ inch thick. Cut circles about 6 to 8 cm/2½ to 3 inches in diameter, using a pastry cutter or wine glass.
4. The success of a puri is in its cooking. The oil should be heated until it begins to smoke, and the puris should be carefully immersed one at a time.
5. After about 6 seconds in the hot oil the puri will begin to surface. Using a frying spoon, gently pat it down to keep it submerged in the hot oil until it puffs up.
6. Turn it over and allow it to cook for a couple of seconds more. This whole frying process should take about 15 to 20 seconds per puri.

Priya Wickramasinghe
Cardiff

IRISH SODA BREADS

The mixing of soda bread is done lightly and quickly, like scones. This ensures light fluffy results.
Freezes well, up to 6 months.

Brown
275 g/10 oz wholewheat flour
175 g/6 oz strong plain white flour
2 teaspoons sugar (optional but not traditional)
1 teaspoon bicarbonate of soda
1 teaspoon salt
1 teaspoon cream of tartar*
About 300 ml/½ pint milk*
*It is usually made with sour milk which makes its own contribution to the rising. If fresh milk is used then add cream of tartar, but not otherwise.

1. Put wholewheat flour in a large bowl and sieve in all the other dry ingredients.
2. Mix to a soft dough with the milk, adding extra if required. The dough should be slack but not wet.
3. With floured hands knead until smooth, then flatten the dough into a circle about 3·5 cm/1½ inches thick. Put on a greased baking tin, score a large cross over the top.
4. Bake in a moderatley hot oven, Gas 5, 375°F, 190°C, for about 40 minutes. The bread should feel light when fully cooked.
Eat fresh.

Mrs June Hodgson
Loch Corrib, Ireland

Using Granary Flour
450 g/1 lb granary flour
225 g/8 oz strong plain white flour, or 175 g/6 oz of this plus 50 g/2 oz bran
1 teaspoon bicarbonate of soda
1 teaspoon cream of tartar
1 teaspoon salt
2 teaspoons sugar
Just under 600 ml/1 pint milk or milk and water mixed

1. Put granary flour in a large bowl. Sieve in white flour, bicarbonate of soda, cream of tartar and salt. Add bran, if used.

2. Now gradually mix with milk until dough is soft but not wet.
3. Turn out on to a floured board and knead fairly quickly until smooth.
4. Flatten the dough into a large circle about 3·5 cm/1½ inches thick. Place it on a greased baking tin. Score over the top a large cross (this ensures even distribution of heat).
5. Bake in a moderately hot oven, Gas 5, 375°F, 190°C, for about 50 to 60 minutes. Test with a skewer to check that it is fully cooked. The skewer will come out clean if the bread is ready.

BANANA LOAF

Sliced and thinly-buttered, this is delicious. A good use for over-ripe bananas.

Freezes well packed in a polythene bag with all air excluded.

2 ripe bananas
50 g/2 oz margarine
150 g/5 oz castor sugar
2 eggs
225 g/8 oz self-raising flour*
A pinch of salt

***If you prefer wholewheat flour this works with half wholewheat and half white. If you cannot buy self-raising wholewheat, add ½ teaspoon baking powder.**

1. Mash bananas.
2. Cream margarine and sugar.
3. Beat in eggs.
4. Add flour, salt and banana and mix well.
5. Put in a greased and floured 675 g/1½ lb loaf tin, or slightly larger.
6. Bake in middle of a moderately hot oven, Gas 5, 375°F, 190°C, for about 1 hour, until loaf is golden brown, springy to touch and shrinking slightly from sides of tin.
7. Turn loaf out on to a wire rack to cool.

Anne Wallace
Stewarton, Ayrshire

GRANDMA BASTON'S FRUIT BREAD

This quantity makes 3 large loaves but easy to make one third or two thirds of this quantity.

They keep well and freeze well.

350 g/12 oz currants
350 g/12 oz raisins
225 g/8 oz sultanas
900 g/2 lb plain white flour
1 dessertspoon baking powder
A pinch of salt
350 g/12 oz butter or margarine
450 g/1 lb moist brown sugar
3 beaten eggs
About 150 ml/¼ pint milk
½ teaspoon bicarbonate of soda
50 g/2 oz mixed peel, grated or fine-chopped
50 g/2 oz glacé cherries, chopped

1. The day before baking put currants, raisins and sultanas in a basin of hot water to cover. Leave to steep for 2 or 3 hours.
2. Then squeeze out excess moisture and spread fruit in a large baking tin. Put it to dry in a warm place, stirring about a bit from time to time.
3. Sieve flour, baking powder and salt into a large bowl.
4. Rub in fat and add sugar.
5. Mix in eggs and enough milk to achieve a fairly stiff mixture. Continue mixing until consistency is smooth.
6. Mix bicarbonate of soda with 1 tablespoon milk and add.
7. Lastly, add fruit, peel and cherries. Stir well.
8. Grease three 1 kg/2 lb loaf tins and line the bottoms with greaseproof paper. Divide the mixture between them.
9. Bake below middle of a moderate oven, Gas 4, 350°F, 180°C, for 2½ to 3 hours until well-risen and firm to the touch.

Mrs Patricia Chantry
Hook, Goole, N. Humberside

MALTED WHOLEWHEAT TEABREAD

350 g/12 oz wholewheat flour
2 level teaspoons baking powder
½ level teaspoon salt
50 g/2 oz muscovado sugar
50 g/2 oz sultanas
50 g/2 oz dates
2 rounded tablespoons malt extract
50 g/2 oz butter or margarine
150 ml/¼ pint plus 1 tablespoon milk
2 beaten eggs

1. Mix flour, baking powder and salt in a large bowl.
2. Add sugar and sultanas.
3. Chop the dates and mix in.
4. Gently heat malt and butter or margarine together until fat has just melted.
5. Add milk to beaten eggs.
6. Combine malt mixture with egg and milk mixture and stir into dry ingredients.
7. Mix together to form a soft dough.
8. Turn mixture into a greased 1 kg/2 lb loaf tin, or into two greased 450 g/1 lb tins. Level the surface of the mixture.
9. Bake in a warm oven, Gas 3, 325°F, 160°C, for 1 hour. Then turn out to cool on a wire rack.

Wrap in foil and keep one day before eating and the bread will be nice and moist. Freezes well.

Serve sliced and buttered.

MUFFINS

Made on a girdle or griddle or in a heavy frying pan.

125 g/4 oz plain white flour or half wholewheat and half white
½ teaspoon cream of tartar
¼ teaspoon bicarbonate of soda
15 g/½ oz sugar
20 g/¾ oz melted butter or margarine
2 teaspoons of beaten egg
About 4 tablespoons milk
A knob of suet to grease girdle, or a *very* little lard

1. Mix dry ingredients, sifting in cream of tartar and bicarbonate of soda.
2. Mix in butter, egg and enough milk to make a soft dough.
3. Using a floured board, roll out to 1 cm/½ inch thick. Cut rounds.
4. Heat girdle, grease lightly and cook muffins for 3 to 4 minutes each side until nicely golden brown.

Good to eat hot or cold.

Freeze well.

OATMEAL SCONES

50 g/2 oz medium oatmeal
50 g/2 oz plain wholewheat or white flour
A pinch of salt
1 teaspoon soft brown sugar (or more, to taste)
½ teaspoon cream of tartar
¼ teaspoon bicarbonate of soda
15 g/½ oz dripping or bacon fat
About 3 tablespoons milk, to mix

1. Put oatmeal, wholewheat flour, salt and sugar in a bowl.
2. Sift in cream of tartar and bicarbonate of soda to be sure there are no lumps.
3. Rub in fat.
4. Mix to a soft dough with milk.
5. Using a floured board, roll out about 7 mm/¼ inch thick and cut rounds.
6. Cook on a hot, lightly-greased girdle or heavy frying pan for about 4 minutes each side. Cool in a towel.

SAVOURY DROP SCONES OR PANCAKES

Can be made on a girdle, griddle, bakestone or hot-plate—whatever name you give it—or in a heavy frying pan.

225 g/8 oz plain white or whole-wheat flour
1 teaspoon cream of tartar
½ teaspoon bicarbonate of soda
A pinch of salt
1 dessertspoon finely-chopped onion
1 egg
About 150 ml/5 fl oz milk

To grease girdle: a knob of beef suet or a very little lard or margarine

1. Put flour in a bowl. Sieve in cream of tartar, bicarbonate of soda and salt. Mix in chopped onion.
2. Mix to a thick pouring batter with egg and milk.
3. Heat girdle and grease it if necessary.
4. Drop spoonfuls of batter on girdle. When bubbles appear, turn over and cook other side.
5. Cool scones in a towel. This stops them drying out.

Freeze well.

WELSH CAKES

Makes 40 to 50, but they freeze well

Or you can make half quantity, using 1 small egg and very little milk.

These are cooked on a bakestone, as it is known in Wales, or a girdle, as used in Scotland. A heavy-based frying pan gives best results if you have neither of these.

450 g/1 lb self-raising flour
A pinch of salt
125 g/4 oz lard
125 g/4 oz margarine
175 g/6 oz granulated sugar
50 g/2 oz currants
1 beaten egg
About 3 tablespoons milk
A little extra lard to grease pan

1. Sift flour and salt into a basin.
2. Rub in lard and margarine.
3. Add sugar and currants.
4. Mix to the consistency of pastry dough with beaten egg and milk.

5. Roll out on a floured board to approximately 7 mm/¼ inch thick. Cut with a 6·5 cm/2½ inch plain scone cutter.
6. Heat bakestone, girdle or heavy frying pan and grease it lightly with lard. It is wise to test heat by cooking one cake on its own. If it is too hot, cakes burn before inside is cooked. Cook cakes on both sides until just golden. Grease pan very lightly between batches.
7. Put on wire rack to cool. Store in a tin or plastic box.

Traditionally eaten cold, but they are hard to resist straight from the pan, especially when children are about. They are never buttered.

Mrs Beryl Hawkins
Little Mill W.I., Gwent

POTATO SCONES

Enough for 4 people

Freeze well.

Cooked on a girdle or griddle or heavy frying pan.

15 g/½ oz melted butter or margarine
A pinch of salt
225 g/8 oz cold mashed potato (no lumps)
About 50 g/2 oz plain flour, white or wholewheat

1. Add melted butter or margarine and salt to mashed potatoes.
2. Mix in flour gradually until a working dough is produced.
3. Roll out very thinly. Cut rounds, prick well with a fork.
4. Use a knob of beef suet to grease the girdle lightly.
5. Cook scones on hot girdle for about 3 minutes each side.
6. Cool in a towel.

Eat fresh with butter. Excellent with bacon. Fry in bacon fat with the bacon.

SCONE DROPS

Makes 12 to 15

200 g/7 oz self-raising flour
25 g/1 oz porridge oats
125 g/4 oz margarine
75 g/3 oz sugar
50 g/3 oz mixed dried fruit
6 glacé cherries, chopped
1 large beaten egg
A little milk

1. Mix flour and oats in a bowl.
2. Rub in margarine.
3. Add sugar, dried fruit and cherries.
4. Mix in the beaten egg, using a fork. Add a dessertspoon of milk if too stiff to mix.
5. Put rough heaps on a greased baking sheet.
6. Bake near top of a moderately hot oven, Gas 5, 375°F, 190°C, for 10 to 15 minutes.

Nice hot or cold. Freeze and reheat well.

Margaret Heywood
Todmorden, Yorkshire

WHOLEWHEAT SCONES

175 g/6 oz wholewheat flour
50 g/2 oz plain flour
1 teaspoon cream of tartar
½ teaspoon bicarbonate of soda
¼ teaspoon salt
50 g/2 oz dark brown sugar, try muscovado
1½ tablespoons safflower or sunflower oil
1 egg
75 to 100 ml/3 to 4 fl oz milk

1. Mix dry ingredients, sifting cream of tartar and bicarbonate of soda with plain flour and salt.
2. Beat oil, egg and milk together.
3. Mix this into the dry ingredients adding a little more milk if necessary, sufficient to make a soft elastic dough.
4. Turn dough on to a floured board and knead it lightly.
5. Roll out just over 2 cm/1 inch thick. Cut into rounds. Place the scones on lightly-greased baking sheets.

6. Bake in a very hot oven, Gas 8, 450°F, 230°C, for 10 to 12 minutes, when scones will be browned and nicely risen.

Note: wholemeal scones tend not to rise as much as plain white ones.

7. Slide scones on to a wire rack to cool.

Anne Wallace
Stewarton, Ayrshire

CORN MUFFINS

Makes 12

175 g/6 oz wholewheat flour
125 g/4 oz cornflour
3 teaspoons baking powder
½ teaspoon salt
1 egg
2 tablespoons honey
300 ml/½ pint milk
2 tablespoons oil
Half a 200 g/7 oz tin of sweetcorn
75 g/3 oz grated cheese

1. Mix flours, baking powder and salt.
2. In another bowl mix egg, honey and milk. Then mix this thoroughly into flours.
3. Stir in oil, sweetcorn and cheese.
4. Grease a tray of 12 deep bun tins. Spoon in mixture.
5. Bake near top of a hot oven, Gas 7, 425°F, 210°C, for 10 to 12 minutes.

Delicious piping hot with cheese or soups, or with New England Casserole (*see page 82*).

Sarah Brown
Scarborough, Yorkshire

SUSSEX HEAVIES

Not a bit heavy, just simple nicely-flavoured fruit scones.

225 g/8 oz self-raising white flour, or half white and half wholewheat*
A pinch of salt
25 g/1 oz castor sugar
50 g/2 oz lard
50 g/2 oz mixed currants and raisins

175 ml/6 fl oz sour milk, or fresh milk 'soured' with juice of half a lemon

*Use ½ teaspoon baking powder if you cannot buy self-raising wholewheat flour.

1. Mix flour, salt and sugar (plus baking powder if needed).
2. Rub in lard and add dried fruit.
3. Mix to a soft dough with most of the liquid.
4. Using a floured board, roll out and cut into 5 cm/2 inch rounds. Brush with remaining sour milk. Place on greased baking sheets.
5. Bake near top of a hot oven, Gas 7, 425°F, 220°C, until golden brown, about 10 minutes.

Mrs Gaye Goodall
Steyning, West Sussex

HONEY BISCUITS

These are like exceptionally good digestive biscuits and are particularly nice with cheese.

Makes about 24 biscuits

225 g/8 oz wholewheat flour
½ level teaspoon salt
100 g/4 oz margarine or butter
2 tablespoons clear honey

1. Mix flour and salt in a bowl.
2. Rub in margarine or butter.
3. Mix with honey.
4. Using a floured board, roll out thinly and cut into rounds with a 5 cm/2 inch cutter.
5. Bake in a cool oven, Gas 2, 300°F, 150°C, for 20 minutes.

OATCAKES

Makes 20 oatcakes 6·5 cm/2½ inches in diameter

100 g/4 oz vegetable margarine
50 g/2 oz soft brown sugar
100 g/4 oz wholewheat flour
100 g/4 oz porridge oats
A little milk

1. Cream margarine and sugar.
2. Mix in flour and oats and work into a paste. Moisten if necessary with a teaspoon of milk.
3. Using a floured board, roll out about 7 mm/¼ inch thick and cut into rounds. Put on a greased baking tray.

4. Bake just above middle of a moderately hot oven, Gas 5, 375°F, 190°C, for 20 minutes, until pale brown.
5. Take straight off baking tin on to a wire rack to cool.

Sarah Brown
Scarborough, Yorkshire

Chapter 10

Cakes,
Biscuits
and
Cookies

FATLESS SPONGE

This quantity is sufficient for one 20 cm/8 inch tin 7·5 cm/3 inches deep. Or for two 15 cm/6 inch sandwich tins.

The mixture can also be used for a sponge flan, sponge drops and sponge fingers.

3 eggs
75 g/3 oz castor sugar
75 g/3 oz plain flour

1. Grease tin and put a circle of greaseproof paper in the bottom.
2. Using an electric mixer or a hand whisk, whip eggs and castor sugar together until very, very thick. It takes at least 5 minutes in an electric mixer.
3. Using a sieve, sprinkle about one third of the flour over surface of egg mixture. Fold this in carefully with a spatula using a figure of eight movement. Do this twice more, taking care to cut through the mixture only with sharp edge of spatula in order to keep mixture as fluffy as possible.
4. When flour has been incorporated, pour mixture into tin(s).
5. Bake a 20 cm/8 inch cake in centre of a warm oven, Gas 3, 325°F, 160°C, for about 40 minutes until cake is well-risen, golden, firm to touch and just shrinking from sides of tin.

In 15 cm/6 inch sandwich tins bake about 30 minutes.

Chocolate Fatless Sponge

When flour has been weighed out, remove 2 teaspoons and replace this with 2 teaspoons sifted cocoa (not drinking chocolate). Proceed as before.

Sponge drops

Using a dessertspoon, drop in blobs on a baking tray lined with non-stick paper. Bake at the above temperature for about 12 minutes or until golden. Do not overbake.

Sponge fingers

Using a piping bag with 7 mm/¼ inch plain nozzle, pipe 7·5 cm/3 inch strips on to a baking tin lined with non-stick paper. Use a knife to make a clean cut through the sponge mixture. Bake at the above temperature for about 12 minutes or until golden. Take care not to overbake.

4-5-6 SPONGE CAKE

This mixture will make an 18 cm/ 7 inch sandwich, or one small cake and 4 or 5 Madeleines

125 g/4 oz soft margarine
150 g/5 oz castor sugar
175 g/6 oz self-raising flour
2 large eggs
1 or 2 drops vanilla essence
1 tablespoon boiling water

1. Cream margarine and sugar until light and fluffy.
2. Sieve flour into another bowl.
3. Add eggs one at a time, beating with a spring whisk or an electric whisk between each egg.
4. Fold in flour as lightly as possible and lastly the vanilla essence and boiling water. With the last of the flour, the consistency should be not quite dropping from the spoon.
5. Grease two 18 cm/7 inch sandwich tins and line bases with a circle of greaseproof paper.
6. Bake for about 15 to 20 mintues in a moderately hot oven, Gas 6, 400°F, 200°C. When done, the cakes should be golden, firm on top and springy.
7. Turn out immediately on to a wire rack.
8. When cool, sandwich together with jam or lemon curd (*see page 177*). Sprinkle castor sugar on top.

Mrs Joan Gould
Hook, Goole, N. Humberside

Madeleines

4-5-6 sponge mixture
2 tablespoons raspberry jam
Desiccated coconut
4 or 5 glacé cherries

1. Grease 4 or 5 dariole moulds or castle pudding tins and stand them on a baking tray.
2. Three quarters fill with above mixture.

3. Bake for 15 minutes as above or until risen and golden brown.
4. Turn out of tins to cool on a wire rack.
5. Coat with melted raspberry jam all over and cover with coconut. Set a cherry on top.

Mrs Joan Gould
Hook, Goole, N. Humberside

CHOCOLATE SPONGE SANDWICH

Made all in one bowl.

175 g/6 oz self-raising white flour
175 g/6 oz castor sugar
175 g/6 oz margarine, softened
1 level tablespoon cocoa
1½ level teaspoons baking powder
3 eggs
2 tablespoons warm water

1. Grease two round 20 cm/8 inch sandwich tins and line the base of each with a circle of greaseproof paper.
2. Put all the ingredients together in a warm bowl, sifting in the cocoa and baking powder. Mix well until smooth. Beating is not required.
3. Divide mixture between tins, and level tops.
4. Bake above middle of a warm oven, Gas 3, 325°F, 160°C, for 30 minutes until cakes are risen and firm to the touch.
5. Turn cakes straight out of tins on to a wire rack to cool.

Sandwich filling

50 g/2 oz soft margarine
100 to 175 g/4 to 6 oz icing sugar
1 large teaspoon cocoa
1 teaspoon hot water
1 teaspoon sherry or liqueur (optional)

1. Beat margarine in a bowl.
2. Sieve in 100 g/4 oz of the icing sugar and the cocoa.
3. Add other ingredients, including 1 extra teaspoon hot water if sherry is not used.

4. Beat until smooth, sieving in extra icing sugar if necessary.
5. Fill sponge with about half of this quantity.
6. Use the rest to spread on top, saving a little to pipe decorations around edge. Nuts or flaked chocolate can also be used to decorate.

CHOCOLATE BUTTER CREAM

100 g/4 oz plain cooking chocolate
100 g/4 oz butter or table margarine
150 g/6 oz icing sugar

1. Break up chocolate in a bowl and put it to melt over a small pan of simmering water. Do not let water touch bowl.
2. Cream butter or margarine and icing sugar.
3. When light, add melted chocolate and beat again.

This filling is worth making in this quantity as it keeps in a cool place or refrigerator for quite some time and can be used as required to fill or top cakes or biscuits. If too firm to spread beat up with a very little boiling water when using.

Anne Wallace
Stewarton, Ayrshire

SIMPLE LEMON CRUNCH TOPPING FOR A PLAIN SPONGE

Juice of 1 whole lemon (about 2 tablespoons)
125 g/4 oz granulated sugar

Allow the sponge to cool slightly on a wire tray.

Then mix the lemon juice very swiftly with the sugar and before it dissolves the sugar spread evenly over the sponge. The lemon sugar should stay on top of the sponge and the juice should sink into the cake. This gives a lovely crunchy lemon topping with little effort, but it must be done swiftly.

RASPBERRY AND COCONUT TOPPING FOR A PLAIN SPONGE

For a 20 cm/8 inch sponge use:

2 level tablespoons raspberry jam
25 g/1 oz desiccated coconut

Spread jam over top of cooled sponge and sprinkle coconut evenly over the surface.

APPLE CAKE

Looks and tastes superb.

200 g/7 oz self-raising flour
A pinch of salt
150 g/5 oz butter, or half margarine half butter
75 g/3 oz castor sugar
1 egg
350 g/12 oz cooking apples
A squeeze of lemon juice
2 tablespoons apricot jam
2 tablespoons granulated or demerara sugar
A little icing sugar

1. Grease and line a 20 cm/8 inch cake tin, which should be at least 4 cm/1½ inches deep.
2. Sieve flour and salt.
3. Cream butter and castor sugar until light and fluffy.
4. Beat in the egg.
5. Fold in flour and salt.
6. Using a lightly-floured board, gently pat or roll out three-quarters of the mixture and fit it into prepared tin.
7. Peel, core and slice apples and squeeze lemon juice over to keep their colour. Arrange overlapping slices on the cake mixture.

8. Heat jam and brush it over apples. Sprinkle with the 2 tablespoons of sugar.
9. Take small pieces of the remaining mixture, roll into strips with floured hands and arrange a lattice pattern over the apples.
10. Bake above middle of a warm oven, Gas 3, 325°F, 160°C, for 1 hour.
11. Take cake out of tin on to a wire rack to cool.
12. Dust with icing sugar and serve cool or cold.

Mrs Aileen Houghton,
Kemsing, Nr. Sevenoaks, Kent

CHESHIRE PARKIN

Keeps well—freezes well.

225 g/8 oz coarse oatmeal
75 g/3 oz wholewheat or white flour
50 g/2 oz demerara sugar
1 teaspoon ground ginger
A bare ½ teaspoon bicarbonate of soda
A pinch of salt
225 g/8 oz syrup or treacle
125 g/4 oz margarine
70 ml/2½ fl oz milk

1. Mix the dry ingredients together.
2. Melt the syrup and fat in a pan and add to dry ingredients.
3. Stir in milk to make a soft consistency.
4. Grease a 20 cm/8 inch round sandwich tin, or an 18 cm/7 inch square tin and line it with greased, greaseproof paper. Put in the mixture.
5. Bake in the middle of a moderate oven, Gas 4, 350°F, 180°C, for 1¼ hours when parkin will be firm to the touch.
6. Leave in tin to cool.

Best kept 2 days before eating.

Judith Adshead
Mottram St. Andrew, Cheshire

DEVONSHIRE BLOCK CAKE

This recipe is easily reduced to make a smaller cake. It also freezes well so that the whole quantity can be made and the cake cut in 3 or 4 pieces to freeze. Very good flavour; improves with keeping.

175 g/6 oz butter or margarine
175 g/6 oz sugar
125 g/4 oz black treacle
3 large eggs
1 tablespoon milk
450 g/1 lb currants or sultanas or a mixture of both
125 g/4 oz mixed peel
350 g/12 oz plain flour

1. Work butter or margarine to a cream.
2. Beat in sugar and treacle.
3. Add eggs one at a time, beating well.
4. Add milk.
5. Mix in currants, sultanas, peel and lastly the flour.
6. Use a greased tin 18 cm/7 inch square or two 1 kg/2 lb loaf tins and line with greased, greaseproof paper.
7. Put mixture into tin and bake in middle of a cool oven, Gas 2, 300°F, 150°C, for 2½ hours, when cake will be a rich brown and firm to the touch. Look in oven after 1½ hours and, if cake is already very brown, reduce heat to Gas 1, 275°F, 140°C, and lay a doubled sheet of greaseproof paper over top.

Mrs Becky Blackmore
Exeter, Devon

DUNDEE CAKE

Keeps very well.

175 g/6 oz soft margarine
175 g/6 oz light soft brown sugar
½ teaspoon almond essence
200 g/7 oz plain flour
1 level teaspoon baking powder
175 g/6 oz sultanas
175 g/6 oz currants
50 g/2 oz chopped cherries
25 g/1 oz ground almonds
3 large eggs
Whole blanched almonds

1. Grease an 18 cm/7 inch square tin or a 20 cm/8 inch round tin and line it with greased, greaseproof paper.

2. Cream together margarine, sugar and almond essence.
3. Into another bowl sift flour and baking powder. Into this mix prepared fruit and ground almonds.
4. In a third bowl beat the eggs.
5. Fold egg a little at a time, and fruit likewise, into the creamed mixture. Do not beat.
6. Turn into tin. Level the top.
7. Bake in a warm oven, Gas 3, 325°F, 160°C, for about 1¾ hours, when cake will be brown and firm to the touch. During baking whole almonds are carefully placed on cake. Do this while top of cake is still just moist but not too soon or they will either sink into the mixture or burn before cake is cooked.
8. Leave in tin to cool.

HEAVY CAKE

In Cornwall this was made in the fishing villages south of Truro. When the seine net was being hauled in and the men shouting 'heave' with every pull, the wives would know the men would soon be in for tea and would make this quick flat cake to be eaten warm or cold.

225 g/8 oz flour*
¼ teaspoon salt
50 g/2 oz lard
75 g/3 oz sugar
175 g/6 oz currants
About 75 ml/2 to 3 tablespoons milk
50 g/2 oz butter
*If you prefer wholewheat flour it is best made with two thirds wholewheat and one third white flour, otherwise *too* heavy!

1. Mix flour and salt in a bowl and rub in lard.
2. Add sugar and currants. Mix to a soft dough with milk.
3. Using a floured board, roll out to a long strip about 15 cm/6 inches wide and 3 times as long, about 45 cm/18 inches.
4. Dot half of the butter over the top two-thirds of the pastry. Fold the bottom third, without fat, upwards. Then fold the top third down over it.

5. Give the pastry a half-turn so that folds are at sides.
6. Roll out again into a thin strip and spread the rest of the butter as before, repeating the folding in the same way.
7. Roll out finally into a square about 1 cm/½ inch thick. Criss-cross the top with a knife, like a net. Brush with a little milk.
8. Bake above middle of a moderately hot oven, Gas 6, 400°F, 200°C, for 25 to 30 minutes. Remove on to a wire rack to cool.

Eat fresh.

Mrs Jean Daybell
Cornwall Women's Institute

KENTISH HOP-PICKERS CAKE

Makes 2 cakes in ½ kg/1 lb loaf tins

Moist and spicy. Inclined to sink in middle. Keeps well.

275 g/10 oz self-raising flour
1 teaspoon ground ginger
1 teaspoon mixed spice
175 g/6 oz margarine
100 g/4 oz soft brown sugar
100 g/4 oz sultanas
100 g/4 oz currants
50 g/2 oz mixed peel
425 ml/¾ pint milk
1 tablespoon black treacle
1 level teaspoon cream of tartar
½ level teaspoon bicarbonate of soda

1. Sift flour and spices into a bowl.
2. Rub in margarine.
3. Add sugar and fruit.
4. Warm milk with treacle and dissolve in it the cream of tartar and bicarbonate of soda.
5. Mix liquid into dry ingredients with a wooden spoon. The mixture should drop from the spoon.
6. Grease and line two ½ kg/1 lb loaf tins and put in the mixture.
7. Bake in middle of a warm oven, Gas 3, 325°F, 160°C, for about 1½ hours until cakes are firm to the touch.
8. Leave cakes to cool in tins.

Mrs Zina Barnard
Whitstable, Kent

PORTLAND RICE CAKE

A recipe from 'What's Cooking in Dorset' published by the Dorset Federation of Women's Institutes.

225 g/8 oz self-raising flour
½ teaspoon bicarbonate of soda
½ teaspoon cinnamon
½ teaspoon nutmeg
125 g/4 oz ground rice
75 g/3 oz butter or margarine
175 g/6 oz lard
75 g/3 oz soft brown sugar
450 g/1 lb currants
50 g/2 oz mixed peel
2 beaten eggs
300 ml/½ pint milk
1 teaspoon vinegar

1. Sift together flour, bicarbonate of soda, cinnamon and nutmeg.
2. Stir in ground rice.
3. Rub in butter and lard.
4. Add sugar, currants and peel and mix well.
5. Add eggs, milk and vinegar and beat into mixture.
6. Grease a 23 cm/9 inch square tin and line it with greased, greaseproof paper. Put in the mixture and smooth the surface.
7. Bake in the lower part of a cool oven, Gas 2, 300°F, 150°C, for 1 hour. Then reduce heat to Gas 1, 275°F, 140°C for a further 30 minutes, when cake will be firm to the touch and golden brown in colour.
8. Leave it to cool in the tin.

Mrs S. Patterson
Buckland Newton, Dorset

SHEARING CAKE

Cacen Gneifo—a seed cake traditionally baked in Wales at sheep-shearing time. Keeps quite well in a tin for over a week.

Easy to make half this quantity.

450 g/1 lb plain white flour, or half wholewheat half white
1 teaspoon grated nutmeg
1 rounded teaspoon baking powder

A pinch of salt
225 g/8 oz butter or margarine
350 g/12 oz soft brown sugar
1 tablespoon caraway seeds
Grated rind and juice of 1
lemon
300 ml/½ pint milk
2 beaten eggs

1. Sift together white flour, nutmeg, baking powder and salt. Mix in whole-wheat flour if used.
2. Rub in butter or margarine.
3. Add sugar, caraway seeds, lemon rind and juice.
4. Pour in milk slowly, mixing well all the time. Finally, mix in well-beaten eggs.
5. Grease a 23 cm/9 inch round cake tin and line base and sides with greased greaseproof paper. If making half quantity an 18 cm/7 inch round tin is suitable or a ½ kg/1 lb loaf tin.
6. Pour in cake mixture.
7. Bake in middle of a moderate oven, Gas 4, 350°F, 180°C, for 30 minutes, then reduce temperature to cool, Gas 2, 300°F, 150°C, for another 1½ hours when it will be golden brown and firm to the touch.
If making half quantity, bake as above but it will need only 1 hour when temperature has been reduced.
8. Leave cake in tin till slightly cooled. Then turn it out on to a wire rack.

Mrs Eileen Trumper
Llanvair Kilgeddin, Gwent

SOMERSET CIDER CAKE

A moist cake. Keeps well in an airtight tin.

125 g/4 oz butter
125 g/4 oz soft brown sugar
2 beaten eggs (must be at room temperature)
225 g/8 oz plain flour
1 teaspoon bicarbonate of soda, use a measure
Half a nutmeg, grated
About 225 ml/8 fl oz dry cider

1. Cream butter and sugar until really light and fluffy.
2. Beat in eggs a little at a time.
3. Sift together flour, bicarbonate of soda and nutmeg. Fold it in.
4. Add cider slowly to form a soft dropping consistency.
5. Grease an 18 cm/7 inch round tin and line bottom with greased greaseproof paper.
6. Put mixture into tin and bake near top of a moderately hot oven, Gas 5, 375°F, 190°C, for 1 to 1¼ hours or until brown on top, shrinking from sides of tin and springy to the touch.

Mrs Angela Mottram
Axbridge, Somerset

ABERNETHY BISCUITS

50 g/2 oz sugar
3 tablespoons milk
225 g/8 oz self-raising flour
A pinch of salt
75 g/3 oz margarine
50 g/2 oz cooking fat such as Cookeen

1. Put sugar and milk in a small pan over low heat and stir until dissolved. Allow to cool.
2. Sift flour and salt into a bowl, rub in fats and bind to a dough with the cooled liquid.
3. Using a floured board, roll out dough to 7 mm/¼ inch thick. Cut round biscuits and place them a little apart on baking trays. Or, make small balls of the dough, place on baking tray and flatten them with fingertips. Prick each biscuit with a fork.
4. Bake near top of a moderatley hot oven, Gas 5, 375°F, 190°C, for 15 minutes when biscuits will be pale golden brown.
5. Slide off baking trays on to a wire rack to cool.

Anne Wallace
Stewarton, Ayrshire

ORANGE CRISPS

Makes about 20 biscuits

125 g/4 oz butter
50 g/2 oz castor sugar
Grated rind of 1 orange
150 g/5 oz self-raising flour

To finish: extra castor sugar

1. Rub butter into other ingredients until mixture resembles fine crumbs. Work together into a dough.
2. Roll small balls about 2.5 cm/1 inch in diameter. Put them 5 cm/2 inches apart on greased baking trays. Flatten with a fork dipped in cold water.
3. Bake above middle of a moderate oven, Gas 4, 350°F, 180°C, for 10 to 12 minutes until pale gold in colour.
4. Remove from baking trays on to a wire rack. Sprinkle with castor sugar while still hot.

From Cheshire W.I. 'Cook Book'

GRASMERE GINGERBREAD

175 g/6 oz wholewheat flour
50 g/2 oz porridge oats
½ level teaspoon bicarbonate of soda
1 level teaspoon cream of tartar
2 level teaspoons ginger
175 g/6 oz margarine
175 g/6 oz brown sugar, nice with muscovado
50 g/2 oz mixed peel, finely-chopped (optional)

1. Put flour and oats in a bowl and sift in bicarbonate of soda, cream of tartar and ginger. Mix well.
2. Rub in margarine, stir in sugar and mixed peel.
3. Press mixture into a greased Swiss roll tin, 28 by 18 cm/11 by 7 inches. They will be thin biscuits.
4. Bake in a warm oven, Gas 3, 325°F, 160°C, for about 30 minutes until firm and brown.
5. Allow to cool in tin for 5 minutes then cut into fingers.

GRANDMA'S GINGER BISCUITS

100 g/4 oz golden syrup
75 g/3 oz lard
50 g/2 oz sugar
1 teaspoon ginger
½ teaspoon bicarbonate of soda
225 g/8 oz self-raising flour

1. Put all ingredients except flour into a fairly large saucepan and heat gently until lard is melted.
2. Remove from heat and stir in flour, 2 tablespoons at a time.
3. Roll mixture into walnut-sized balls. Put them on a greased baking tray 5 cm/2 inches apart.
4. Bake above middle of a warm oven, Gas 3, 325°F, 160°C, for 10 minutes.
5. Leave on tray for a few minutes to firm up. Then lift on to a wire rack to cool.

Mrs Kathleen Smith
Armley, W. Yorkshire

MRS OADES' GINGER CRISPS

Makes about 300 g/¾ lb biscuits

225 g/8 oz plain flour
25 g/1 oz castor sugar
1 teaspoon ground ginger
1 level teaspoon bicarbonate of soda
100 g/4 oz golden syrup
50 g/2 oz butter or margarine

1. Sift dry ingredients into a bowl.
2. To be precise with golden syrup, put a small pan on to scales, weigh it and then weigh syrup into it.
3. Melt fat and syrup together over low heat.
4. Mix this very thoroughly into dry ingredients.
5. Line a ½ kg/1 lb loaf tin with greaseproof paper.
6. Press the soft mixture into tin. Make top level and smooth. Leave for several hours, or overnight, in a cool place or refrigerator.

7. Turn biscuit loaf out of tin and use a sharp knife to cut very thin biscuits, about 7 mm/¼ inch thick or less.
8. Put biscuits on greased baking trays or use non-stick baking paper to line tin.
9. Bake in middle of a warm oven, Gas 3, 325°F, 160°C, until golden. 3·5 mm/⅛ inch thick biscuits take about 12 minutes.
10. Leave on baking tin for 5 minutes to firm up, then put biscuits on to a wire rack to cool.

KRISPIE BISCUITS

Makes about 40 biscuits

150 g/5 oz margarine
150 g/5 oz castor sugar
50 g/2 oz sultanas
1 beaten egg
175 g/6 oz self-raising flour
50 g/2 oz Rice Krispies

1. Put margarine and sugar in a large pan over low heat.
2. When margarine has melted, remove pan from heat and add sultanas, beaten egg and flour. Mix well. Allow to cool and firm up.
3. Put the Rice Krispies in a flat dish and, using a teaspoon, drop in the biscuit mixture. Toss each teaspoonful about so that it is well-covered.
4. Grease baking trays or line with non-stick baking paper. Space biscuits 5 cm/2 inches apart. Press each biscuit down with a fork.
5. Bake in middle of a warm oven, Gas 3, 325°F, 160°C, for 15 to 20 minutes until golden.
6. Leave on baking trays for 10 minutes to firm up. Then slide off on to a wire rack to cool.

SHORTBREAD BISCUITS

Try the variations in flavours and finishing given below.

Can be done by hand or with an electric mixer. Freeze well.

225 g/8 oz unsalted or slightly salted butter
100 g/4 oz castor sugar
350 g/12 oz plain white flour, sifted

To finish: extra castor sugar

1. Use softened butter, do not let it melt and become oily. Put it in a warm bowl.
2. Beat in sugar and flour and work mixture together thoroughly.

If using an electric mixer, warm the bowl, put all ingredients in together and beat until mixture looks like damp breadcrumbs.

3. Form into a fat sausage about 4 cm/1½ inches thick. Roll this on a board sprinkled with castor sugar. Then put into refrigerator for one hour to firm up.
4. Then, using a sharp knife, cut thin slices from the roll, 7 mm/¼ inch thick or less.
5. Place on greased baking trays, or trays lined with non-stick baking paper.
6. Bake above middle of a cool oven, Gas 2, 300°F, 150°C, for about 30 minutes until golden. Take care not to overbake or they will develop a bitter taste.
7. Remove from oven and dredge with castor sugar while still hot. Leave on trays to stiffen up. Then slide off on to a wire rack to cool.
8. When cold, store in airtight tins and remove from tins just before serving.

Variations

1. Delicious made with wholewheat flour, but it is not so easy to make perfectly-shaped biscuits.
2. Unusual fragrance by incorporating ¼ teaspoon dried or ¼ teaspoon fresh rosemary, finely chopped. Work it in at paragraph 3.
3. Another unusual flavour using ¼ teaspoon caraway seeds.
4. **Dorset Shortbread.** The 'sausage' is rolled in demerara sugar at paragraph 3 above. Do not dredge with castor sugar at paragraph 7. Although this recipe is different this method of finishing is typical of traditional

Dorset shortbread. This method was contributed by members of Dorset Women's Institute.

SHORTBREAD TOFFEE PIECES

Shortbread

100 g/4 oz margarine
50 g/2 oz castor sugar
150 g/5 oz self-raising white or brown flour

Toffee

100 g/4 oz margarine
100 g/4 oz castor sugar
2 tablespoons golden syrup
Half a 383 g/13·5 oz tin of condensed milk

Topping

100 g/4 oz plain cooking chocolate

1. **Shortbread base.** Cream margarine and sugar. Mix in flour. Spread in a greased 28 by 18 cm/11 by 7 inch Swiss roll tin.
2. Bake above centre of a moderate oven, Gas 4, 350°F, 180°C, for 20 minutes. Allow to cool in tin.
3. **Toffee.** Melt margarine, sugar, syrup and condensed milk in a pan and cook gently, stirring, until the mixture leaves the sides of the pan.
4. Pour over the cooled shortbread and leave to cool again.
5. **Topping.** Heat an ovenproof bowl. Break chocolate into it in small pieces and let it melt in the hot bowl. Spread melted chocolate over toffee. Allow to cool.
6. Turn out on to a board and cut into small pieces.

SHORTCAKE BISCUIT STARS

Swiftly made with an electric mixer but can also be done by hand.

225 g/8 oz softened margarine
50 g/2 oz icing sugar

225 g/8 oz plain white flour or half white and half wholewheat

To decorate: glacé cherries (optional)

1. Cream margarine until soft and fluffy.
2. Sift in icing sugar. Beat again.
3. Add flour and beat until smooth.
4. Using a forcing bag with a large star nozzle, pipe star shapes on to a greased baking tray. Put a tiny piece of cherry on top of each star.
5. Bake in the middle of a cool oven, Gas 2, 300°F, 150°C, for 30 minutes until golden. Do not overbake or biscuits will develop a bitter flavour.

BLAKENEY FRITTERS

Makes 10

75 g/3 oz plain flour
40 g/1½ oz margarine
25 g/1 oz sugar
1 large egg-yolk
Jam

1. Put flour in a bowl and rub in margarine.
2. Add sugar and egg-yolk and work mixture into a paste.
3. Roll little balls of mixture and put them on a lightly-greased baking sheet.
4. Make a hole in each with the end of a wooden spoon. Brush over with a little white of egg.
5. Bake above middle of a moderate oven, Gas 4, 350°F, 180°C, for 30 minutes until just turning golden.
6. Slide off on to a wire rack to cool. Fill the hole in each biscuit with jam.

Mrs Phyl Drinkwater
for Blakeney W.I., Glos.

BRIGHTON ROCKS

Certainly not rock-like.

Made small the yield is 35, easy to make half this quantity.

They freeze well.

100 g/4 oz butter or margarine
100 g/4 oz castor sugar
2 beaten eggs
50 g/2 oz currants
50 g/2 oz ground almonds
225 g/8 oz plain flour
1 teaspoon rose-water or lemon
juice

1. Cream butter and sugar.
2. Save 1 tablespoon of egg for glazing
and beat in the rest with rose-water or
lemon juice.
3. Work in currants, ground almonds
and flour.
4. Form into walnut-sized balls and
place on greased baking trays. Brush
with a little beaten egg.
5. Bake in middle of a hot oven, Gas 7,
425°F, 210°C, for about 10 minutes
until just golden.
6. Cool on a wire rack.

Mrs Ruth Brooke and Mrs Gaye Goodall
Hove and Steyning, West Sussex

CHOCOLATE AND CHERRY COOKIES

100 g/4 oz margarine
50 g/2 oz soft brown sugar
1 level tablespoon honey
25 g/1 oz glacé cherries,
chopped small
25 g/1 oz chocolate chips
100 g/4 oz plain white flour or
half wholewheat half white

1. Beat together margarine, sugar and
honey until fluffy.
2. Mix in cherries, chocolate chips and
flour and work together.
3. Place teaspoons of the mixture well
apart on a greased baking tray.
4. Bake in middle of a moderate oven,
Gas 4, 350°F, 180°C, for 15 to 18
minutes until golden.
5. Leave on baking tray for 1 minute
to firm up. Then lift on to a wire rack
to cool.

CHOCOLATE CLUSTERS

No cooking.

Makes 20

A 150 g/5·3 oz block of plain
cooking chocolate
1 level tablespoon golden syrup
2 teaspoons water
75 g/3 oz raisins
75 g/3 oz salted peanuts*
25 g/1 oz mixed peel, finely-
chopped

*Can be made with unsalted nuts
but rub off brown skins.

1. Place a bowl over a saucepan of
boiling water. Do not allow bowl to
touch the water. Allow bowl to warm
up. Then turn off heat.
2. Break up chocolate and put it in the
bowl with the golden syrup and the
water. Allow to melt and blend
together, stirring occasionally.
3. Stir in raisins, peanuts and mixed
peel.
4. Put small teaspoons of the mixture
on to a sheet of waxed paper (from a
cornflakes packet).
5. Leave to set in a cool place before
removing from paper.

CHOCOLATE PEPPERMINT SQUARES

Another recipe from 'What's Cooking
In Dorset', published by the Dorset
Federation Of Women's Institutes.

100 g/4 oz margarine
50 g/2 oz castor sugar
3 level teaspoons baking powder
100 g/4 oz plain flour
50 g/2 oz desiccated coconut

Butter Cream

50 g/2 oz margarine
75 g/3 oz icing sugar
1 small teaspoon peppermint
essence
Drop of green colouring

Topping

175 g/6 oz plain cooking chocolate

1. Beat margarine until soft and cream with the castor sugar.
2. Sift in baking powder and flour.
3. Add coconut and mix well.
4. Press mixture into a greased tin approximately 20 cm/8 inches square.
5. Bake in lower part of a warm oven, Gas 3, 325°F, 160°C, for about 30 minutes when cake will be soft but springy to the touch, slightly risen and golden.
6. Allow to cool in tin until firm, crisp and biscuit-like. Then cover with butter cream.

Butter Cream

1. Beat margarine till soft.
2. Sift in icing sugar adding essence and colouring carefully.
3. Spread over cold cake base.
4. Melt chocolate in a small bowl over a pan of simmering water. Do not let water touch bowl.
5. Spread warm chocolate over butter cream.
6. Cut into squares with a sharp knife when chocolate has almost set. Leave in tin until set.

Mrs Joane Robinson
Cranborne, Dorset

COCONUT BROWNIES

A rich chewy cake.

50 g/2 oz plain cooking chocolate
100 g/4 oz butter or margarine
2 large eggs, lightly-beaten
½ teaspoon vanilla essence
225 g/8 oz sugar
50 g/2 oz self-raising flour
¼ level teaspoon salt
50 g/2 oz desiccated coconut

1. Break chocolate in pieces. Put it with butter in a pan and heat *very* gently until both are melted.
2. Remove from heat and, using a wooden spoon, gradually beat in the eggs. The mixture will thicken.

3. Add vanilla and sugar, then flour, salt and coconut. Mix thoroughly.
4. Grease an 18 cm/7 inch square shallow tin and line base with greased foil. Pour in mixture.
5. Bake above middle of a moderate oven, Gas 4, 350°F, 180°C, for 50 to 60 minutes when the cake will be crisp at the edges and feel firm in the middle.
6. Leave to cool a little, trim the edges and loosen cake from sides of tin with a knife. Leave to go firm then turn out and remove foil.
7. When quite cold cut into 9 or 12 pieces.

Margaret Heywood
Todmorden, Yorkshire

COCONUT DROPS

225 g/8 oz self-raising flour*
100 g/4 oz margarine
175 g/6 oz castor sugar
50 g/2 oz desiccated coconut
2 medium-sized beaten eggs

***Can be made with half white and half wholewheat flour. If you cannot buy self-raising wholewheat flour, add ½ level teaspoon baking powder. Delicious also with light soft brown sugar.**

1. Put flour in a bowl and rub in margarine.
2. Mix in the rest of the ingredients. Mixture will be firm but not stiff.
3. Roll mixture into balls and place, well apart, on a greased baking tray. Press each biscuit lightly with a fork.
4. Bake near top of a moderately hot oven, Gas 5, 375°F, 190°C, for 10 to 12 minutes or until pale brown. For a crisper result leave in oven till a shade darker.

Mrs Elsie Kaye
Saltmarshe, N. Humberside

COCONUT KISSES

Makes about 30 double kisses!— easy to make half quantity

2 egg-whites
150 g/5 oz castor sugar
100 g/4 oz desiccated coconut

160

Butter Icing

25 g/1 oz butter or margarine
50 g/2 oz icing sugar
Almond essence and pink
colouring
Or, pistachio essence and green
colouring

1. Line baking sheets with oiled
greaseproof paper.
2. Whisk egg-whites till firm. Then
add half of the sugar and whisk again.
3. Fold in coconut and remaining
sugar.
4. Put small teaspoons of the mixture
on to prepared baking sheets.
5. Bake in the 2 middle shelves of a
cool oven, Gas 2, 300°F, 150°C, for 35 to
40 minutes until golden brown.
6. Meanwhile, prepare butter icing.
Beat butter and sifted icing sugar
together, flavouring and colouring as
suggested.
7. Take coconut kisses off baking
sheets to cool on a wire rack. When
they are cold, sandwich in pairs with
butter icing.

These keep well after filling, stored in
airtight containers.

Anne Wallace
Stewarton, Ayrshire

DATE BARS

No baking in oven.

100 g/4 oz margarine
100 g/4 oz sugar
225 g/8 oz chopped dates
225 g/8 oz sweet biscuits, broken
into pieces

1. Melt margarine and sugar in pan.
2. Add chopped dates, mix well and
cook 2 or 3 minutes.
3. Remove from heat and add broken
biscuits. Mix well.
4. Press into a shallow, greased, Swiss
roll tin. Leave to cool.
5. Cut into bars when cold.

May be iced with melted chocolate
before cutting into bars. Or dip the
ends into melted chocolate.

Sybil Norcott
Irlam, Nr. Manchester

DEMERARA BRANDY SNAPS

Makes about 24

50 g/2 oz plain white flour
50 g/2 oz golden syrup
50 g/2 oz demerara sugar
50 g/2 oz butter
1 teaspoon ground ginger
2 teaspoons lemon juice

To finish

Whipped cream
A pinch of sugar
Brandy

1. Put flour to warm in a warm oven,
Gas 3, 325°F, 160°C, for 10 minutes.
2. Weigh a saucepan and weigh into it
the golden syrup. This is the easiest
way to measure syrup without getting
sticky.
3. Melt syrup, sugar and butter.
Remove from heat.
4. Mix in warmed flour, sift in ginger
and add lemon juice. Stir well.
5. Put teaspoons of the mixture on to
well-greased baking trays, or trays
lined with non-stick baking paper.
Keep them 15 cm/6 inches apart
because they spread out very thinly
while baking.
6. Bake in a warm oven, Gas 3, 325°F,
160°C, for 10 minutes or until nicely
golden.
7. Leave for 1 or 2 minutes to firm up
a little. Then quickly roll each brandy
snap into a tube around the handle of
a wooden spoon. Leave to cool.
8. Mix sugar and brandy to taste into
whipped cream. Using an icing bag
with a 1 cm/½ inch star pipe, fill each
brandy snap.

Mrs Amy Cannon
Goole, N. Humberside

JAPS

3 egg-whites
A pinch of cream of tartar
160 g/5½ oz castor sugar
125 g/4 oz ground almonds
20 g/¾ oz custard powder
4 drops almond essence

Butter Cream Mousse (*see next recipe*) flavoured with coffee or rum

To Finish

40 g/1½ oz desiccated coconut, toasted*
25 to 50 g/1 to 2 oz plain cooking chocolate
*To toast coconut, spread it in a baking tin and put under a moderately hot grill until golden. Stir often. It burns easily.

1. Whisk egg-whites with cream of tartar until stiff. Add 125 g/4 oz of the castor sugar and whisk again.
2. Add all at once the ground almonds, remaining sugar, custard powder and essence. Fold in carefully.
3. Put this mixture in a piping bag with a 1 cm/½ inch plain pipe.
4. Pipe in small heaps on a well-greased baking tray or a baking tray lined with non-stick paper.
5. Bake in middle of a moderate oven, Gas 4, 350°F, 180°C, for about 20 minutes until just coloured.
6. Cool on a wire tray.
7. Sandwich with the butter cream mousse.
8. Coat sides with more butter cream and roll cakes in toasted coconut.
9. Melt chocolate in a small jug standing in a pan of simmering water and dribble it over the finished cakes.

Mrs Joan Hudson
Finsthwaite, Ulverston, Cumbria

BUTTER CREAM MOUSSE

This is much less sweet than ordinary butter cream and is excellent for filling cakes. The quantity given here would fill two cakes.

50 g/2 oz castor sugar
65 ml/2½ fl oz water
2 egg-yolks
100 g/4 oz unsalted or slightly salted butter
Coffee essence or rum to flavour

1. Dissolve sugar in water and boil till the syrup is sticky and will pull a thread between finger and thumb. Cool slightly.

2. Beat egg-yolks, pour syrup over them and whisk until thick.
3. Cream butter and beat mousse mixture into it by degrees.
4. Flavour with coffee essence or rum.
Keeps for a week in a covered container in refrigerator.

Mrs Joan Hudson
Finsthwaite, Ulverston, Cumbria

MERINGUES

Using an electric whisk.
Notes: Do not use fresh eggs. Be careful to use a grease-free bowl. Store meringues in a tight-lidded tin. Remove from tin at last minute. Sugar attracts moisture and the meringues will go soft if uncovered.

2 large egg-whites
A pinch of salt
A pinch of cream of tartar
125 g/4 oz castor sugar*
*Try also grinding demerara sugar to castor sugar consistency in electric grinder.

1. Whisk the egg-whites. When frothy, add salt and cream of tartar. Continue to whip at high speed until stiff.
2. Now lower the speed and add castor sugar, 2 tablespoons at a time, and continue beating well between each addition until all the sugar is used up and the mixture is thick and peaks easily.
3. Line a baking tray with foil or non-stick baking parchment.
4. Put the meringue mixture into a large icing bag with a 1 cm/½ inch star nozzle. Many different shapes can be made:

Meringue Baskets. Swirl round in a circle about 5 cm/2 inches across. Then pipe round edge to make a small wall. This amount will make about 10 baskets.

Meringue Rounds. For a Pavlova-type cake. Draw three 20 cm/8 inch rounds on the paper or foil. Starting at the centre, pipe round and round until you meet the pencilled edge. This amount will make three rounds.

Bake below middle of a very cool oven, Gas ¼, 225°F, 110°C, for 1½ hours or until dry and firm.

SEMOLINA HALVA

For 4 people

300 g/11 oz coarse semolina
100 g/4 oz butter or ghee (*see page 38*)
600 ml/1 pint milk
275 g/10 oz sugar
50 g/2 oz blanched almonds, coarsely-chopped
A few drops of almond essence
¼ teaspoon saffron powder, dissolved in ¼ teaspoon water

1. Using a heavy-based pan, dry roast semolina over low heat until pale brown, stirring frequently or it will burn.
2. Add the butter, milk and sugar and stir continuously over low heat to prevent semolina sticking to pan.
3. When quite stiff, add almonds, essence and saffron.
4. Mix thoroughly and pat on to a buttered tray to about 7 mm/¼ inch thick.
5. Cut into 2·5 cm/1 inch squares.

Keep in a cool place and eat within a day or two of making.

Priya Wickramasinghe
Cardiff

SHERRY SLICES

No cooking.

225 g/8 oz marzipan

Filling
¾ cup digestive biscuit crumbs
½ cup desiccated coconut
½ cup mixed dried fruit, chopped
¼ cup chopped nuts
½ cup raspberry jam
1 tablespoon icing sugar
1 dessertspoon cocoa
1 to 2 tablespoons sherry

To finish: about 175 g/6 oz plain cooking chocolate

1. You need a tin about 23 cm/9 inches square.
2. Divide marzipan in half. Using a board dusted with icing sugar or corn-flour, roll each piece out to 23 cm/9 inches square. Put one piece in tin.
3. Mix all the filling ingredients, spread over marzipan and put on the marzipan top.
4. Break chocolate into a small basin and stand it over a pan of simmering water to melt. Do not let basin touch water.
5. Spread melted chocolate over and leave till cold.
6. Slice into small fingers.

Judith Adshead
Mottram St. Andrew, Cheshire

Chapter 11

Preserves and Home-made Sweets

JAMS AND JELLIES

There are two stages in the making of jams and jellies. *First*, there is the gentle simmer in water which breaks down the fruit and extracts the natural setting agent, pectin. With jellies the fruit needs to be crushed well with a potato masher while it is simmering. The initial simmering also softens the fruit. If the sugar is added too soon it makes tough-skinned fruit chewy. *Second*, after the sugar has been added, comes the fast rolling boil to obtain a set quickly which will give the preserve the best flavour and the brightest colour.

Always use dry, fresh fruit, slightly under-ripe, and try to make the preserve on the same day as the fruit is picked. The pectin content does decrease even if the fruit is left overnight. Frozen fruit, if it has been frozen in perfect condition, is excellent but will also have lost a little pectin, and to counteract this add a little extra fruit—e.g., in marmalade making add an extra orange to the recipe weight.

Good Pectin Content

Blackcurrants
Cranberries
Damsons
Gooseberries
Some Plums
Quince
Freshly picked Raspberries
Redcurrants
Seville Oranges

Medium Pectin Content

Fresh Apricots
Early Blackberries/Brambles
Greengages
Lemons
Limes
Loganberries
Sweet Oranges

Poor Pectin Content

Late Blackberries
Cherries
Elderberries
Grapefruit
Marrows
Medlars
Pears
Rhubarb
Strawberries
Tangerines
Tomatoes

The Pectin Test

Half-way through the jam making, before the sugar has been added, it is possible to test the pulp for pectin:

1. Take a teaspoon of juice from the pan of simmered fruit, put it in a glass and cool it.
2. Add three teaspoons of methylated spirit. Shake gently.

If plenty of pectin is present, a clear jelly clot will form. If a medium amount of pectin is present several small clots will form. If a poor amount of pectin is present, no real clot will be formed.

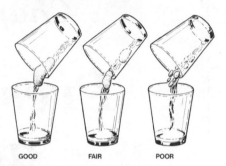

GOOD FAIR POOR

If after further cooking no clot is formed, additional pectin should be added:

50 to 100 ml/2 to 4 fl oz per $\frac{1}{2}$ kg/1 lb of fruit—e.g., to 1·8 kg/4 lb fruit, add 2 tablespoons lemon juice, or $\frac{1}{2}$ level teaspoon citric or tartaric acid, or 150 ml/$\frac{1}{4}$ pint redcurrant or gooseberry juice.

Testing for a Set

Do this when the sugar has been added and boiling has started:

After 10 minutes if fruit is in the high pectin list
After 15 minutes if it is in medium pectin list
After 20 minutes if in poor pectin list

There are several ways.

1) **Volume test.** If you know the expected yield of your fruit—e.g., the recipe says you will get, say, 2·5 kg/5 lb of jam, then measure out in water that amount. Take a 1 lb jam jar (not a 12 oz jar), fill it five times and pour this into your pan. Use a wooden spoon handle, stand it upright in the water and mark this level with a pencil. Keep the spoon handy. Then, when you are testing for a set, draw pan off heat. Wait until bubbling subsides and stand spoon in the jam. When the volume has returned to the level of the pencil mark, the jam is ready to pot.

2) **Cold plate test.** Have some plates cooling in the refrigerator, and take a tea-spoon of jam and drop it on the cold plate. Wait a minute and, if it wrinkles when

pushed, the jam is ready. If not, go on boiling a little longer.

3) **Flake test.** Dip a clean wooden spoon in boiling jam. Allow the cooling jam to drop from the spoon. If the drops run together and form a flake or curtain it is ready to pot.

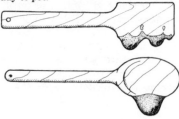

4) **Temperature test.** Use a sugar thermometer. It is important to dip the thermometer in hot water immediately before using it in the jam. Submerge the bulb fully in the boiling jam but do not let it touch bottom of pan. When the thermometer registers 220°F or 150°C the jam is ready to pot.

To Pot the Jam

1. Have your jam pots washed, dried and warming on a low heat in the oven. You should be able to hold them by the rim.
2. Draw the pan off heat, stir in a knob of butter. This helps disperse the foam. If it still persists, scoop it off into a bowl and use it in the kitchen—it is just jam with a lot of air in it.
3. Now, with a heatproof glass or metal jug, fill jam pots to the brim and cover either with a metal twist top lid or seal with a waxed tissue. Make sure that no bubbles of air are trapped underneath.
4. Wipe jars when hot.
5. When cold, cover with dampened cellophane jam pot covers, placing them dry side down. Stretch the cellophane and fix with an elastic band.
6. Label with name of preserve, and the date, and store in a cool, dark, airy place.

Strawberry jam and marmalade may be left to stand for a few minutes before potting to prevent fruit rising in the jars.

Jelly is best potted in small jars so that it is eaten up quite quickly. In large jars it tends to 'weep'.

Aluminium or stainless steel pans are best, then they can be used for pickles and chutneys as well.

Always use a roomy pan for jam and jelly making. The preserve rises very high during the final boiling and spits fiercely. Aim to have your pan not more than half full before you start.

Granulated sugar is excellent but proper preserving sugar crystals are said to give a brighter result when making jelly. Castor and brown sugar produce a lot of extra froth. It is best to warm sugar before adding to pan of fruit. It will then dissolve quickly.

Jelly bags can be bought, but a piece of sheeting or even old blanket can be used. In each case scald it before using by pouring boiling water through it and wringing it out. If jelly is to be clear the bag of pulp must not be squeezed. Allow at least 2 hours for juice to drip through.

BLACKBERRY AND APPLE JAM

No seeds.

Yields about 2·25 kg/5 lb jam for every 1·4 kg/3 lb sugar used

1·8 kg/4 lb blackberries
300 ml/½ pint water
675 g/1½ lb cooking apples, weigh after peeling and coring
Sugar (*see paragraphs 3 and 4 below*)

1. Simmer blackberries very gently in half of the water until tender. Then sieve to remove the seeds.
2. Meanwhile, prepare apples and slice finely. Simmer them in remaining water till soft and pulpy.
3. Combine blackberry purée and apple pulp and weigh it.
4. Weigh out an equal quantity of sugar and put it in a bowl to warm in a very cool oven, Gas ¼, 225°F, 110°C.
5. Boil the pulp until it is thick. Then add the warmed sugar and stir without boiling till it is dissolved.
6. When it is completely dissolved bring to boil and boil rapidly till setting point is reached. It may be only a few minutes (*see notes, page 166*).
7. Fill warmed jars to the brim. Put on at once a well-fitting waxed tissue waxed side down. This is to seal the jam and protect it from the atmosphere.
8. Wipe the jars and put on outer covers, either while hot or when cold, *never* in between.
9. Label with name and date and store in a cool, dark, dry well-ventilated place.

167

GREEN EGG PLUM JAM

Look out for these plums in mid-August and buy green ones if you can. This is important as it produces a nice tangy jam with a good green colour.

Yields about 2¼ kg/5 lb

1·4 kg/3 lb plums
300 ml/½ pint water
1·4 kg/3 lb sugar

1. Wash plums and remove stalks.
2. Simmer them in the water in a large pan until skins are really tender. Skim off stones as they rise to the surface.
If liked a few plum kernels may be cracked out of the stones and added to the jam at this stage.
3. Meanwhile, put sugar in a dish in a very cool oven, Gas ¼, 225°F, 110°C, for about 20 minutes to warm. Put clean jars in oven to warm at same time.
4. Add warmed sugar to pan of fruit, stir until dissolved without letting it boil.
5. Then boil rapidly, stirring occasionally, until setting point is reached (*see page 166*). Begin testing after 6 minutes.
6. Pot, seal, cover and store as directed on *page 167*.

Mrs Olive Odell
Hartlebury, Worcestershire

POTTED RASPBERRY JAM

Yields 3·6 kg/8 lb—easy to make less

Keeps for only 5 to 6 months. This preserve does not set like ordinary jam. The fruit rises and there is a layer of jelly at the bottom. However, its flavour is superb and it is good for sponges, tarts, etc. Give it a stir in jar before using.

1·8 kg/4 lb raspberries, in perfect condition
1·8 kg/4 lb castor sugar, dissolves more easily than granulated

1. Do not wash raspberries. They must be perfectly dry. Put sugar in another bowl. Put both bowls in the oven. Put clean jars to warm in oven at same time.
2. Heat oven to cool, Gas 2, 300°F, 150°C, for about 25 minutes or until the juice starts to run. Switch off heat.
3. Now mix the sugar and raspberries and stir until sugar has dissolved.
4. Pot into warm jars, put on a waxed tissue and leave till cold before covering jars (*see notes, page 167*).

RHUBARB AND ORANGE JAM

Yields about 3·4 kg/7½ lbs

Good as a filling for a plate-pie.

1·8 kg/4 lb rhubarb
2·3 kg/5 lb sugar
2 oranges
1 lemon
450 g/1 lb seedless raisins*

*As an economy raisins may be replaced by 450 g/1 lb bananas. Slice them just before they are added at paragraph 4 below.

1. Wash and trim rhubarb. Cut it into 2·5 cm/1 inch lengths. Put into preserving pan or large saucepan and sprinkle over the sugar.
2. Grate rind from oranges and lemon. Squeeze juice.
3. Add raisins, juice and rind. If using bananas, do not put them in at this stage. Mix with a wooden spoon and allow to stand for 1 hour.
4. Bring to the boil, stirring to ensure there is no undissolved sugar. If using bananas add them now, thinly-sliced. Cook slowly for about 45 minutes, stirring occasionally until liquid evaporates from the fruit and jam is thick. Do not boil this jam hard or rhubarb goes to a mush.
5. Meanwhile, prepare clean jam jars. Put them to dry and warm in a very cool oven, Gas ¼, 225°F, 110°C. Although this jam is not boiled hard to reach setting point it still keeps well as long as it is potted in the usual way, as follows.

6. Fill warmed jars to the brim with the hot jam. Immediately put on well-fitting waxed tissues, waxed side down. This seals the jam and protects it from the atmosphere.
7. Wipe jars and put on outer covers, either while jam is hot or cold, but *never* in between.
8. Label with name and date and store in a cool, dark, dry, well-ventilated place.

Mrs Doreen Allars
Welbourn, Nr. Lincoln

STRAWBERRY JAM

A recipe particularly suitable for frozen fruit which does not set easily. Fresh fruit can be used.

1·8 kg/4 lb strawberries
2·25 kg/5 lb sugar
10 ml/2 teaspoons alum, can be bought at chemists

1. Allow fruit to thaw a little. Then put it in a large saucepan with the sugar and bring to the boil, stirring all the time until sugar has dissolved.
2. Boil briskly for 10 minutes.
3. Meanwhile, put clean jars to warm in a very cool oven, Gas ¼, 225°F, 110°C.
4. Take pan off heat and allow bubbling to stop.
5. Stir in alum, then return pan to heat and bring to the boil again. Remove from the heat.
6. Allow jam to cool for 10 minutes so that fruit will remain evenly suspended when potted.
7. Pot jam following notes *on page 167*.

Anne Wallace
Stewarton, Ayrshire

MINCED SEVILLE MARMALADE

Yields about 3·2 kg/7 lb

1 kg/2 lb Seville bitter oranges*
1 large lemon
2·3 litres/4 pints water
1·8 kg/4 lb granulated sugar
15 g/½ oz butter

*If using oranges taken from the freezer add one extra orange.
1. Scrub fruit and remove green stalk ends.
2. Cut each orange in two. Squeeze out all pips and put them in a piece of muslin tied with a long string.
3. Cut lemon in two and squeeze out juice.
4. Put water in a large deep pan. Add lemon juice and bag of pips tied to handle of pan.
5. Put orange shells through mincer or a food processor, then into pan. Leave overnight.
6. Next day, simmer this mixture in pan with the lid on for 15 minutes. Then remove lid and simmer uncovered for about 1 hour, to reduce mixture by about half.
7. Meanwhile put sugar to warm in a very cool oven, Gas ¼, 225°F, 110°C, prepare clean jars and put them to warm in oven too.
8. Test marmalade for pectin strength (*see page 166*).
9. Add warmed sugar. Stir well. Do not let it boil before sugar has dissolved. Then turn up heat and bring to a fast rolling boil, lid off pan. Stir occasionally.
10. After 15 to 20 minutes test for a set (*see page 166*).
11. When setting point has been reached, remove pip bag. Remove pan from heat. Add butter to disperse scum. Stir again.
12. Let marmalade stand for about 5 minutes to cool a little. Otherwise peel may rise in jars, leaving a gap at bottom. Then stir again to distribute peel and pour into warmed jars. Fill to brim.
13. Put on a well-fitting waxed tissue to seal surface and complete according to notes *on page 167*.

Very economical marmalade.

In place of 1 kg/2 lb Seville oranges use:

450 g/1 lb Sevilles
450 g/1 lb peel from sweet oranges and grapefruit

169

This peel can be frozen at any time of year until enough is collected to make marmalade or until Sevilles season returns.

Proceed with recipe as before.

JELLY MARMALADE
Yields 2·25 kg/5 lb

Grapefruit

2 grapefruit ⎱ combined weight
3 lemons ⎰ 900 g/2 lb
2·6 litres/4½ pints water
1·4 kg/3 lb sugar

Orange

900 g/2 lb Seville oranges
2·6 litres/4½ pints water
Juice of 2 lemons or 1 teaspoon citric or tartaric acid
1·4 kg/3 lb sugar

1. Score the fruit in quarters then scald. To do this, pour boiling water over and leave for 5 minutes. Then drain.
2. Remove peel and cut white pith away from rind. Shred the rind finely.
3. Cut pith and fruit coarsely, put in a saucepan with 1·4 litres/2½ pints of the water (plus lemon juice or acid for Orange Jelly). Put on lid, bring to boil and simmer for 2 hours.
4. Meanwhile, put shredded rind in another pan with 600 ml/1 pint water, put on lid and simmer 1½ hours or until tender.
5. Drain liquid from shreds into pan of pulp.
6. Set up jelly bag (*see notes on page 167*).
7. Empty pan of pulp into jelly bag and allow to drip for 10 to 15 minutes.
8. Return pulp to pan with remaining 600 ml/1 pint of water. Cover pan and simmer for 20 minutes more.
9. Pour this into jelly bag and let it drip without squeezing bag for at least 2 hours.
10. Meanwhile, put sugar to warm in a very cool oven, Gas ¼, 225°F, 110°C, and put small clean jars to warm at same time.

11. Put juice into a roomy pan, bring to the boil, turn down heat and add sugar. Stir until it is dissolved.
12. Then add shredded rind and boil rapidly until setting point is reached (*see notes on page 166*).
13. Quickly skim off froth, then allow jelly to cool until a skin forms, 5 to 10 minutes.
14. Stir gently and pot following notes *on page 167*.

GRAPEFRUIT AND GINGER CHEESE

An interesting way to use the peel remaining after making Grapefruit Jelly (*see previous recipe*). It may be sliced and eaten as a dessert with whipped cream or a few chopped nuts, or with plain biscuits or wholemeal scones and butter.

It is best potted in straight-sided jars, moulds or even old mugs, so that when served it can be turned out on to a plate.

Peel from 2 grapefruit and 3 lemons used for Grapefruit Jelly
Sugar
About 1 level teaspoon ground ginger

For potting
A little glycerine

1. Sieve the pulp.
2. Weigh the purée. It will probably be 350 g/12 oz.
3. Put the same weight of sugar in a dish into a very cool oven, Gas ¼, 225°F, 110°C, for 20 minutes to warm. Put clean, straight-sided jars or moulds into oven to warm at same time.
4. Heat purée in a pan. Remove from heat and add sugar, stirring until it is completely dissolved.
5. Add up to 1 level teaspoon ginger, according to taste. Bring to the boil then simmer, stirring occasionally, for about 10 minutes until mixture coats back of spoon thickly.

6. Smear glycerine inside warmed jars. This helps release cheese from jars when it is turned out.
7. Pour hot cheese into jars, press waxed tissues, waxed-side down, on to the hot surface to seal it. Cover and store as directed for jams (*see page 167*).

Can be eaten a week after making. Best used within 6 months.

Mrs R. Punt
Wychbury W.I., Worcestershire

PLUM BUTTER

Any plums, including greengages and damsons, may be used.

Plums
A little water
Honey
Ground allspice
Ground nutmeg

1. Put plums in a pan with a very little water, barely 1 cm/½ inch deep.
2. Cover pan with a well-fitting lid and allow plums to simmer until they are tender.
3. Put plums through a sieve to make a purée.
4. Measure purée in a measuring jug and put it back in pan.
5. Now measure out honey to exactly half the quantity of purée. Add this to the pan with just enough of the spices to flavour it gently.
6. Cook slowly, stirring often, until it is thick and creamy with no loose liquid.
7. Meanwhile, prepare clean jars with air-tight lids and put jars to dry and warm in a very cool oven, Gas ¼, 225°F, 110°C.
8. Pour hot, plum butter into warmed jars. Put on air-tight lids at once.
9. Label with name and date.

This will not keep for more than a few weeks.

CRANBERRY AND ORANGE PRESERVE

Delicious with roast turkey. Sets like jelly.

450 g/1 lb granulated sugar
450 g/1 lb fresh or frozen cranberries
Finely-grated rind and juice of 1 orange
Water

1. Put sugar to warm in oven on lowest heat, Gas ¼, 225°F, 110°C. Put clean 225 g/½ lb jars into oven at same time.
2. Pick over fruit and discard any that is bruised. Put cranberries into a roomy saucepan.
3. Mix orange juice with water to make 300 ml/½ pint. Add to pan with rind.
4. Bring to the boil over gentle heat and simmer for 10 minutes, stirring occasionally. Cranberries will cook down to a thick pulp. Draw pan off heat.
5. Push pulp through a nylon sieve to make a purée, scraping as much as possible from under the sieve.
6. Put purée in a clean pan, add sugar and stir over low heat until sugar is dissolved.
7. Now turn up heat and boil for 4 to 5 minutes.
8. Pour hot preserve into prepared jars. Finish as indicated *on page 167*.

MEDLAR JELLY
Yields about 1·1 kg/2½ lbs

1·8 kg/4 lbs medlars
1 large lemon or 2 teaspoons citric acid
About 1·7 litres/3 pints water
Sugar

It is a good idea to use small jars for jelly because when it has been opened for a little time it begins to go runny.

1. Wash and cut up medlars and put into a preserving pan or large saucepan with enough water to cover. Simmer slowly, till it is reduced to a pulp.

2. Strain through a scalded jelly bag. To be sure of getting a clear jelly it is best not to squeeze the bag.
3. Measure the juice and return it to the pan. To every 600 ml/1 pint juice weigh out 350 g/12 oz sugar.
4. Put sugar in a bowl to warm in a very cool oven, Gas ¼, 225°F, 110°C. Prepare clean, small jars and put them to dry and warm in coolest part of oven.
5. Add citric acid (if lemon has not been used) and bring pan of juice to the boil. Add warmed sugar. Stir without letting it boil until sugar is dissolved.
6. Boil rapidly until setting point is reached (*see page 166*). It usually takes about 25 minutes.
7. Skim off the scum with a metal spoon. Then fill the jars without delay before jelly starts to set.
8. Put on at once well-fitting, waxed tissues, waxed-side down. This is to seal the jelly and protect it from the atmosphere.
9. With jelly it is easier to put outer cover on jars when it is set, but wait until it is quite cold.
10. Label with name and date and store in cool, dark, dry well-ventilated place.

Mrs Doreen Allars
Welbourn, Nr. Lincoln

MINT JELLY

Made from gooseberries.

Yields about 450 g/1 lb

Often made with apples. However the combination of mint and gooseberries is lovely, especially with lamb.

Not a clear jelly.

450 g/1 lb small green gooseberries
Water
Sugar
A bunch of fresh mint, about 10 to 12 fresh stalks, tied together
1 or 2 drops of green food colouring (optional)

1. There is no need to top and tail gooseberries. Just wash and put them into a pan.
2. Just cover with water and cook gently until very mushy.
3. Strain through a nylon sieve, pressing gently but not pushing the pulp through.
4. Measure this juice and for every 600 ml/1 pint add 450 g/1 lb sugar.
5. Put sugar to warm in a very cool oven, Gas ¼, 225°F, 110°C. Put small clean jars to warm also.
6. Put juice, sugar and mint in a pan. Heat gently, stirring until sugar is dissolved.
7. Bring to the boil and boil rapidly, stirring occasionally until setting point is reached (*see notes on page 166*).
8. Remove mint and add green food colouring, if used.
9. Pour carefully in warm jars and finish according to notes *on page 167*.

PICKLES, CHUTNEYS AND SAUCES

Fruits for pickling need to be firm and sound but not of the finest quality. Vegetables should be young, fresh and crisp. Cheaper fruit, provided it is firm, usually forms the basis for chutney.

Aluminium and stainless steel pans are best. Use only wooden spoons, a nylon sieve and stainless steel knives.

Fruit and vegetables for chutney are chopped or minced and cooked to soften in a covered pan with very little water. A pressure cooker is ideal. Vinegar is not usually added at first as it can have a hardening effect and so prolong cooking, thus making the product less economical.

Once all ingredients are combined, chutney is cooked gently until thick, stirring often so that it does not catch. When a spoon drawn through the mixture leaves its trail, and does not at once fill with excess liquid, the chutney is ready to pot.

Pot into clean, dry, warm jars, filling to the brim.

Covers for jars need to be vinegar-resistant—e.g., metal twist top with plastic inner coating, soft plastic snap-on type, or hard plastic screw-on type. Cellophane jam pot covers are not suitable because vinegar will evaporate. Plain metal tops will corrode and rust and impart a metallic taste.

Allow chutneys to mature for 1 or 2 months before using.

Spiced vinegar for pickles can now be bought, but there are 2 methods for home-made:

Best Spiced Vinegar

7 g/¼ oz each of cinnamon bark, whole allspice, whole cloves and whole mace
6 peppercorns
1·1 litre/2 pints white vinegar

Tie spices loosely in a piece of muslin and leave in the vinegar for 2 months, stirring often. Allow to settle for 3 days before straining ready for use.

Quickly Spiced Vinegar

1. Put vinegar and spices in a bowl and cover with a plate.
2. Stand basin in a pan of water. Bring water slowly to boiling point.
3. Remove bowl from heat and leave to stand for 3 hours.
4. Strain and cool.

TO PICKLE NASTURTIUM SEEDS

These are a substitute for capers. Useful for sauces including Sauce Tartare.

1. Pick the green seeds when tiny, about the size of dried peas.
2. Soak for three days in salted water, changing the water daily.
3. Drain and pat dry.
4. Use jars with vinegar-proof lids. Coffee jars with plastic lids can be used.
5. Pack seeds into jars with a little finely-chopped onion if wanted.
6. Cover with cold spiced vinegar (*see above*) and leave for one week to mature.

SWEET PICKLED PRUNES

These can be eaten immediately, do not need to mature. Keep for a year. Good with cold meat and a good alternative to black olives on pizza.

225 g/8 oz dried prunes
225 g/8 oz soft brown sugar
300 ml/½ pint malt vinegar
150 ml/¼ pint water
A 5 cm/2 inch piece of cinnamon

1. Put prunes in a basin, add sugar, vinegar, water and cinnamon. Cover and leave overnight.
2. Next day, turn everything into a saucepan. Simmer until the prunes are tender, about 10 minutes. Leave to cool.
3. Lift out the prunes, split and remove the stones.
4. Pack prunes into jars.
5. Return the pan of syrup to the heat. Simmer for one minute and pour over the prunes to cover.
6. Put on vinegar-proof lids, label and store.

UNCOOKED CHUTNEY

Yields nearly 1·4 kg/3 lb
This chutney is ready to eat as soon as it is made. Good fill-in between seasons. Best eaten within 6 weeks.

250 g/8 oz each of dates, sultanas, apple, onion
250 g/8 oz soft brown sugar, try muscovado
300 ml/½ pint spiced vinegar (*see opposite*)
5 g/1 teaspoon salt
A pinch each of pepper, mustard and cayenne pepper

1. Using coarse plates of mincer, mince the dates, sultanas, apple and onion.
2. Mix well with all other ingredients.
3. Use clean dry jars with vinegar-proof lids. Fill jars, cover and store in a cool dry place.

Anne Wallace
Stewarton, Ayrshire

KENTISH APPLE CHUTNEY

Yields about 1·8 kg/4 lbs

Traditionally made late in winter with stored apples. A mild, sweet, firm chutney, quick to make.

1 kg/2 lb apples
600 ml/1 pint spiced pickling vinegar (*see page 173*)
450 g/1 lb sugar
1½ teaspoons salt
1 teaspoon ground allspice
125 g/4 oz preserved ginger
350 g/12 oz sultanas

1. Peel, core and chop apples into small pieces.
2. Put vinegar, sugar, salt and allspice into a large saucepan and bring to the boil, stirring to dissolve sugar. Add apples. Simmer for 10 minutes.
3. Meanwhile, wash syrup from ginger, dry and chop into very small pieces. Add to pan with sultanas.
4. Simmer until chutney thickens, stirring occasionally so that it does not burn. It is thick enough when a spoon drawn through the mixture leaves its trail and does not at once fill with liquid.
5. Meanwhile, choose jars with vinegar-proof lids. Coffee jars with plastic lids are ideal. Put clean jars to warm in a very cool oven, Gas ¼, 225°F, 110°C.
6. Allow chutney to cool slightly before putting it into jars. Put on waxed paper discs and, when chutney is quite cold, put on vinegar-proof lids.
7. Label with name and date and store in a cool, dry, well-ventilated cupboard.

Allow to mature 6 weeks before eating.

Mrs Jill Marshall
Hythe, Kent

DATE CHUTNEY

This chutney is made in small quantities to be eaten as soon as it is made. Keeps well.

225 g/8 oz dates
350 ml/12 fl oz malt vinegar
6 tablespoons demerara or muscovado sugar
4 cloves of garlic, finely-chopped
1 teaspoon fresh ginger, finely-chopped
50 g/2 oz sultanas
2 teaspoons paprika
1 teaspoon salt

1. Chop dates quite small.
2. Put vinegar and sugar in a pan, stir over low heat to dissolve sugar, then bring rapidly to the boil.
3. Reduce heat and add dates, garlic and ginger.
4. Cook on a low heat for 5 minutes, stirring all the time.
5. Add the sultanas, paprika and salt and cook for a further 5 minutes.

Do not overcook or it will turn to caramel.

Priya Wickramasinghe
Cardiff

ELDERBERRY CHUTNEY

450 g/1 lb elderberries
450 g/1 lb onions
450 g/1 lb cooking apples or windfalls—weigh them after peeling and coring
125 g/4 oz dried fruit—raisins, sultanas or both
1 teaspoon mixed spice
1 teaspoon ginger
1 teaspoon salt
¼ teaspoon cayenne pepper
300 ml/½ pint malt vinegar
350 g/12 oz sugar

1. Remove elderberries from stalks. To do this, hold them over a large basin and strip off berries with a table fork. (A large basin is necessary because berries tend to fly everywhere.)
2. Peel and finely chop onions. Chop apples finely. Put in a large pan.
3. Add dried fruit, spices, salt, pepper and half the vinegar.
4. Bring to the boil and simmer until ingredients are soft.

5. Add sugar and remaining vinegar. Stir over low heat until sugar is dissolved.
6. Then simmer until chutney is thick. It is thick enough when you can draw a wooden spoon through the mixture and the trail of the spoon remains without filling with excess liquid. Stir frequently to prevent sticking.
7. Meanwhile, prepare clean jars with vinegar-proof lids. Coffee jars with plastic lids are ideal. Warm the jars in a very cool oven—Gas ¼, 225°F, 110°C.
8. Fill jars to the brim with hot chutney and put on waxed paper discs, waxed-side down. Leave to cool.
9. When quite cold, put on the vinegar-proof lids. Label jars with the name and date.
10. Store in a cool, dark, dry, well-ventilated cupboard.

Mrs Lynda M. White
Wroot, Nr. Doncaster

ORANGE CHUTNEY

Yields 2·25 to 2·7 kg/5 to 6 lbs

Delicious with cold pork or hot sausages.

450 g/1 lb onions, peeled and sliced
Water
1 kg/2 lb apples, peeled, cored and sliced
2·3 litres/4 pints good malt vinegar
1·8 kg/4 lb sweet oranges
450 g/1 lb sultanas or raisins
15 to 20 fresh green or red chillis, de-seeded, or 8 dried red chillis*, deseeded and tied in a muslin bag
2 dessertspoons cooking salt
2 teaspoons ground ginger
1 kg/2 lb white sugar

*Fresh chillis are quite mild. It is the dried chillis which are peppery and 4 would be enough if you don't like chutney too hot.

1. Cook onions until tender, in water just to cover. Strain (saving liquid for soup).

2. Add apple and about a cupful of the vinegar and continue cooking gently until mushy. Remove from heat.
3. Meanwhile, scrub oranges and peel them. Remove white pith from outer skin and discard. Reserve the peel.
4. Put peel and orange flesh through mincer, removing as many pips as possible.
5. Mince sultanas or raisins and the chillis, if fresh ones are used.
6. Put dried chillis and other ingredients, except sugar, into the pan with about half the remaining vinegar. Simmer until thick, stirring occasionally.
7. Add sugar and rest of vinegar. Stir to dissolve sugar and simmer again until thick. Stir occasionally or it will stick and burn.
8. Remove muslin bag if dried chillis are used. Finish, pot and store as indicated *on page 172.*
9. Allow to mature for 6 weeks before using.

PLUM CHUTNEY

Yields 1·8 kg/4 lb

Can be made with all types of plums but dark-skinned varieties give it the best colour. Cider vinegar gives chutney a lovely flavour.

1·1 kg/2½ lb plums
450 g/1 lb onions, finely-chopped
Water
900 g/2 lb cooking apples
600 ml/1 pint cider vinegar
A piece of root ginger
1 dessertspoon each of whole cloves, whole allspice and peppercorns
450 g/1 lb soft brown sugar
3 level teaspoons salt

1. Wipe, halve and stone the plums.
2. Put onions in a saucepan, cover with water and boil for 5 minutes to soften them. Drain (saving liquid for soup, etc.).
3. Peel, core and chop apples. Put these and the plums in a large pan with half of the vinegar. Bring to the boil and cook for 20 minutes to a soft pulp.

4. Meanwhile, bruise the ginger by hitting it with a hammer. Then tie it with the other spices in a piece of muslin.
5. Put spice bag with vinegar and sugar into another pan. Bring to the boil and simmer for 5 minutes, stirring all the time. Draw pan off heat and let the vinegar infuse for 30 minutes. Then remove spice bag.
6. Add with onions and salt to apples. Bring to the boil and simmer for about 2 hours until chutney is thick and pulpy. Stir frequently in case it sticks and burns.
7. Finish, pot and store as indicated *on page 172.*
8. Allow to mature for 4 weeks before using.

TOMATO RELISH

1·6 kg/3½ lbs firm ripe tomatoes, skinned (*see page 72*) or use two 675 g/1½ lb tins of tomatoes
1 kg/2 lbs onions, finely-chopped
1 teaspoon salt
1 kg/2 lb sugar
90 g/3¼ oz demerara sugar
25 g/1 oz fresh ginger, finely-chopped
7 g/¼ oz chilli powder
600 ml/1 pint malt vinegar

1. Chop tomatoes and place all ingredients, except vinegar, in a pan. Stir over low heat until sugar is dissolved. Cook gently for about 1 hour to a thick consistency, stirring occasionally.
2. Add vinegar and cook for another 10 minutes.
3. Pour the chutney while hot into warmed, clean, dry jars with vinegar-proof lids.
4. Put on the lids when chutney is cold. Label and store in a cool, dry place.

Priya Wickramasinghe
Cardiff

BROWN PLUM SAUCE

Yields about 1·75 litres/3 pints

Keeps very well.
A simple recipe.

1·1 kg/2½ lb red plums
3 medium-sized onions, sliced
125 g/4 oz sultanas
15g/½ oz root ginger
25 g/1 oz pickling spice
1·2 litres/2 pints malt or white vinegar
225 g/8 oz granulated sugar
50 g/2 oz salt
25 g/1 oz dry mustard
1 teaspoon ground nutmeg
1 level teaspoon turmeric

1. Wipe and stone plums and put them in a large pan. Don't worry if stones are firmly anchored—pick them out later.
2. Add onions and sultanas.
3. Bruise the ginger by hitting it with a hammer. Tie it with pickling spice in a piece of muslin. Put it in pan.
4. Add half of the vinegar and boil for 30 minutes.
5. Meanwhile put sugar to warm in a very cool oven, Gas ¼, 225°F, 110°C. Put clean bottles into oven to warm at same time. (Choose bottles with vinegar-proof lids.)
6. Remove spice bag and stir in all the other ingredients. Stir to dissolve sugar and bring to boiling point.
7. Simmer for 40 to 60 minutes, stirring occasionally, then leave to cool.
8. When cool, push contents of pan through a nylon sieve. Remember to scrape all the purée off underside of sieve.
9. If the sauce is too thin, simmer and reduce the volume by evaporation until it is thicker but still of pouring consistency.
10. Pour into warmed bottles, right to the brim and put on clean lids immediately. Label and store.
11. Leave for 4 weeks to mature.

LEMON OR ORANGE CURD

Yields about ½ kg/1 lb

2 lemons or oranges
75 to 100 g/3 to 4 oz butter
225 g/8 oz granulated sugar
2 eggs and one extra yolk

1. Scrub fruit and grate it, removing only the zest. *Or*, peel fruit very finely with potato peeler. Squeeze juice.
2. Put rind and juice with butter and sugar into an earthenware jar or basin. Stand this in a pan of simmering water. A double saucepan is ideal. Take care that water in outside pan never splashes into mixture. Keep water simmering and stir until sugar dissolves.
3. Meanwhile, put clean jars to warm in a very cool oven, Gas ¼, 225°F, 110°C.
4. In another basin fork up the eggs, removing the germ. Do not whisk.
5. Pour fruit mixture over eggs, through a strainer if whole pieces of rind were used, and return to the double cooker.
6. Cook until curd thickens, stirring in one direction. It may take 30 to 45 minutes before it is really thick. Stir every 4 or 5 minutes. Curd thickens a little more in jars as it cools.
7. Pour into warmed jars. Put a waxed tissue on top.
8. When quite cold put on jam pot covers.

Keeps for 6 weeks. Best kept in a refrigerator.

GOOSEBERRY CURD

Yields 900 g/2 lb

700 g/1½ lb young green gooseberries*
300 ml/½ pint water
100 g/4 oz butter
325 g/12 oz sugar
3 eggs

*If you cannot get young gooseberries, 1 or 2 drops of green food colouring can be used.

1. There is no need to top and tail gooseberries. Put them in with the water in a pan, bring to boil and simmer until pulpy.
2. Meanwhile, put clean jars to warm in a very cool oven, Gas ¼, 225°F, 110°C.
3. Push gooseberries through a nylon sieve, taking care to scrape purée from underside of sieve.
4. Put butter and sugar into a double saucepan or into a basin standing in a pan of simmering water. Stir to dissolve sugar. Add gooseberry purée.
5. In another bowl, beat eggs but do not whisk. Stir in hot gooseberry mixture, then return to double cooker.
6. Cook, stirring all the time until mixture thickens.
7. Pour into warmed jars. Put a waxed tissue on top.
8. When quite cold, put on jam pot covers.

Can be eaten straight away. Keeps for 6 weeks. Best kept in a refrigerator.

Delicious as a filling for tartlets and sponges. Also in meringue baskets, but fill them, of course, at the very last minute.

MINCEMEAT

As mincemeat is liable to ferment, it is best if potted in a large jar and kept in refrigerator.

225 g/8 oz seedless raisins
125 g/4 oz sultanas
125 g/4 oz eating apples, peeled
125 g/4 oz mixed peel
50 g/2 oz grated suet
225 g/8 oz currants
Grated rind and juice of 1 lemon
125 g/4 oz soft brown sugar
1 tablespoon golden syrup
1 teaspoon mixed spice
1 teaspoon cinnamon
¼ teaspoon grated nutmeg
4 tablespoons brandy or whisky

1. Mince the raisins, sultanas, apple, peel and suet using the coarse mincing plates. Leave the currants whole.
2. Put all ingredients together and mix well.

3. Pot as suggested in previous recipe with a good lid, and keep in refrigerator.

COCONUT ICE

350 g/¾ lb sugar
150 ml/¼ pint milk
125 g/4 oz desiccated coconut
1 or 2 drops of vanilla essence

The same ingredients are used again for a second batch, which is coloured pink.

1. Put sugar and milk in a saucepan and stir over low heat until sugar is dissolved. Then boil for 5 minutes.
2. Pour into a basin and add coconut and vanilla. Beat until mixture becomes thick.
3. Spread in a buttered dish or tin.
4. Make the second batch, using a few drops of red food colouring. Spread it on top of white.

Nathalie Jowett
Yea, Victoria, Australia

CREAM TOFFEE

A toffee with a soft texture.

175 g/6 oz butter
300 g/12 oz demerara sugar
2 tablespoons golden syrup
A 400 g/14 oz tin of condensed milk

1. Melt butter, sugar and golden syrup. Stir over low heat to dissolve sugar.
2. Add condensed milk.
3. Stirring often, boil for about 10 minutes until the soft ball stage—that is, when a few drops are put into a jug of iced water and the mixture forms a soft ball between the fingers. If it dissolves immediately continue to boil for a further 3 or 4 minutes.
4. Pour into a greased Swiss roll tin 28 by 18 cm/11 by 7 inches.
5. When cold, cut into squares and wrap each one in waxed paper. Because of the soft texture of this toffee it must be wrapped or all the pieces will stick together.

CREAMY CHOCOLATE

Makes about 30

150 g/5 oz plain cooking chocolate
50 g/2 oz butter
A few drops of vanilla essence
175 g/6 oz sweetened condensed milk
100 g/4 oz icing sugar
1 level tablespoon cocoa

1. Break the chocolate into pieces and put in a basin with the butter. Place the basin over a pan containing a little hot water. Heat the water gently to melt chocolate and butter.
2. Remove basin from heat, add vanilla essence and beat in the condensed milk.
3. Add icing sugar sieved with cocoa and beat until creamy.
4. Place a teaspoonful of mixture in paper sweet cases (waxed or foil ones are best) and leave to set.

Margaret Heywood
Todmorden, Yorkshire

FRUIT JELLIES

Blackcurrant, gooseberry and raspberry jellies can be made from the fresh fruit.

Fruit of your choice
Sugar
Lemon juice

1. Make a purée of the fruit by simmering it in the minimum of water to soften. Then rub through a sieve to remove skins and pips.
2. Measure the purée. To every 300 ml/½ pint allow 175 g/6 oz sugar and the juice of half a lemon.
3. Put purée, sugar and lemon juice in a pan. Heat gently, stirring to dissolve sugar before it boils.
4. Boil carefully, stirring most of the time to prevent burning. Test every minute or two after it gets thick by putting a little into a cup of cold water. When this forms a firm ball in the water it is ready.
5. Pour mixture into a wetted baking tin.

6. When the jelly is set, turn it out on to greaseproof paper covered in sugar and leave till completely cold.
7. Cut into suitable shapes. Toss in sugar.

Anne Wallace
Stewarton, Ayrshire

GLACÉ FRUITS

Fresh fruits such as strawberries, orange or mandarin segments, clusters of two grapes, etc., are dipped in caramel, giving them a shiny crisp coating. Canned fruit can also be used, including maraschino cherries, provided the syrup is dried off carefully before they are dipped in the caramel.

Lovely for a party, but cannot be made too far ahead as they go sticky in a day or so, particularly if weather is humid.

The quantity of syrup given is enough to coat about 20 pieces of fruit. You will need tiny crinkled paper sweet cases which can be bought at good stationers. Also, several wooden cocktail sticks for dipping. It is useful but not essential to have a sugar thermometer.

Syrup for caramel
100 g/4 oz sugar
60 ml/2½ fl oz hot water
5 ml/1 teaspoon glucose

1. Brush baking trays lightly with oil.
2. Prepare fruit, making sure it is clean and thoroughly dried.
3. Put sugar in the hot water in a pan, stirring over a low heat until dissolved.
4. Bring to boil and add glucose.
5. Boil to 290–300°F, 145–150°C, or until just before syrup turns brown.
6. Set pan on a wet cloth to stop it boiling.
7. As soon as syrup has stopped bubbling start dipping fruits, holding them by the stems or spearing them with a pair of wooden cocktail sticks.
8. Put each dipped fruit on oiled tray to set. Then place in small paper cases.

Anne Wallace
Stewarton, Ayrshire

PEANUT BUTTER BON-BONS
Makes about 24

100 g/4 oz seedless raisins, chopped
100 g/4 oz icing sugar, sieved
100 g/4 oz peanut butter
25 g/1 oz melted butter or margarine
50 to 75 g/2 to 3 oz plain cooking chocolate

1. Put raisins in a bowl with sugar and peanut butter. Mix to a paste with melted butter or margarine.
2. Shape into balls about the size of a grape and leave on foil or waxed paper to harden overnight.
3. Put chocolate to melt in a small bowl set over a pan of simmering water.
4. Dip the top of each bon-bon in melted chocolate and, when set, put in paper sweet cases.

Margaret Heywood
Todmorden, Yorkshire

RUSSIAN TOFFEE
Makes about 600 g/1¼ lbs

For this it is helpful, but not essential, to have a sugar thermometer.

50 g/2 oz butter
100 g/4 oz sugar
100 g/4 oz golden syrup
400 g/1 large tin condensed milk
25 g/1 oz redcurrant jelly
A few drops of vanilla essence

1. Put butter, sugar and syrup in a large saucepan over a low heat, and stir until sugar is completely dissolved.
2. Bring to boiling point and add condensed milk and redcurrant jelly.
3. Continue to boil to 265°F, 130°C, hard ball stage, stirring all the time.

If using a thermometer, be sure to have it by the pan in a container of very hot water, so that it is hot before it enters the toffee. Hard ball stage can be tested without a thermometer by

179

dropping a teaspoon of the mixture into a cup of cold water. When you feel it between thumb and fingers it is a hard ball but still chewy.

4. Add vanilla and pour into a greased 18 cm/7 inch square tin.
5. When set, mark into squares. When cold, cut and wrap in waxed paper.
6. Store in an airtight container.

Anne Wallace
Stewarton, Ayrshire

TOFFEE APPLES

For this you need a large heavy-based pan, wooden lolly sticks and a large greased baking tin.

12 small eating apples
450 g/1 lb white or brown sugar
50 g/2 oz butter
1 tablespoon golden syrup
2 teaspoons vinegar
150 ml/¼ pint water

1. Wash and dry the apples. Push a stick into each stalk end.
2. Put all remaining ingredients into a large pan. Stir over gentle heat until sugar is dissolved, then boil rapidly for 5 minutes. Stir just a little.
3. The syrup in the pan has to boil until it comes to the hard ball stage. This means that when a little of the syrup is dropped into a jug of ice-cold water it forms a hard ball and this tells you when your toffee is ready. Go on boiling until this point is reached.
4. Remove pan from heat and, as quickly as possible, dip the apples. Twirl them around in toffee for a few

seconds, shake off the surplus and put on to the greased baking tin to set.

If the toffee starts to set in the pan, heat it gently again.

SPANISH QUINCE PASTE

1·8 kg/4 lb quinces
300 ml/½ pint water
Sugar

To finish: castor sugar

1. Wash the quinces. Cut them in quarters and put them in a saucepan with the water.
2. Simmer until soft, then put them through a sieve.
3. Weigh the pulp and put it in a large, clean pan.
4. Weigh an equal quantity of sugar and mix it in.
5. Stir over low heat until sugar dissolves. Continue cooking until mixture becomes very thick. Stir continuously.
6. Pour into shallow tins lined with sheets of greaseproof paper.
7. Leave it in a warm place, such as an airing cupboard, for 3 or 4 days. It will dry out a little and be easy to handle.
8. Peel off the paper and cut the paste into pieces. Roll them in castor sugar and store between layers of grease-proof paper in an airtight tin or plastic box.

Can be eaten as a dessert with cream cheese.

Miss Elisabeth Gruber
Winchester

Chapter 12

Beer, Wine and Other Drinks

YEAST STARTER

175 ml/6 fluid oz water
1 dessertspoon malt extract
1 dessertspoon sugar
A pinch of citric acid
A pinch of yeast nutrient
The yeast, as indicated in recipe

1. Put water in a small pan, stir in malt extract, sugar and citric acid. Bring to the boil, then turn off heat.
2. Cool this solution a little, then pour it into a small pop bottle, 300 ml/½ pint. Plug neck of bottle with cotton-wool and cool to 21°C, 70°F.
3. Add yeast. If it is a liquid yeast culture, shake the phial before emptying it into the bottle. Replace cotton-wool plug and leave in a warm place.
4. The yeast will ferment vigorously and will be ready to use in 3 to 4 days.

PALE ALE

Makes 25 litres/5 gallons

1·4 kg/3 lb dried light malt extract
450 g/1 lb crushed crystal malt
50 g/2 oz Golding hops
40 g/1½ oz Northern Brewer hops
450g/1 lb soft light brown sugar

Yeast: British Ale

For priming bottles: granulated sugar

1. Make up a yeast starter 3 to 4 days before starting to make the pale ale. Follow instructions *above*.
2. Warm up about 10 litres/2 gallons of water. When hot, stir in the malts and hops and boil for 45 minutes.
3. Strain into fermenting bin.
4. Rinse the hops and malt with 1 or 2 kettles full of hot water.
5. Add the sugar and stir to dissolve.
6. Make up volume to 25 litres/5 gallons with cold water.
7. When cool, 18 to 20°C, 65 to 70°F, pitch the yeast starter.
8. Cover bin loosely. Leave in a warm place to ferment for about 4 to 5 days.

9. If the bin has an air-tight lid with an air lock, use this. Otherwise, syphon pale ale into containers, such as 4·5 litre/1 gallon jars, or larger vessels if you have them, to which an air-lock can be fitted.
10. Leave containers in a warm place and let pale ale ferment to a gravity of 1·005 or less.
11. Syphon into proper beer bottles. Be sure to use real beer bottles. Other bottles are not strong enough to take the build up of gas during the secondary fermentation.
12. Prime bottles with ½ teaspoon sugar per pint (575 ml) and screw in stoppers tightly or fit new crown corks.
13. Keep in a warm place for 3 to 4 days to allow priming sugar to ferment and so give the pale ale condition.
14. Ready to drink 3 to 4 weeks after bottling but improves if kept 2 to 4 months.

MILD ALE

An ale which is halfway between a bitter and a stout, dark in colour, a favourite tipple with many folk.

To make 25 litres/5 gallons

1·8 kg/4 lb malt extract
125 g/4 oz crushed black malt
50 g/2 oz Fuggles hops
350 g/12 oz soft dark brown sugar

Yeast: Top-fermenting, British Ale

Soft water is necessary for this. If you do not live in a soft water area 1 teaspoon bicarbonate soda and 1 teaspoon salt can be added to a 25 litre/5 gallon brew. However, it is best to consult a local home-brew shop about the most suitable quantity in your area.

Follow the method given for Pale Ale. This ale, however, does not require further maturing after the 3 to 4 weeks in the bottle.

SWEET STOUT

To make 25 litres/5 gallons

**1·5 kg/3 lb dried dark malt
extract
225 g/8 oz crushed black malt
225 g/8 oz crushed crystal malt
450 g/1 lb soft dark brown sugar
50 g/2 oz Fuggles hops
10 to 15 sweetening tablets**

Yeast: Top-fermenting

Soft water is necessary (*see Mild Ale*).

Follow method given for Pale Ale, adding sweetening tablets when wort is still hot.

Dennis Rouston
Kippax, W. Yorkshire

top with water. Fit airlock or cover with a piece of polythene held in place with a rubber band.
5. Leave in a reasonably warm place, about 20°C, 70°F, until wine is all but clear.
6. Syphon wine off sediment into a clean jar, topping up with cold water, refitting airlock or polythene cover.
7. After about 3 months the wine will be clear. If there is any sediment on the bottom of the jar, syphon into a clean jar and it should be ready to drink. But it will improve with keeping.
8. Once a jar is opened for drinking, the wine should be bottled, otherwise it will oxidise and the flavour and appearance will be spoilt.

Ted Adcock
Northolt, Middlesex

WHITE DRY TABLE WINE

A handy recipe as the *main ingredients come from the super-market.* Ready to drink in 3 to 4 months but improves with keeping.

Makes 4·5 litres/1 gallon

**Two 675 ml/24 fl oz bottles pure apple juice
One 675 ml/24 fl oz bottle pure grape juice
3 level teaspoons (15 g) tartaric acid
1 teaspoon Pectolase, or similar
½ teaspoon yeast nutrient
600 g/21 oz granulated sugar**

Sauternes yeast

1. Make up a yeast starter 4 to 5 days before you want to make the wine. Follow instructions *on page 182.*
2. Then put all ingredients, including yeast starter, into a fermentation bin or bucket with water to make volume up to 4·5 litres/1 gallon. Stir to dissolve sugar, etc. Cover loosely.
3. Stir daily for 3 to 4 days.
4. Syphon into a 4·5 litre/1 gallon jar and top up to within 2·5 cm/1 inch of

WHITE DRY TABLE WINE—QUICK

Makes 13·5 litres/3 gallons

Gives you plenty of drinkable table wine in 6 to 8 weeks, but it does improve with keeping.

**Three 1 litre/35 fl oz cartons of apple juice
½ litre/1 pint Riesling grape concentrate (use Southern Vineyards 'Grandier')
2·5 kg/5½ lb granulated sugar
2 teaspoons each tartaric acid, yeast nutrient, Pectolase and Bentonite**

Chablis or Sauternes yeast

1. Make up a yeast starter, at least 3 to 4 days before you want to make the wine, following instructions *on page 182.*
2. Put all the other ingredients into fermentation bin with water to make volume up to 13·5 litres/3 gallons. Stir well to dissolve.
3. Add the yeast starter. Ferment in the bin for 14 days, stirring occasionally. Keep bin covered loosely.

183

4. Syphon into 4·5 litre/1 gallon jars. Top up with cold water to within 2·5 cm/1 inch of top, fit airlock or a piece of polythene held in place with a rubber band.
5. After 3 to 4 weeks the wine should be clearing. Rack off (i.e., syphon wine off sediment) into clean jars.
6. Rack off the sediment again when clear and it should be ready to drink.
7. Once a jar is opened for drinking the wine should be bottled otherwise it will oxidise and the flavour and appearance will be spoilt.

Keith Simpson
Hartburn, Darlington

FARMHOUSE KITCHEN 'NOUVEAU'

A nice, light, rosé type of wine, with a fresh, clean taste and a pleasant bouquet, that just asks to be drunk young.

Because the various fruits ripen at different times, pick when ripe and freeze, then make the wine at your leisure.

Makes 4·5 litres/1 gallon

700 g/1½ lb blackberries
250 g/8 oz elderberries
125 g/4 oz blackcurrants
12 raspberries
Boiling water
1 kg/2·2 lb sugar
115 ml/4 fl oz white or rosé grape concentrate
1 teaspoon tartaric acid
1 teaspoon yeast nutrient
1 Campden tablet

Bordeaux or Port yeast

1. Make up yeast starter 3 to 4 days before beginning to make the wine. Follow instructions *on page 182.*
2. Put fruit into a large basin and pour over about 1 litre/2 pints of boiling water.
3. Put on rubber gloves and squeeze fruit.

4. Strain juice through muslin into a polythene fermenting bin or bucket.
5. Repeat this process twice—i.e., pour boiling water on to pulp, squeeze and strain. Then throw the pulp away on to the compost heap.
6. Add the sugar and stir to dissolve.
7. Make up the volume of juice to 4·5 litres/1 gallon with cold water. Let it cool to 18 to 20°C, 65 to 70°F.
8. Add the grape concentrate, tartaric acid, yeast nutrient, Campden tablet and the yeast starter.
9. Cover bin loosely with a cloth or lid.
10. Stir daily for 3 to 4 days, then pour into a 4·5 litre/1 gallon jar, top up to 2·5 cm/1 inch from top with cold water.
11. Fit airlock or cover top with a piece of polythene secured with a rubber band.
12. Leave in a warm place, not the airing cupboard, to ferment.
13. After about 3 months, rack off (i.e., syphon wine off sediment) into a clean jar, topping up to 2·5 cm/1 inch from top with water.
14. Rack again once or twice more at 3-month intervals. The wine should be ready to drink in less than a year.
15. Once a jar is opened for drinking, the rest of the wine should be bottled. Otherwise it may oxidise, and flavour and appearance could be spoilt.

Dennis Rouston
Kippax, Yorkshire

THREE WINES SAME METHOD

Each recipe makes 4·5 litres/1 gallon

White table wine

Dry or Sweet

This recipe gives a dry wine in the Muscadet style. If sweetened with white grape concentrate as suggested in the method, it gives it a Vouvray style.

1 kg/2 lb gooseberries, fresh,
frozen or tinned
250 g/8 oz very ripe bananas,
peeled
625 g/1 lb 6 oz sugar
225 ml/8 fl oz white grape
concentrate
3 level teaspoons tartaric acid
½ teaspoon yeast nutrient

Sauternes yeast

Red table wine

This recipe gives a dry red wine in the
Valpolicella style, but can be blended
with the white wine for a Rosé. It can
then be sweetened with white grape
concentrate for an Anjou-style Rosé.

570 g/1 lb 4 oz blackberries
150 g/5 oz elderberries
225 g/8 oz very ripe bananas,
peeled
650 g/1 lb 7 oz sugar
225 ml/8 fl oz red grape
concentrate
2 level teaspoons (10 g) tartaric
acid
½ teaspoon yeast nutrient

Bordeaux or Port yeast

Dessert wine

This wine will become medium-sweet
in the Madeira-style. The sweetness
can be adjusted with white grape
concentrate to give a Malmsey-style.

200 g/7 oz dried rosehip shells
(soak for 1 hour in warm water)
125 g/4 oz dried figs (soak for 1
hour in warm water)
225 g/8 oz very ripe bananas,
peeled
1 kg/2·2 lb sugar
10 g/2 level teaspoons tartaric
acid
½ teaspoon yeast nutrient

Madeira yeast

Sugar syrup made up with 900 g/2 lb
sugar stirred over low heat to dissolve
in 600 ml/1 pint water is added during
fermentation. At paragraph 7 in the
method begin to take gravity readings.
When gravity reaches 1·005 start
feeding in 50 ml/2 fl oz syrup once a

week until fermentation stops. This
could take a month or more.

Method

For this you need a liquidiser.

For each of the above wines you need:

2 Campden tablets
1 teaspoon Pectolase, or similar

1. Prepare a yeast starter and activate
with the suggested yeast 3 to 4 days
before it is required for the wine.
2. Liquidise the fruit with the
minimum of water.
3. Add 1 crushed Campden tablet and
1 teaspoon Pectolase. Cover with a
cloth and leave overnight.
4. Next day dissolve sugar by heating
gently in about 1 litre/1½ pints water,
stirring. Pour over fruit pulp, add the
grape concentrate, tartaric acid and
yeast nutrient.
5. Make up volume to about 4·5
litres/1 gallon then add yeast starter.
6. Ferment on the pulp for 3 to 5 days.
Stir daily.
7. Strain and put into a 4·5 litre/1
gallon jar. Top up with water to
within 2·5 cm/1 inch of top. Fit airlock
or a piece of polythene held with a
rubber band. If possible keep jar at a
controlled temperature of 20°C, 70°F,
while fermenting proceeds.
8. When wine has finished
fermenting, remove to a cool place, add
1 crushed Campden tablet and leave
for 2 to 3 days.
9. Then rack (i.e., syphon it off
sediment). If it throws another
sediment rack again.
10. Once a jar is opened for drinking,
the wine should be bottled. Otherwise
it will oxidise and the flavour and
appearance will be spoilt.
11. If you require the sweeter version,
add white grape concentrate as the
bottle is needed.

Ted Adcock
Northolt, Middlesex

185

DAMSON WINE

Makes a very nice steady sipping wine for a cold winter's evening. Sugar content can be varied to give a dry or sweet wine.

Makes 4·5 litres/1 gallon

1·8 kg/4 lb damsons
4·5 litres/1 gallon boiling water
125 ml/4 fl oz red grape concentrate
1 teaspoon yeast nutrient
1 teaspoon tartaric acid
1 teaspoon Pectolase or similar
1 kg/2 lb sugar, for a dry wine
Or, 1·5 kg/3¼ lb sugar, for a sweet wine

Port yeast

1. Make up a yeast starter 3 to 4 days before beginning to make wine. Follow instructions *on page 182.*
2. Then chop up damsons, removing stones and put chopped fruit into a fermentation bin or bucket.
3. Pour over boiling water, stir in ¼ kg/1 lb of the sugar and allow to cool.
4. Add other ingredients, including yeast starter.
5. Cover loosely with a cloth or lid and let it ferment on the pulp for 4 to 5 days. Stir at least twice daily.
6. Strain, taking care not to squeeze fruit or it may produce a hazy wine. Return liquor to bin.
7. Over the next 4 to 5 days add sugar, about ¼ kg/1 lb at a time, until the required amount has been used. Stir to dissolve.
8. Syphon into a 4·5 litre/1 gallon jar. Fit an airlock or a piece of polythene secured with a rubber band. Leave in a reasonably warm place.
9. Rack (i.e., syphon wine off sediment) at 3 to 4 month intervals until wine is clear and ready to drink.

It may take a year or more to mature before it will be drinkable, but it is well worth waiting for. Once a jar is opened for drinking the rest of the wine should be bottled. Otherwise flavour may be spoilt.

Dennis Rouston
Kippax, W. Yorkshire

RHUBARB WINE

A medium-sweet wine, which is not only good to drink, but also very useful for blending with other wines. With a freezer, it can be made at your leisure.

2·75 kg/6 lb rhubarb
125 ml/4 fl oz white grape concentrate
1 teaspoon Bentonite
1 Campden tablet
1 teaspoon yeast nutrient
1·35 kg/3 lb sugar

Sauternes yeast

1. Pick the rhubarb as early as possible until the end of June—while it is still pink or red.
2. Trim and wipe clean, cut long sticks in half, put into polythene bags to weigh ½ kg/1 lb. Then put into freezer.
3. Make up a yeast starter 3 to 4 days before beginning to make wine. Follow instructions *on page 182.*
4. Put a strainer over your fermentation bin, put a frozen packet of rhubarb into the strainer. Let it thaw.
5. When the rhubarb has thawed squeeze the last few drops out—throw away the pulp (or use it for a pie).
6. Repeat until 2·75 kg/6 lb rhubarb is used.
7. Add to the rhubarb juice the white grape concentrate, Bentonite, Campden tablet and yeast nutrient and 450 g/1 lb of the sugar. Stir to dissolve. Then stir in yeast starter.
8. Add water to make up volume to 4·5 litres/1 gallon. Cover the bin loosely with a cloth or lid.
9. Stir daily. On third day add 450 g/1 lb sugar. Stir to dissolve.
10. On the fifth day add the last 450 g/1 lb sugar. Stir to dissolve.
11. Next day syphon into a 4·5 litre/1 gallon jar, top up to within 2·5 cm/1 inch of top. Fit airlock or a piece of polythene secured with a rubber band. Leave to ferment in a reasonably warm place.
12. Syphon wine off sediment at 3 month intervals.

Should be ready to drink in 9 months. After opening a jar to drink, bottle the rest of the wine. Otherwise it may oxidise and flavour as well as appearance could be spoilt.

Dennis Rouston
Kippax, West Yorkshire

CIDER

A nice drink. Also very useful in the kitchen for cooking. A press is required which can be bought or made, or it is possible to hire one. Ready to drink in a month or so.

To make 4·5 litres/1 gallon

10 kg/20 lb windfall apples, a mixture of eaters and cookers is ideal
Granulated sugar
1 teaspoon tartaric acid

Sauternes yeast

1. Make up a yeast starter 3 to 4 days before starting to make the cider. Follow instructions *on page 182.*

2. Wipe the apples clean. Do not bother to cut out the bruises.
3. Mince them using coarsest mincer blades.
4. Put the minced apples into a coarse-woven bag, hessian is ideal. Then press, collecting the juice in your fermenting bin. Make up volume to 4·5 litres/1 gallon with water.
5. Measure the gravity with an hydrometer and add sugar until the gravity is 1·055. (15 g/½ oz sugar raises the gravity of 4·5 litres/1 gallon by one degree.)
6. Add tartaric acid and the Sauternes yeast starter. Stir to dissolve acid and sugar.
7. After 3 to 4 days syphon into a 4·5 litre/1 gallon jar, fit airlock or a piece of polythene held in place with a rubber band. Ferment to 1·005.
8. Then syphon off sediment into another jar and if the cider is nice and clear syphon into clean, strong, screw-topped cider or beer bottles. Returnable cider or beer bottles are suitable but the non-returnable are not strong enough. Add 1 level teaspoon sugar per pint. Screw down the top. If it is not clear leave it to settle before bottling.

The cider should be ready to use after a month or so.

CYSER

An old fashioned drink with more of a punch than cider, but a still drink, not sparkling. Matured for a year. As for cider you need a press (*see introduction to previous recipe*).

10 kg/20 lb windfall apples, a mixture of eaters and cookers is ideal
1 kg/2 lb honey
1 teaspoon tartaric acid
1 teaspoon yeast nutrient

Sauternes yeast

1. Make up a yeast starter 3 to 4 days before starting to make the cyser. Follow instructions *on page 182.*
2. Wipe the apples clean. Do not bother to cut out the bruises.

187

3. Mince them using coarsest mincer blades.
4. Put the minced apples into a coarse-woven bag, hessian is ideal. Then press as for cider, collecting juice in a fermenting bin.
5. Heat up 2 litres/3 pints of the apple juice to 60 to 65°C, 140 to 150°F.
6. Stir honey into hot juice. When dissolved, add to remaining juice. Leave to cool.
7. Add tartaric acid, yeast nutrient and Sauternes yeast starter. Put bin in a warm place.
8. Allow to ferment in the bin for 3 to 4 days.
9. Syphon into a 4·5 litre/1 gallon jar, fit airlock or a piece of polythene held in place with a rubber band. Any liquid over, put into a small bottle and plug neck with cotton wool.
10. Rack at 3 to 4 month intervals (i.e., syphon off the sediment). Top up jar to within 2·5 cm/1 inch of top with liquid from the little bottle. The cyser should be ready to drink in about a year.

Once the jar is opened for drinking the rest should be bottled or it may oxidise and deteriorate in flavour and appearance.

Dennis Rouston
Kippax, Yorkshire

BLACKCURRANT SYRUP

The same method can be used for blackberries, loganberries, raspberries and strawberries.

Blackcurrants
Sugar
Campden tablets

Use really ripe, clean, dry fruit.

1. Put fruit in an earthenware jar or a tall straight-sided jug. Crush it with a wooden spoon or pulper.

2. Cover the container with a thin cloth and leave in a warm room to ferment just a little. It will take 3 to 5 days. Other fruits mentioned above may only take 1 day to ferment, so keep an eye on it.
3. When bubbles of gas are forming on the surface, tip fruit into a scalded jelly bag. Allow it to drain overnight.
4. Next day press the bag thoroughly to remove any remaining juice.
5. Measure juice and to every 600 ml/1 pint add ½ kg/1 lb sugar. Stir until sugar is dissolved.
6. Strain syrup through jelly bag to make sure it is clear but this step is not essential.
7. For every 600 ml/1 pint of syrup add 1 Campden tablet dissolved in 1 tablespoon warm water.
8. Use really clean bottles. To be sure of this put them in a large pan of water. Bring to the boil, take bottles out and drain. Boil the caps for 15 minutes just before use.
9. Fill bottles to 1 cm/½ inch of the top.
10. Once opened, keep bottles in a cool place or refrigerator.

WILLAWONG LEMON CORDIAL

3 to 4 lemons
450 g/1 lb white sugar
1 dessertspoon tartaric acid
600 ml/1 pint boiling water

1. Peel lemons finely to produce rind with no pith.
2. Squeeze lemons.
3. Put rinds, juice, sugar and tartaric acid into a bowl. Pour over boiling water. Stir till dissolved. Leave to cool, preferably overnight.
4. Strain and bottle.
5. Keep in a cool place or refrigerator.
6. Dilute with water to taste.

Nathalie Jowett
Yea, Victoria, Australia

INDEX

S